HEROES & VILLAINS
of CHESTER
and beyond

HEROES & VILLAINS
of CHESTER
and beyond

800 years of history in 30 lives

PETER COTGREAVE

For G.W.C and E.M.C.,
because I am no longer the last of the line

First published in 2019
by Palatine Books,
Carnegie House,
Chatsworth Road
Lancaster LA1 4SL
www.palatinebooks.com

British Library Cataloguing-in-Publication data
A catalogue record for this book is available from the
British Library

Paperback ISBN 13: 978-1-910837-24-5

Designed and typeset by Carnegie Book Production
www.carnegiebookproduction.com

Printed and bound by Cambrian Printers

Front cover illustrations: Thomas Eaton Cotgrave in 1862
(courtesy of Gillie Turner), Elizabeth Lady Forbes in 1800
(courtesy of Rosemary Walker) and Chester, the Cross looking
towards Watergate Street by Louise Raynor (1832–1924),
Wikicommons
Back cover illustration: print of a map of Cheshire, *c.*1850

A note on names, dates and money

For the people whose lives are the main focus of the book, I have tried to spell their surnames in the same way they spelled them themselves. If I have found no surviving examples of their signature or handwriting, I have opted for the version most often used by the people around them. For first names, I have tried to do the same, but there is often some confusion – there are for example, plenty of men where it is impossible to know whether they called themselves Randle or Randolph or Ranulph, or even if they were consistent. For peripheral characters, I have used what seems to me to be the most usual modern version of their name.

For all dates, I have assumed that the year starts on 1 January. This modern reckoning means that for some events before changes to the calendar in 1752, what I have written will disagree with what is recorded on original documents, which dated the beginning of the year from 25 March.

I have tried to avoid too many attempts to compare historical sums of money with current values. Economists have invented all sorts of different ways of doing the calculations, and they produce vastly different answers, and are sometimes (often) confusing. Where I have been tempted to say anything, I have tried to compare a sum with the rough amount that an average employed person – like a journeyman working in Chester – might have earned at the time.

References

A comprehensive list of references to original documents and secondary sources, for each Chapter, is given at the end of the text. I have not broken up the flow of the stories by giving a separate reference to each individual fact, but I would welcome any inquiries from anyone trying to identify the source of any particular statement. Contact may be made via possessingantiquity.com.

Contents

This crumpled photograph of William and Mary Cotgreave in about 1895, with their four surviving children standing behind them, inspired me to want to know more. As a child, I knew people who remembered the woman at the back, Emma Cotgreave, who was born in 1862.

This lichen-covered post marks the corner of the field called Far Cotgreaves, a dimly-remembered echo of the location of 'Cotegrave,' the origin of Thomas de Cotegrave's name.

for preserving old documents. It is not popular enough with historians to justify shelf space in the main storage facilities at the National Archives at Kew; if you want to see it, you must wait three days for it to arrive. But its current home is remarkably appropriate; it is in Winsford in Cheshire, in an area where Thomas de Cotegrave himself owned a salt works. After three quarters of a millennium, the document on which Cotegrave's name first appears is housed in the place he lived, the very place that he and his neighbours understood so well that they were called upon to decide which villages, farms, barns, mills, ponds, fields and copses could be considered of equal value.

Thirteen jurors are named in the list, but the document is damaged and there is a space where there was originally another. Eighth in the sequence is *Th'm de Coteg'aue* and this seemingly inconsequential detail is the earliest surviving record of the Cotgreave family. Everyone in the world called Cotgrave, Cotgreave Cotgrove or Coatgrieve – hundreds of people alive today and thousands over the centuries – has inherited Thomas's name in one way or another, directly or indirectly. His descendants have included every kind of person imaginable: murderers, priests, farmers, businesspeople, magistrates, husbands, thieves, fraudsters, politicians, tailors, paupers, shoemakers, wives, painters, slave-owners, sailors, soldiers, fishermen, philanthropists, misers, grandparents, prostitutes, tax collectors, gardeners, mayors, sheriffs, wives, cricketers, cyclists, golfers and footballers. They have lived in just about every corner of the globe from the frozen highlands of Scotland to the rainy tropics in Nigeria. Cotgreaves were in the vanguard of settlement as Europeans moved west in America and they explored the Andaman Islands in the Eastern seas. They were among the earliest settlers on the island of Saint Helena in the mid-Atlantic, far from any other people, and they spread to almost every corner of the bustling, crowded Indian subcontinent. There is no location, no subject, and no occupation that does not prove to have a Cotgreave connection if you look hard enough. Thomas de Cotegrave started something enduring when he walked into Chester Castle, and his posterity weaves a story from the thirteenth century to the twenty-first.

Considering how long ago he lived, and that he was not a major landowner or political figure, it is possible to piece together a reasonably complete sketch of Thomas de Cotegrave's life. His father, who was called Richard FitzWilliam, was born in about 1190, putting Thomas's own birth sometime in the early thirteenth century. His mother (or at least his father's wife, who could have been Thomas's stepmother) was called Mabel, but is otherwise invisible in the records. His grandfather, who was a major landowner in Cheshire, is recorded in original documents as William de Malpas, but historians later remembered that he had been known as William Belward. Richard FitzWilliam was Belward's youngest son, and inherited a relatively small estate, which in time Thomas de Cotegrave had to share with his brothers. Thomas was the oldest of his generation and received a manor called Cotegrave, one sixteenth share of the manor of Duckington and other smaller pieces of land and property.

Cotegrave acquired a coat of arms that displayed three hunting horns, and this led later historians to propose that perhaps the family worked as the Earl of Chester's huntsmen. But this is nothing more than speculation that springs from the frustration of wanting to know more about someone whose life we can only see dimly and in parts.

Fixed, hereditary surnames were a novelty at the time, and Thomas's brothers were known as William de Overton, because he inherited lands in a place of that name, and Richard Little, presumably because he was short (unless it was a joke, like the large man called 'Little John' in the Robin Hood stories). They had a sister whose married name was Morville Taillard and perhaps another called Millicent Praers.[1] Cotegrave himself took his name from a settlement about five miles from Chester.[2] It no longer exists, although as recently as the mid nineteenth century, the name persisted in two fields called Near Cotgreaves and Far Cotgreaves. Thomas de Cotegrave owned, bought and sold lands in the same parish and was trusted by his neighbours as a reliable witness when they did the same. He seems to have died in the 1270s and from around 1280, his name is replaced in the records by that of his son William de Cotegrave.

Not much is known about the working of the county court that Thomas attended in December 1259. It was a forum not just for prosecuting criminals and resolving private disputes, but also for all sorts of aspects of local administration. Attending the court was a duty, supposedly compulsory for adult men, at least those who qualified for jury service because they owned sufficient land.

One way in which the court certainly differed from a modern one was that, as a juror, Thomas de Cotegrave did not turn up on the day ignorant of the details of the case he was there to decide. He was known to the parties; the two warring sisters had in fact chosen the jurors as men they knew and trusted. Indeed, in Thomas's case, they were related. The father whose lands Beatrice and Idonea were disputing had been called David de Malpas, and he was Cotegrave's uncle. The other jurors were all landowning men of high social standing in the county community. Alan de Windhul, the first on the list, was witness to a charter in about 1250, Richard Hermitage was a clerk who was seneschal of Halton, Robert Winnington, Patrick Heswall, Randle Horton, Hugh Berniston and William the Welshman all had surnames relating to places in the local area, and all are mentioned in surviving thirteenth century deeds.

1 Later documents named other sisters but it is hard to be sure if they are accurate.
2 A seventeenth century copy of deed dated 1304 in the name of Thomas's son calls the place 'Cotegreve in Brune Stapelford' (which is now called Bruenstapleford).

What is so special about what these men did in that draughty courtroom in 1259 is just how familiar it would have been in any age. It is remarkable because it is so unremarkable. The names were spelled differently and the handwriting takes a while to get used to, the official language needs a bit of effort from the modern reader, no doubt the clothes would look vaguely unfamiliar to modern eyes, the smells would have been stronger, or at any rate very different, and the technology was obviously a great deal less sophisticated. But apart from the fact that there were no women in the room, these differences are all superficial; this event is noteworthy principally for its antiquity and for the fact that it introduced the written record of a family that happens to have persisted under the same name for a very long time. That is why in the eighteenth century, Thomas's descendent Sir John Cotgreave could choose as his motto *Antiquam obtinens* – 'possessing antiquity'.

On that day in early December 1259, two siblings were fighting over their father's estate and refused to be sensible, so a jury had to sort out their differences. Something almost identical would happen repeatedly to the Cotgreaves through the ensuing centuries. In 1579 William Cotgreve would sue Eleanor Cotgreve over the title to lands just a few miles from the ones that Thomas de Cotegrave had adjudicated. Anne Cotgreave would take Thomas Cotgreave to court in 1647, and he would countersue, for land and property mentioned in the will of Ralph Cotgreave. In 1726, another Ralph and John Cotgreave would fight again over exactly the same land that Anne and Thomas had contested 79 years earlier. Margaret and Gilbert Cotgrave would fight out the ownership of the house in John Cotgrave's estate, half a world away on the Atlantic island of St Helena in 1706. The Court of Chancery would hear two different cases called 'Cotgreave versus Cotgreave' in the nineteenth century – both concerned with interpreting someone's will to establish which member of the family should inherit which property in Cheshire. Each of these cases would have seemed unremarkable to Thomas de Cotegrave; he and his neighbours could have judged them just as they did the case in the thirteenth century.

Repeatedly throughout the ensuing 800 years, men called Thomas Cotgreave would do their civic duty by turning up for jury service, often in the same building where those two pieces of parchment were delivered by Thomas de Cotegrave and his colleagues. Another Thomas de Cotegrave in Yorkshire in 1302, Thomas Cotgrave at Chester Castle in 1663, Thomas Cotgreave at Stafford in 1750, Thomas Charles Cotgreave in 1890 and Thomas Frank Cotgreave in 1900 in Shropshire, just a few miles from Chester. 641 years after Thomas de Cotegrave assembled with a group of his neighbours to sort out a problem where the law needed to create a tidy answer out of messy facts, his direct descendent did precisely, unerringly, exactly the same thing.

Just nineteen generations separated Thomas de Cotegrave in 1259 and Thomas Frank Cotgreave in 1900 – with a bit of imagination, you could see the two of them sitting around a table with all of the intervening generations. If the two men discussed what had happened to their family in between, there would have been much that baffled one or the other or indeed both of the Thomases. But in their jury service, they would have shared a fixed and specific frame of reference that gave them a starting point from which to plot the history of a group of people who happened to share their surname and genes. Those individuals were not famous – at most a few of them achieved modest prominence amongst a local or specialist audience – but their collective existence, as a family, tells the fascinating story of eight centuries of Cheshire people.

SECTION ONE

ART AND SCIENCE

Art and literature are important parts of human culture, and science – in its broadest form including medicine and engineering – touches everyone's life.

This section tries to understand the purpose of artistic and scholarly works, including a Tudor woman's portrait and a seventeenth century dictionary. It describes a nineteenth-century struggle to make a success of an engineering invention, and how a Victorian man used his artistic talent to recover some dignity when his life fell apart. The stories of a small girl and a middle-aged woman reveal the difficulties of effective healthcare in the days before modern medicine. Finally, there is the tale of one man's relentless crusade to bring the practical and emotional benefits of the written word to the widest possible audience.

CHAPTER 2

1579

A portrait of Eleanor Cotgrave

In a museum in the Deep South of America hangs a painting of a pale, thin 34-year-old English woman. It is almost certainly the work of Robert Peake, a young artist who would go on to become famous for his pictures of the Royal Family. The woman in the portrait – identified as 'Madame Savage' – has auburn hair and is wearing a high ruffed collar on a black dress that is covered with images of roses; she also has a brooch in the form of a rose and a golden chain studded with pearls and jewels, long enough to loop around her neck three times.

This is Eleanor Cotgrave, who was born in about 1545 at the end of her mother's 30-year childbearing career.[1] She would not have remembered her father, a draper called John Cotgreve,[2] who died when she was two, but she knew that he had come from a modest but comfortable background and that by hard work, political judgment (or perhaps luck), clever land deals and civic service, he had made a provincial name for himself in Cheshire. Eleanor grew up partly in Chester and partly in London, where her mother moved after John's death.

It was probably through her oldest brother, who worked for the King's uncle, that Eleanor came into contact with the court, where she met and married Sir Richard Pecksall. Pecksall was a major landowner, a knight, and former sheriff of Hampshire, who served the Queen as Master of the Buckhounds, an hereditary post that had been filled by his ancestors for at least two centuries. Eleanor cannot have brought much of a dowry to the marriage – her father had hardly been rich and there were at least six daughters to provide for. For Richard Pecksall, the young woman held

---

1 She spelled her own first name Elyoner, but I have modernised it to Eleanor.
2 See Chapter 22; he always spelled his name Cotgreve, but Eleanor appears to have favoured Cotgrave.

MADAM · SAVAGE   1 5 7 9

Eleanor Cotgrave in 1579, when she was married to Sir John Savage
[Reproduced by generous permission of the Louisiana State University
Museum of Art (59.9.2)].

the prospect of producing a male child, an heir, after he had fathered four
daughters but no sons with his aristocratic first wife. But throughout what
would eventually be four marriages, and although in her 20s she thought
it 'verye likelie' that she would have children, Eleanor had none, and she

was to become a significant hindrance to Pecksall's inheritance rather than a boon.

The day before he died in 1571, Richard Pecksall made a will in which he left modest legacies to three of his grown-up daughters, cut the eldest out altogether, gave a promise of riches to his grandson – but only in the distant future – and left the whole of his vast estate to his young and beautiful wife. The suspicion clearly was that as Sir Richard lay dying, Eleanor sat on the edge of the expensive counterpane and incited him to commit an act of deathbed folly. It was alleged that the will had been written when the old knight lay 'in greate extremitie ... at the pointe of deathe and paste memory'. Eleanor took immediate possession of the document and refused to show it to anyone else, but she was not the only one suspected of undue influence. One of her stepdaughters accused one of the will's witnesses of using 'dyverse and sundry lewde unconscionable and indirecte waies and meanes' to turn Sir Richard against his daughters.

In any case, it turned out the will could not be implemented – as a 'tenant in chivalry,' Pecksall was required to leave at least a third of his estate to his proper heirs. Consequently, his four daughters quickly managed to get their hands on some of the property. Even so, one third, split four ways, was not a great deal each. So for years afterwards, they tried through lawsuits to recover the rest of what they believed was right-fully theirs. There was no way they were going to allow control of their father's inheritance to pass to a grasping young woman who was not even the mother of any of his children. Eleanor knew she needed a powerful ally to protect her interests, and since her own family was not in the right league, the best way was to find a new and influential husband.

Having been married to a rich knight, Eleanor Cotgrave was not going to accept an inferior second husband, and she quickly wed Sir John Savage, a Cheshire magnate with a knowledge of how to use the legal system. Eleanor and Sir John almost certainly knew one another already, partly because they would have met in London society but also because of their Cheshire connections. The couple clearly worked extremely well as a business partnership, and together they successfully defended their right to hold on to the Pecksall lands and fortune. They refused even to yield much up to Pecksall's grandson when he came of age and was supposed to inherit large parts of the estate. It was later claimed that the grandson had refused to marry one of Savage's daughters, and his life was so blighted by his disinheritance that he became a drunken womaniser who ended up having to do public penance at St Paul's Cathedral for his sins. Forty years after Richard Pecksall's death, when his principal residence at Beaurepaire in Hampshire was surveyed, it belonged to 'the

Worshipful Edward Savage Esq,' who was Sir John Savage's son by his first marriage, and who providentially happened by then to be married to Eleanor Cotgrave's niece.

Eleanor's marriage to Sir John Savage lasted more than a quarter of a century until he died in 1597. Manifestly not being at all sentimental, she rapidly wed a third time, to Sir Robert Remington, a younger son of a Yorkshire family, knighted for his role in the battle of Cadiz. Remington died when Eleanor was already well into her 60s, but she must have been addicted to marriage because she acquired a fourth husband – yet another knight – called Sir George Douglas. Little is known about him, but he had travelled into England either with James I when he took the Crown in 1603 or very soon after. 'George Douglasse, a Scotchman' was knighted by the king, who also gave him expensive jewels and awarded either him or his son a plum job in his Privy Chamber.

It is perfectly plain that Eleanor Cotgrave did not love her husbands. If she had any real feelings for Pecksall, she could never have been so persistently mean to his daughters and then casually watched while his disinherited grandson's life fell apart. Eleanor and Robert Remington did not even pretend to like one another. They lived apart for five years and when he died, even though he had no children and did not wish to give his money to his nephews, he made it plain that he hated Eleanor. He left any mention of her to the very end of his will, where he cut her out without a penny because 'her unkinde and unrespective demeanor towardes me … duringe my life hath made me forgettfull of her at my deathe'. It is possible that Eleanor cared about John Savage in her own way; they certainly had a successful business relationship and he called her 'my most dear and loving wife'. But even he made it plain that his real love was really his first wife, demanding to be buried as close to her as possible in Macclesfield church because while she had lived 'one sowle did governe and directe our boddies, soe deere was the unitie and love between us'.

Eleanor Cotgrave's husbands mattered to her not because of who they were but because of what they were, and more importantly what their status said about her. She almost seems to have deliberately collected different kinds of important and influential men. Court officials, rich landowners and swashbuckling soldiers; it did not matter how they derived their status, they all fell for Eleanor Cotgrave. Coming as they did from Hampshire, Cheshire, Yorkshire and Scotland, she could even claim to have conquered the men of the country from North to South, East to West.

Her first husband, Sir Richard Pecksall, had been buried in

Westminster Abbey, and as his widow, Eleanor raised a huge monument, supposedly to his memory. But her own coat of arms shines as brightly from it as his. Of the effigies of his two wives praying for his soul, Eleanor is the only one shown piously holding a Bible. The inscription tells us not only that she was the daughter of John Cotgreve of Chester – fair enough – but also that she went on to marry Sir John Savage, at best irrelevant and at worst insulting on her first husband's tomb. It even boastfully specifies that the obviously expensive edifice had been paid for out of their own money.[3] The whole thing has nothing to do with Pecksall. It is a statement about how Eleanor Cotgrave, the daughter of a Chester tradesman, has arrived and established herself in society's upper reaches. Her boasting must have been insufferable when Queen Elizabeth visited her home in 1601.[4] Something of how others felt compelled to speak about Eleanor Cotgrave is clear from her own brother-in-law's will in the probate registry at Chester, in which he called her 'the Right worshipful Lady Eleanor'.

In 1598, during her second widowhood, Eleanor had taken a liking to a 'little sweet bag' that belonged to one of her nephews, a Cheshire lawyer named William Brock. Realising there was no point in resisting the great lady, he gave it to her, but she could not be seen simply to take it. So she told Brock she would reward him with £50 if ever she were to marry again. Neither of them really meant it (the bag was only worth a few shillings), but Lady Savage signed a bond for twice the promised amount. It was 'for a show to the world', but she came to regret it some years later. Brock knew the whole thing was a joke, but the document ended up in the hands of another relative, who pursued Eleanor through the courts for its face value of £100.

This grand Tudor matron managed to set four different families at war with one another. From the 1580s to the mid-seventeenth century (long after her death), there was an endless stream of legal cases in every court imaginable. Savage versus Pecksall's grandson in the Star Chamber, Remington versus Savage in the Court of Requests, cases in the Exchequer and Chancery involving the Remingtons, the Savages, Richard Pecksall's heirs and even Sir George Douglas, who was only married to Eleanor Cotgrave for the last six months of her life. Even after

---

3   The text in Latin says 'hoc monumentum suis sumptibus libens lubensque posuit,' which means 'has set up this monument willingly and gladly at her [or perhaps his, i.e. Savage's] own expense'.
4   Nobody else noticed that the event had happened, and we only know about it because the bellringers at the local church were paid extra on the occasion.

Eleanor's death, the battle continued, and became violent – in 1621 her niece Polexina Savage was dragged a mile down a dirty lane as Pecksall's descendants tried to evict her from what they said was their property. As late as 1634, more than 60 years after Sir Richard Pecksall's death, Chancery judges were still considering the case of Savage versus Brocas (Pecksall's grandson). Pecksall's family later claimed that they had been ruined by fighting lawsuits costing more than £2,000. They accused Eleanor of destroying their old deeds and muniments to muddy the waters about who should own what. Even the Pecksall family's Victorian biographer, who was happy to call Eleanor a 'bete noir,' admitted that this was going too far, since much of the paperwork she was supposed to have destroyed could still be found nearly 300 years later, and indeed is still extant today.

When Eleanor Cotgrave died in May 1612, the burial record called her simply the 'ladie' of Sir George Douglas. Since the 67-year-old had only married him the previous November, this description was appropriate for less than one percent of her lifespan. But if she chose to define her importance by the powerful men she attracted in her lifetime, she could hardly complain if others defined her solely in relation to her husband once she was dead.

Nothing is known about what happened to Eleanor Cotgrave's striking portrait after it was painted in 1579, until 1910, when it was hanging on the walls of a country house called Sutton Place in Surrey in the South of England. It was bought by the Louisiana State University Museum in 1959, where is it now housed. She is half way around the world from her humble origins in Chester or her boastful and grand existence at court, but Eleanor looks out from the painting as clearly, boldly and defiantly now as she did in life.

From the date of the painting, 1579, it has been suggested that Eleanor's portrait was created to mark the occasion when her second husband became sheriff of Cheshire. But he had been sheriff twice before during their marriage (in 1573 and again in 1574) and he had also been Mayor of Chester. On none of these occasions did he feel the need to commission any paintings. The truth is that nothing in this picture is about Sir John Savage, or anyone or anything else except Eleanor Cotgrave. The coat of arms is hers alone, not the joint version they might have used together. The eyes in this painting are not looking sideways towards a matching pair on a companion portrait of her husband, they are staring out directly and deliberately at the viewer.

Eleanor Cotgrave is looking at you, but only to check that you are looking back at her.

CHAPTER THREE

1611

Randle Cotgrave publishes the first comprehensive French dictionary

Nobody knows why Randle Cotgrave produced one of the most important and interesting books of the seventeenth century. He claimed it was merely to occupy his time because he was otherwise lazy, but since it took him years and his employer had to release him from 'many hours' of his proper duties to work on it, this reason has the ring of very false modesty. It cannot have been for the money that he wrote his *Dictionarie of the French and English Tongues*. He did not become rich, and ended up having to pay for copies of his own book because of what he called the 'base' attitudes of people more interested in money than in scholarship. His dictionary was certainly not written to satisfy his employer, since Cotgrave freely admitted that the work could not be 'of less use' to William Cecil, whose family all spoke French fluently. It may be that Cotgrave simply recognised the need for a good French dictionary when he travelled on the continent, but the only specific place he is known to have visited was in the Low Countries where the locals spoke Germanic languages. It is hardly credible that Cotgrave compiled his book for the fame; almost nobody now knows who he was and there is no evidence that he was well known in his own lifetime.

The only explanation seems to be that Randle Cotgrave developed a love of words, of language and of scholarship. *Dictionarie of the French and English Tongues* was by far the largest and most comprehensive dictionary for translating French into English there had ever been. With over 900 pages it covers 48,000 French words from 'aache,' defined as a doleful cry or lamentation[1] through to 'zummach,' an eagle with a white

---

1   There are seven different entries under the single-letter word 'a' before aache.

Randle Cotgrave's *Dictionarie of the French and English Tongues* (1611) includes a small woodcut depicting him sitting down writing the book.

patch symbolising perfect goodness. It represented years of dedicated scholarship not just on the part of Cotgrave but also of the friends and collaborators on whom he relied for help, and possibly paid scribes or assistants. It revolutionised bilingual dictionaries by including a wide variety of vocabulary that had previously been snootily dismissed as inappropriate or unnecessary and it indirectly recorded a great deal not just about the languages of Renaissance England and France but also about their peoples.

Most of all, it captured the essence of one man, between a fancy scrolled engraving at the front and a short paragraph on grammatical conjunctions at the back.

Randle Cotgrave was born in Chester in about 1570 at a time when his family were on the cusp of having a significant role in the city's life.[2] When Randle was born his father had been the Bishop of Chester's registrar for about five years, and had fought off an attempt to get him sacked; Henry Chetham thought the job should have been his, just because his father had held it in the past. The young Cotgrave was taught at the grammar

2   His exact year of birth is confused by the fact that the ages he gave on various occasions are not consistent, but most of them suggest that he was born within a year or two either side of 1570. His older brother Robert's life is described in Chapter 11.

school in Chester, where he presumably started his interest in languages by learning Latin, although modern scholars think his Latin was not particularly good. Then in his later teens, he was sent to Cambridge, the first member of his family ever to go to university. It was the friends he made here that changed his life. They included Robert Heath who, like Cotgrave, was from the provincial middle classes. Heath would go on to a major legal career, serving as Attorney General, and as the Chief Justice first of the Court of Common Pleas and then of the King's Bench. Randle Cotgrave retained his undergraduate friendships, and he signed a bond for Heath (by then Sir Robert) over 30 years after they had matriculated together at St John's College in Cambridge.

Like many young men at the time, Randle Cotgrave did not complete his university degree, but he was admitted to the Inner Temple in 1591. During the 1590s, he appears to have spent at least some of the time back home in Cheshire, where his signature appears on various title deeds. Some of these involved the Brock family of Upton-by-Chester (who were cousins), and others related to property on the Wirral that his brother Robert would later buy.[3]

Cotgrave did not mean, however, to spend the rest of his life handling routine conveyancing matters in the provinces. He had made influential contacts at Cambridge and intended to use them. One of these was a young man called Richard Cecil, whose grandfather was the Queen's great and all-powerful first minster, Lord Burghley. Cotgrave and Cecil were the same age, had been at St John's together and were admitted to the London Inns of Court within a few weeks of one another. It was no doubt through Cecil that on 31 January 1598 Randle Cotgrave entered into a contract of employment with Elizabeth, Lady Hatton. She was the young widow of a man whose uncle had been the Lord Chancellor. More importantly, she was Richard Cecil's sister.

Entering the service of the Cecil family was the biggest stroke of luck that Randle Cotgrave ever had. He had opened the door to patronage for decades to come, and would later acknowledge that he owed to the Cecils, 'what I have been many years, whatsoever I am now, or look to be hereafter'. After two years working for Lady Hatton (who remarried and became the wife of the Attorney General Sir Edward Coke), he transferred to the household of another of her brothers, William Cecil, who took his grandfather's old title of Lord Burghley in 1605. It was while working for William Cecil that Cotgrave wrote his great work, the *Dictionarie of the French and English Tongues*.

---

3   See Chapter 11.

The project to compile the dictionary seems originally to have been an exercise in updating a much smaller one that had been published in 1593 by a man who used the pseudonym Claudius Holyband. But Cotgrave's desire for comprehensive coverage took over. He began, logically, at the beginning, with entries under the letter 'A' that were based on Holyband's earlier work. Then he abandoned that project because it was too limited in its scope and did not include enough scientific terms about natural history, enough useful, practical words about trade, law and politics or sufficient coverage of the vocabulary of popular literature. He ransacked French books to find thousands of words that had never before been included in any dictionary and he was the first to produce a French dictionary that was properly alphabetical. Long after Cotgrave's death, Guy Miege produced what he thought was a more practical French dictionary, which he described as 'the present use and modern orthography' of French. But his readers complained so much that in the next edition, he had to put back all of the words he had removed from Randle Cotgrave's great work.

But despite its size, its importance, and its critical acclaim, the *Dictionarie* was not really enough for Randle Cotgrave. His ambitions were huge, and he had wanted to create something far greater. He said that his eyes 'failed' to see into reality the outcome that he had imagined, and he had to be pressurized by his friends into publishing at all, rather than eternally waiting for unattainable perfection. According to his French friend Jean L'Oiseau de Tourval, Cotgrave could cite the authors, the books, and the page numbers to illustrate usage of every word in his book, but then his output would no longer be a dictionary but a 'labyrinth'.

Very few of Cotgrave's papers survive, and it is impossible to know exactly how he went about the monumental task of producing such a book, but there is some evidence that he allowed others to compile parts of the work, and two of his letters demonstrate that in the final stages, he sent manuscript sections to friends for them to review – Monsieur Beaulieu, the Secretary of the British Ambassador in Paris, and Monsieur Limery, about whom little is known except that he lived near Paris, was interested in the political and social events of the city, was a Protestant at a time of religious trouble in France and knew the staff at the British Embassy.

If you are adorable, astute, decisive, unobservant, pensioned, elderly or outstanding, or if you have done anything charmingly, avariciously or nastily, then you have Randle Cotgrave to thank for first recording the word to describe it. In the modern age of information technology, we use his words to describe the 'compatibility' of computer parts, to say whether a television programme or video is 'watchable' or if a signal is 'transmittable'. He appears to have been interested in nature and was the first to record the English names of the woodlouse, tigress, rock pigeon, warbler and water-wagtail. Assortment, drinkable, ignore, narrator, omelette, reappear, squeeze, recalculate, subsequently, and ungainly are all English words that Cotgrave is credited with first recording. In all, some 1,397 English words appear for the first time in Cotgrave's dictionary and there are a further 2,764 words where he was the first person to record a particular meaning. Although he knew the dictionary was not perfect, Randle Cotgrave was clearly proud of it, and he presented copies to various members of the nobility, including the Prince of Wales and the Countess of Rutland.

Randle Cotgrave was probably 41 when the *Dictionarie* was published. His interest was not sated, but perhaps his employer's patience was exhausted. He had talked of producing a second edition that would incorporate late comments and amendments from his friends, but it was in fact 21 years before a new edition appeared, and then another 18 before the third.[4]

During these years, he became an invaluable and indispensable part of the apparatus by which the Cecil family managed its vast interests across several counties. William Cecil's aunts, sisters and daughters married into various branches of the nobility, and in time Cotgrave became involved in the legal and business affairs of a host of the Cecil's in-laws, cousins, and connections including Sir William Drury, Sir Thomas Hatton and Sir Martin Lister. A series of court papers reveal how he knew the Earls of Bedford, Oxford and Stamford. He was a solicitor, a term that at the time had a specific meaning of someone who steered business through the complexities of the Court of Chancery. This involved spending a great deal of time in Westminster where the court sat, and in the City of London, where the legal profession was based. He was such a frequent user of the Chancery court than when an investigation was held into its fee structure in 1631, he was one of the regular clients interviewed about the costs involved. His evidence in Chancery cases referred numerous times to working at Exeter House (the Cecil family's London house) and he was quite comfortable attending the chambers of various law officers, including successive Attorneys General. He also had to travel

---

4   Editions appeared in 1632, 1650 and 1660 (by which time Cotgrave was dead); from the second edition onwards, there was an English-French dictionary added by Robert Sherwood.

to the various places where the Cecils and their in-laws owned estates, especially the fens of Lincolnshire, which he said he took little notice of. He frequently travelled into Essex, where he acted for the dowager Countess of Oxford, and he handled the probate of the Earl of Oxford's will. On at least one occasion, in 1624, he had to go to the Netherlands to deliver a large sum of money to his employer. Financial detail was something of a speciality and he regularly reviewed complex accounts for Exeter and his family. He had to work out whether the costs of draining fenland to make it more productive outweighed the profits expected to be derived from farming the improved ground. Many times, he was a trustee of property and estates, taking formal legal possession of manors, farms, houses and intangible property (such as the right to appoint clergymen to particular posts), sometimes as part of complicated deals and on other occasions when the Cecils were arranging marriage settlements. He fiercely defended the Cecil family's honour, hurriedly borrowing £200 rather than allowing his absent employer to be dishonoured by not paying a debt.

In the course of his duties, Cotgrave also made the acquaintance of many retainers and servants of the extended Cecil clan, lodging with Lady Hatton's receiver general and dealing with various surveyors, attendants and hangers-on.

Randle Cotgrave was present in 1640 when the Earl of Exeter made his will, and Cotgrave's signature appears as one of the witnesses. The earl died soon afterwards, and Randle, who was by now 70 years old, continued to work for the dowager countess. He sided with her when she fell out with the third earl (the son of Cotgrave's old university friend Richard Cecil). The dowager would outlive Randle, so it is possible he continued in her service into his old age. Randle Cotgrave's wife Margaret had died in 1639, and with the possible exception of Robert Cotgrave,[5] his brothers were long since dead. It is possible that his only close relative was his son John. He died an old man, probably 83 years of age, in 1653. He left no will, and the vast document collection he kept at his home was lost forever.

Although Randle Cotgrave's published work has been well studied, historians have tended to push the man himself to one side. A recent paper says 'information about [him] is quite limited' and his entry in the *Dictionary of National Biography* states that 'almost nothing is known of Cotgrave's life after 1612'.

In fact, rather a lot is known about him, given that he has been dead for

5   See Chapter 11.

nearly 400 years and his personal archives are long gone. The *Dictionarie* and the surviving legal papers paint a consistent picture of a complex and interesting personality. Both show Cotgrave to have been meticulously concerned with detail. Anyone who could produce a dictionary defining 48,000 words would have to be at least slightly compulsive. But we also know from his own preface and the introduction written by one of his French friends that he wanted to strive for even greater and more perfect completeness and that he could cite every quotation from memory even down to the page number of the book it came from. Cotgrave's evidence in various court cases gives the same impression. He kept paperwork for decades and could lay his hands on the minutest detail. Although he had accurate copies of important documents (and knew they were correct because he could compare them with copies certified under the Great Seal of England), he nevertheless asked officials to make diligent searches for the originals. He kept letters and papers indefinitely and had 'a very great quantitie or number of deedes, evidences and writings'. Sadly, only one of the letters he received appears to have survived, and it is carefully annotated in his distinctive handwriting with the date, the sender and the subject. He could recite financial figures from decades earlier, down to the nearest penny, and he testified with absolute confidence of the precise dates – 30 years before – on which he had started working for Lady Hatton and when he had transferred his employment to her brother the Earl of Exeter. On one occasion, he gave a former workmate an alibi by producing an almanac in which he had made a note, seven years earlier, recording the date when the colleague had arrived in London; Cotgrave even remembered that his friend had on that particular occasion travelled to the capital from Yorkshire via Nottinghamshire. Given that these are merely the details he happened to produce in the witness statements that happen to survive, Cotgrave's memory and document collection must have contained a truly vast array of trivia. A picture emerges of someone almost pathologically obsessed with inconsequential facts, someone who had the potential to be rather boring, the sort of person you would not want to get cornered with at a party.

That would be grossly unfair, because a funny and engaging personality shines through both the dictionary and the surviving archives. In fact, what makes Randle Cotgrave's book so special is not that it marked a major change in the way dictionaries were compiled, or even that in recording so many new words and definitions, it preserved a snapshot of what was important to his age. The best thing about it is that he could not help himself from immortalising his personality on the pages of a work that, on the face of it, should have been objective and academic. When he translated a proverb about it being easier to ride somewhere than to walk, he joked in parenthesis that 'some lazy fellow' must have written it. When he included a saying about how good needed help to flourish over evil, he added that this was particularly true 'in this unjust age' and when interpreting an odd French adage about fighting over an abbot's mitre that you are never going to get, he clearly could not help waxing lyrical about 'castles in the air, moonshine under water'. Describing the colour the French knew as 'verte d'oie' – literally goose green – Cotgrave said it was a yellowish green, but graphically described what he really meant – the colour of 'goose-turd'.

It is equally plain from the legal documents that Cotgrave did not just know a wide range of people, from earls, dukes, ministers, ambassadors and judges down to clerks, farmers and workmen, but that he knew them well, in a way that was only possible because he got on with people. He 'did well know' William Graves, Cecil's overseer, was in 'a place of near correspondence' with John Franklin and 'often in ... company' with another friend. In 1610, when he wrote to his French friend Monsieur Beaulieu, ostensibly for assistance with his dictionary, he used more than half of the letter to ask for help securing a job for a young friend.

The most poignant indication of Randle Cotgrave's humanity is a throwaway comment about the first Earl of Exeter, who had died at the age of 80 in 1623. Randle had not been formally employed by the old peer, but by his daughter and then his son (who became the second earl). But from time to time towards the end of his life, the old man had used Randle Cotgrave's services on various bits and pieces of business. When they had been together in the earl's London mansion, the old man 'was sometimes pleased to talk with [Cotgrave] of matters'. A picture of Randle Cotgrave emerges that marries his compulsive attention to detail about words with a warm affection for using them, by talking in a relaxed and conversational manner.

To use words and meanings that he first recorded, Randle Cotgrave liked to 'gossip' and to 'leaf' through books. He did not do things incorrectly, lukewarmly, nastily, senselessly or roguishly. In short, he was astute, civilized, outstanding, unsurpassable.

CHAPTER FOUR

1838

Ellen Cotgreave drinks some 'ginger wine'

Something very specific is recorded about Ellen Cotgreave's early childhood. That makes her remarkable, perhaps even unique, among the people whose stories are told in this book.

On 10 May 1838, 17-month old Ellen and her older brother George wanted a drink. Her mother, Sarah Cotgreave, went to the cellar of their home at Great Barrow, about 5 miles from Chester. She reappeared with a small bottle, which she said contained ginger wine. Sarah drank some herself, and then shared the remainder among the two children and a woman called Margaret Astbury, who was staying with them. The bottle cannot have been clearly labelled, because Mrs Astbury asked Mrs Cotgreave to check that it really did contain wine.

Although Sarah Cotgreave said she drank the wine without initially noticing anything odd, Margaret Astbury felt very unwell immediately – it was 'as if her throat had been set on fire'. Within a few minutes, all four of the people who had drunk from the bottle were violently ill, and a messenger was sent to fetch a doctor as quickly as possible.

Although known as a surgeon, 28-year-old Robert Bostock Ankers does not appear to have had much medical training. At the time, he assisted his brother, who was in general medical practice, but within a few years, he was known as a 'surgeon and farmer' and then for the rest of his life just a farmer. So perhaps he was not very interested in medicine, or not very good at it. Probably he could not really do much anyway in the circumstances, especially since it must have been almost an hour before he arrived. He administered what he thought 'suitable remedies,' (perhaps an emetic), took the bottle for analysis and left.

Six hours after drinking the poison, Ellen Cotgreave died. Her mother, her brother and Mrs Astbury remained gravely ill for at least a week. By then the dregs of the liquid had been investigated, and it turned out to be Extract of Lead, a chemical occasionally found in tiny amounts in medicines, especially eye drops, but certainly not meant to be drunk in any quantity.

A few days later, the coroner held an inquest in Barrow, and the jury found that the little girl had died accidentally.

Ellen's mother must have recovered fairly soon, because within a year she had given birth to another child; three more followed in the next few years, including another daughter called Ellen. The other child who had drunk the poison, three-year-old George Cotgreave, recovered fully and lived for another 77 years. He called his eldest daughter Ellen.

CHAPTER FIVE

~ 1849 ~

Sibella Cotgrave is admitted to a lunatic asylum

When Sibella Cotgrave was admitted to the Lunatic Asylum at Plympton in Devon in the late 1840s, it was a blessing that her mental condition meant that she probably did not realise where she was. The House of Lords had heard in 1844 that magistrates had repeatedly visited Plympton and complained about the appalling treatment of the patients. One had been placed in restraints for two months, 'merely for breaking windows,' a woman who had given birth a few weeks earlier was 'confined by a straight waistcoat and chained by the arm and leg to a bench,' the bedrooms were wet and 'besmeared with filth,' and there were 17 patients in a room where no more than ten could possibly sit down at the same time. The food was barely any better than the accommodation, consisting of bread, milk and water for breakfast and supper, with a main meal of boiled rice, bread and potatoes three times a week, pease soup with vegetables on a Tuesday and protein just twice a week. 'We can give no other general description,' the examiners said 'than that it was disgusting and offensive' before listing a further catalogue of stinking, cold, dark, cramped accommodation in which pitiful, filthy women and girls were just about kept alive in the same rooms as an 'idiot boy' and a dangerous, criminally mad man. The proprietor – a surgeon called Richard Langworthy – 'ought not to be entrusted with the care of Insane Persons'.

But he was entrusted with the care of Sibella Cotgrave, a married woman in her forties with a teenage son. Her husband was a former naval lieutenant who had joined the Coast Guard. It is hard to believe that Richard Cotgrave knowingly allowed his wife to be so appallingly maltreated and it is possible that, as a private patient, her conditions were

Sibella Cotgrave's husband, Richard, seems to have shut her up in a squalid asylum and put her out of his mind [Reproduced by kind permission of Gillie Turner].

not as bad as the state-funded paupers with whom the Commissioners in Lunacy were concerned. Certainly in Gloucestershire, her relative John Farmer Cotgreave seems to have enjoyed a much better standard of care, when he was declared insane in 1849. There the inspectors found that 'the rooms, and also the bedding ... were generally very clean ... The dinner consisted of bacon, greens, potatoes and suet pudding with half a pint of small beer'. At Fairford Asylum, where he was a patient, the principal complaint was that 'the means of amusement ... should be increased'. Amusement was completely unknown at Plympton.

Born in 1800 into a prosperous Cornish family that had been settled in the same parish for five hundred years, Sibella Brendon had been an appropriate match for Richard Cotgrave. He was just a year older, a naval officer whose father had fought with Nelson, and his family also had a track record of living in rural comfort in Cheshire for half a millennium. Richard and Sibella were married in 1829, when they were both in their

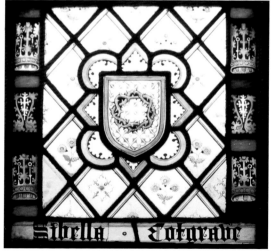

Apparently abandoned by her husband, Sibella Cotgrave's blood relations erected a large and expensive stained-glass window to her memory and that of her son, who was a teenager when she went mad and killed herself.

late 20s, and she may well have found the life lonely. Lieutenant Cotgrave was away at sea for months on end; he was, for example, on a three month tour of South American waters when their son, Richard Edward Forbes Cotgrave was born just over two years after the wedding. Later in the 1830s, Lieutenant Cotgrave transferred to the domestic Coast Guard service. Perhaps he recognised that Sibella did not enjoy the solitary existence when he was away for long periods, or perhaps he was himself fed up with the discomfort, violence and general unpleasantness of a naval career. He had even been required to serve as an untrained surgeon on HMS *Tribune* when many officers and crew were out of action through sickness. One of his brothers, also a naval officer,[1] had lost an eye, while various of his relatives in military service suffered severe injury, near death experiences and fatal tropical infections. The change was good for Richard Cotgrave, who appears to have thrived in his new role as a Coast Guard service. He was highly thought of for his efforts in controlling smuggling, and was praised by the Royal Humane Society for his courage in saving lives.

At some stage, Sibella's mental state worsened and eventually she was admitted to the Lunatic Asylum. Luckily for her, she had made her already made her will. Written on blue paper ten years earlier, Sibella Cotgrave's will was the first in over six hundred years of the family's existence to be made by a married woman whose husband was still alive, because married women had no property of their own to bequeath. Everything belonged automatically to their husbands, wherever it had come from. Sibella Cotgrave could not leave her possessions to anyone in a will because by definition she could have none to leave.

But by the time Sibella had been married, although the law remained unchanged, clever lawyers had invented a method that gave her near guaranteed control over her own money. The marriage settlement was finalised the day before the wedding ceremony and it declared that a significant sum of money should be invested either in Government bonds or in some other secure investment. The legal owners were the trustees and they were to pay Sibella the interest and dividends. The documentation that accompanied the wedding in 1829 went even further, specifying that Sibella could decide what happened to the capital after she died. She could write a will, appoint the trustees of her marriage settlement as her executors, and they would be legally bound to respect the trust and do as she directed. In fact, Sibella Cotgrave left the income on her investments to her husband Richard for the rest of his life, and

---

1   Their father Isaac was also a naval officer, see Chapter 13.

then directed her trustees to dispose of the assets and pass full control of the proceeds to her son when he reached the age of 21 or married.

If Sibella's first experience of serious mental illness was when she moved to Devon early in 1849, at least it did not last long. She was dead within six months. On 17 June that year, she hanged herself, 'being of unsound mind'. The neglectful approach of the proprietor surely contributed, but there are hints that once she was shut up in the asylum, Richard Cotgrave not only put her out of sight but also out of mind. He can hardly have been unaware of the institution's poor record, and when the coroner certified the death, Richard did not take an attentive interest. Nobody was even sure of the absent husband's first name – there is a blank space on Sibella's death certificate where it should be written. Perhaps he was not unusual in neglecting his mad relative; at Fairford, John Farmer Cotgreave's fellow patients 'complained that they never saw or heard from any of their friends'. But her own blood relatives the Brendons cared about Sibella, even if her husband did not. After her death, it was in their local church that a large stained glass window was commissioned in her memory. It is in the parish church at Trusham in Devon, where her niece Sibella Gregory was married to the rector. The Brendons felt a special affinity with Trusham church. They bought a chalice and an alms plate in memory of Sibella Cotgrave's nephew and when the whole church was restored in 1865, the Brendon family 'desired … the exclusive privilege' of renovating the interior.

When Sibella died, her son, Richard Edward Forbes Cotgrave, was a 17-year-old cadet at Addiscombe Military Academy. In the same week that she killed herself, he was recorded as having scored highly both for his 'good conduct' and his ability to speak Hindustani. He was given the local rank of Ensign in the Indian army and was presented to the Queen before travelling out to Mumbai and serving with 'great spirit and zeal'. He reached the rank of full Colonel, retired, and died (wealthy) in his early 40s. He does not seem to have been close to his father – they did not live near one another and when he died, Colonel Cotgrave chose to be buried with more distant relatives, not with Lieutenant Richard Cotgrave, who had passed away just three years earlier.

It cannot be a coincidence that the huge window commemorating Sibella Cotgrave's life shows a very familiar scene of a loving mother with her son. The middle panel shows the Virgin Mary and the infant Jesus. On either side, the shepherds and the three wise men kneel and offer their gifts. Nor is hard to see why later, when the window was enhanced to commemorate Colonel Richard Cotgrave's death (23 years after his mother's) the quotation from St John's Gospel was adapted to include the words 'Young Man' which do not appear in the original – 'Young Man, take up thy bed and walk'.

To accompany the original imagery, Sibella's family, apparently led by her sister Mary, chose as the main Biblical text some words from St Luke: *'Lumen ad revelationem gentium'* – a light to lighten the gentiles. This looks like a clear hint that in former days, before her wretched end in a place that even the Victorians thought was too dark, Sibella Cotgrave had shone a bright and joyous light into the lives of her family and friends.

CHAPTER SIX

1850

Robert Cotgreave takes out a patent

When he looked back on his life, Robert Cotgreave had a great deal to be proud of. He had patented an invention that had received awards and praise from around the world, he had accrued modest wealth and he had accomplished some very fine cartography that was not only useful but which resulted in lasting artefacts of beauty. But somehow, perusing the perfunctory probate court document that wrapped up his earthly affairs a few weeks after his death, it is hard to believe that he died content with his success.

His eldest son and his grandson, both named Robert Cotgreave after him, were dead, and another son's birth had been deliberately obscured. It is possible there was a third son, illegitimate and unacknowledged. He lived with the knowledge that his mother had died in an horrific accident while in his house, that he had never paid off huge debts resulting from failures of the past, and that nobody seemed quite sure how to describe his status: was he a gentleman, or a civil engineer, a land surveyor or a farmer? It must have been particularly sad that nobody ever thought to define him in relation to his invention, once hailed as a brilliant award-winning technological breakthrough, but in which nobody now seemed remotely interested.

Born some time before 1809 on his father's farm at Eccleston in Cheshire, Robert had an older brother who was destined to tend the family land, so he looked for alternative skills early in life. A simple but attractive map that Robert Cotgreave drew of the fields at Stanney, a few miles from his home, is dated 1818, when he was a child of about ten. It is hard to believe the date because few children of that age would have the patience and skill to produce such a plan, but there is no doubt that he must have learned cartographic and surveying skills very well in his youth because he excelled at them as an adult.

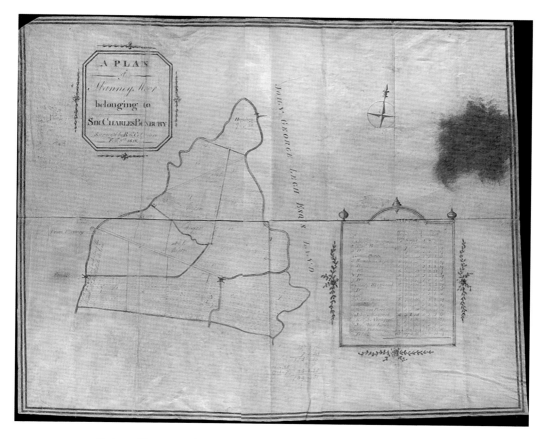

Robert Cotgreave learned his skills as a surveyor in childhood; he
drew this plan of a neighbour's estate in Cheshire when he was about
10 [Reproduced by kind permission of Suffolk Record Office, Bury St
Edmunds branch. Ref E18/711/4].

The rest of his early life seems to have been unremarkable. His father
died when he was 15, in his early twenties he married a local farmer's
daughter, settled down in the village where he had been born and became
a normal member of society, substantial enough in his status to serve on
local juries, but with no realistic pretensions to anything greater.

After bearing three children in four years, his wife died before her
thirtieth birthday and Robert was left a single father with three infants
and a small farm. He also had a talent for land surveying at a moment
in history when such a skill was about to be in great demand. Recent
legislation aimed to rationalise ancient tithes, and to do so, it required

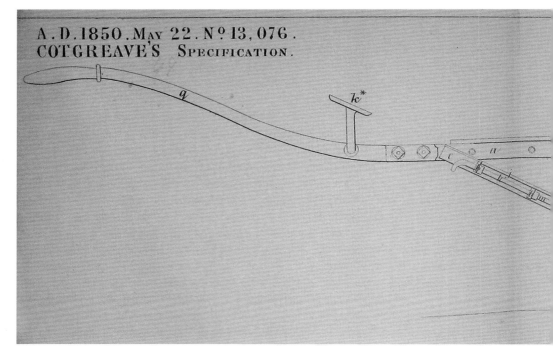

Robert Cotgreave took out a patent on his new design for a draining plough in 1850 [GB Patent 1850 13076].

accurate maps of exactly who owned exactly what pieces of land in each parish. Cotgreave's maps of Tattenhall, Bradley, Cuddington, Malpas and Duckington all survive, along with receipts for the payments he received for the work. They are careful, intricate and skilful, and they are also beautiful.

Despite his surveying success, he was still listed as a farmer in the 1841 census, and that was obviously his main occupation. He was still tied to the land in Eccleston, where he had lived his entire life to date. He was among the founders of the local Association for the Prosecution of the Felons, which offered rewards for help in convicting thieves stealing agricultural products (anything from cattle to potatoes), and he continued to serve on the local coroner's juries, one of the civic duties that almost defined a class of men who formed the matrix of village society.

Having lost his wife, Robert did not entirely eschew female company. In 1841, an unmarried teenager called Mary Durham had a son who in later life claimed that his father had been a Cheshire farmer called Robert

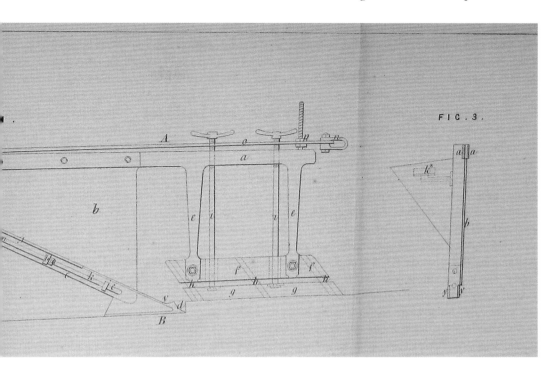

Cotgreave. A few years later, Robert certainly had a son called Alfred with another unmarried woman, Mary Bird, the much younger daughter of a local surgeon.[1]

However, unlike Mary Durham, Mary Bird became a permanent fixture in Robert Cotgreave's life, and they lived together as if they were man and wife. They eventually married in 1860, less than a year before she died. It remains a mystery why they did not simply legitimise their relationship sooner or why, if they had lived together happily for at least 15 years, they suddenly felt the need to stop pretending they were married and actually become so. Perhaps they were worried about her right to inherit his money if their relationship was not sanctioned by law.

As the children grew up, Robert Cotgreave's life began to become more interesting. In 1848, he became the tenant of Rake Farm, a 280-acre holding in his home village of Eccleston that was owned by the Marquis

1   See Chapter 8.

of Westminster. Robert was now employing 13 men as well as a dairy maid and household servants. Tragedy struck the following year when his 76-year-old mother was standing close to the hearth at Rake Farm. Her clothes caught a spark from the fire, she was engulfed in flames and quickly died.

The size of his holding and the number of men he had to toil the land afforded Robert the time to work on perfecting the invention that would obsess him in the coming years. It was a plough that was very effective at cutting the trenches required to sink the pipes that were essential to enhance the drainage of wet fields. Using this plough was easier and quicker than other drainage methods, taking one tenth of the time of traditional approaches and being accomplished for half the price. Nobody had believed that a horse drawn plough could dig deep enough trenches, but everyone who saw Robert Cotgreave's contraption in action was rapidly convinced. Cotgreave organised a demonstration in which during a single day, he cut the ditches, laid the pipes, and backfilled the holes over one complete acre and dug half the trenches for a second acre. The plough was not hampered by large stones when they got in the way, it was said to be effective in all weathers except when the ground was frozen hard, and it could handle all types of soil. The speed and accuracy with which it laid the pipes was 'surprising'. Robert's landlord, Lord Westminster, was impressed, and he began to garner testimonials from around the world. He had 'vindicated his county,' with Cheshire said to be well known for failing to adopt new agricultural technologies. He received appreciative correspondence from Massechussetts while the *Farmers' Magazine* in London and the American Institute in New York both published accounts of the plough's remarkable success. Visitors came from Sweden, France and Switzerland to examine the plough.

In 1850, Robert had done something unusual; he took out a patent on his clever invention in the hope that he could profit from its success. The plough was clearly taking over his life and he was neglecting his agricultural livelihood. He gave up the tenancy of Rake Farm when he was over £700 in arrears with his rent and moved 200 miles to Ipswich, where he knew nobody, because that was the home of one of the country's foremost manufacturers of farm machinery. Robert's prototypes had presumably been produced by local blacksmiths in Cheshire, but now the company of Ransomes and Sims began making what became known as Cotgreave's Subsoil Plough. They introduced new levels of professionalism, and especially a more aggressive approach to promoting sales. The company printed handbills advertising the plough and made sure the contraption was exhibited at agricultural shows, where it began to win awards. These activities were valuable as promotional propaganda in their own right, but they also guaranteed coverage in major publications such as the *Times* and the *Illustrated London News*. Robert Cotgreave was said to be working as a surveyor in Ipswich in 1855, but he was surely doing this unenthusiastically to make ends meet while his mind was concentrating on the future of the Subsoil Plough. But as he sat with his awards from the Royal Agricultural Society and his newspaper clippings, Cotgreave failed to realise that the plough did not have a future.

By the late 1850s, in the face of competing alternatives, interest in the plough had died away; Robert Cotgreave moved to Bolney in Sussex and then within a year or so moved again to London. He married the woman he had lived with for decades and settled in Lambeth with her and their son Alfred. She died within a year of the marriage, so Robert and Alfred Cotgreave gravitated back to Cheshire and appear to have been living back in or near Eccleston by the mid 1860s.

Robert's eldest son, also called Robert Cotgreave, was apprenticed to a draper in Chester, but he died of tuberculosis, leaving Robert senior with a married daughter (he appears to have been living with her) and a single son. The son, William Parker Cotgreave, married in 1866 and rapidly gave Robert a grandson, who was also called Robert. But the child died in infancy, so that within four years, the elder Robert, now in his mid 50s, had seen his son Robert Cotgreave die aged 32 and his grandson of the same name die when he was two. He acquired other grandchildren and he was no doubt delighted to spend time with them.

As he aged, Robert Cotgreave took lodgings in the city of Chester, he may well have continued to work as a land surveyor, something he never quite gave up and which linked the disappointed elderly man with the eager child he had once been, decades ago when he had carefully measured and mapped the fields at Stanney.

Robert Cotgreave died in the outskirts of the city in 1874, at the age of 66, almost certainly of tuberculosis.[2] His body was taken the couple of miles to Eccleston, the village where he had been born and where he had lived the first two thirds of his life. It was here that he had abandoned a badly-run, debt-ridden farm, here that his first wife had died in her 20s and here that his mother had been consumed by a conflagration in his own home. But it was also here that he learned the surveying skills that had kept him in work, and here that he had first created the masterpiece which had generated such praise and such interest from across the world.

---

2   His death certificate names the cause as Phthisis, which generally means pulmonary TB.

CHAPTER SEVEN

1854

Charles Cotgreave enters the Grand National

In record offices, lawyers' safes, libraries and homes around Britain, there are documents bearing many thousands of words written by Charles Cotgreave. None of them are his letters, diaries, personal papers or accounts, nothing that reveals anything about his thoughts or his personality. But it is a fair bet that on the afternoon of 1 March 1854, his heart rate reached a peak, his adrenalin levels soared, and he experienced overwhelming excitement, before suffering sudden, crushing, shocking disappointment.

Cotgreave's start in life was neither especially positive nor unusually poor. His father, also called Charles, was a master shoemaker and a freeman of the city of Chester.[1] But there were 12 children, seven of them boys. The most Charles junior could reasonably expect was that his father would use his contacts among the municipal leaders to get him a job and perhaps provide some very modest financial investment to start his career. After that, he would have to grasp whatever opportunity came along. There was unlikely to be a second chance.

Charles Cotgreave senior understood that literate, office-based work would prove more profitable and comfortable than manual labour, even skilled work such as his own. His eldest son worked in a solicitor's office, managing the affairs of many of the local dignitaries, another became a clerk in the diocesan probate court and one of the youngest worked in an office as a teenager, before using his education to get ahead in the newly-invented railway industry where he became a carriage inspector.[2] Charles

---

1   See Chapter 25.
2   William Cotgreave, see photograph, p. x.

Alfred Cotgreave looks very serious in this photograph, but he had a sense of humour, and according to one historian deserved to have been born in the age of television [Reproduced from Cotgreave's *Views and Memoranda of Public Libraries* (1901)].

the idea of driving a horse and cart. He claimed to have no previous relevant experience[2] but was determined to have a go. Egged on by drunken friends, Alfred convinced a farmer (who was himself drunk) to let him take control of a horse and trap. As Alfred showed off in front of his friends, his inebriation rapidly became clear and they 'came to grief'.

But however much fun he was having, this was not the life for Alfred Cotgreave. He married in 1870, and perhaps his new wife urged him not to leave her alone while he travelled on lengthy voyages, or maybe he just realised he would be happier doing something else.

It is hard to imagine a bigger change of direction but when Cotgreave abruptly ended his incipient naval career, it was to become a librarian. In January 1874, Mrs Durward, who looked after the Royal Exchange Library in Manchester, was unwell. It was plain that she would be off work for at least four weeks. For reasons they did not record (cost was probably one), the shareholders of the private establishment decided that the 26-year-old former seaman Alfred Cotgreave was a suitable stand-in; they offered him a one-month contract. It was the start he needed. Mrs

---

2   If that were true, it would surely mean that he had not grown up at his parents' home – no teenage boy whose father ran a farm of 280 acres in the mid nineteenth century can have escaped a task so integral to the business as controlling horses.

Although he ran a number of libraries, Alfred Cotgreave failed in his application to become librarian in his native city of Chester. When he compiled a book about Britain's public libraries, he included more photographs of Chester library than those in other towns [Reproduced from Cotgreave's *Views and Memoranda of Public Libraries* (1901)].

Durward's illness continued, the job was extended, and Alfred performed extremely well. Officers of the Library Committee wanted him stay permanently, but the rules did not allow it once Mrs Durward was well enough to return to her desk.

This brief experience gave Cotgreave his first basic familiarity with librarianship and he made the most of it. By the following year, he had a proper job as a one of the network of assistants who staffed Birmingham's public libraries. By 1879, he was writing papers that were accepted for presentation at the Library Association's Annual Conference, the major event in the calendar of an endeavour that was growing rapidly.

It is difficult now to appreciate quite how new and important the library movement was at the time. The first legislation that enabled English authorities to use local taxes to pay for free libraries had been passed in 1850 when Alfred Cotgreave was a child. The vast majority of towns and boroughs did not yet have public libraries but new and impressive institutions were beginning to open all over the country. Librarianship was a fertile, unbroken ground where an ambitious youngster could make his mark. And Alfred Cotgreave turned out to be an ambitious youngster with a mark to make. When he stood up to deliver his paper at the Birmingham meeting of the Library Association, the youth from Chester unveiled the detailed plans and careful thinking behind an invention that he believed would revolutionise the way people used libraries, and which he thought might make him rich – the Cotgreave Library Indicator.

Free libraries, with a large stock of books and a mass readership, needed a simple and effective way of recording whether a particular

Alfred Cotgreave relentlessly promoted his inventions and methods. This advertisement for his magazine rack appears in his own book, *Views and Memoranda of Public Libraries* (1901).

volume was available or whether it was already on loan to someone. The idea of readers selecting from open shelves had not yet caught on, so users had to ask the staff whether the library had a copy of any book they wanted and if so, whether someone else had already borrowed it. Cotgreave's 'indicator' provided a supposedly simple way of ascertaining how many copies of a book were in the library's stock, whether any were out, and if so who had them. Over the years, his crusade to convert librarians to the use of indicators in general and the patented Cotgreave Indicator in particular would come to dominate the wider perception of his character. It was this relentless quest for publicity for the indicator that prompted the modern comparison with television celebrities, persistently pushing themselves forward to the world.

Alfred Cotgreave evidently did well at Birmingham. The Libraries Committee increased his wages by 17 per cent in recognition of his workload and achievements.

From Birmingham, Alfred was invited to take up the post of Librarian just down the road at the new Wednesbury Free Library. Excitingly, this would be a blank canvas for him because the library had not yet opened. It was in the process of being planned. The Free Library and Public Baths Committee had 'a most careful and lengthened consideration of the applications' before recommending Mr Alfred Cotgreave should be employed. He took up the post in December 1877 and set about overseeing the construction of the library building, purchasing books, soliciting donations, cataloguing the stock and letting contracts to supply newspapers.

The official opening took place in March 1878, when local dignitaries and their wives gathered in the Library's Reading Room, along with 'a large assemblage of the general inhabitants' of Wednesbury. This boded well for Alfred's belief that Free Libraries would genuinely serve the interests of the masses. The Chairman of the Library made an eloquent speech, and then told the crowd, 'It is well that you should know the librarian'. He asked Cotgreave to step forward and say when books would start to be issued. 'I propose to open the Library at ten o'clock tomorrow,' came Alfred's short but confident reply.

It was soon clear that the library would be a major success. An Assistant Librarian was appointed, 290 books a day were being borrowed and the Committee was not merely expressing great satisfaction with Alfred Cotgreave's work but proving that they meant it by giving him a pay rise from £100 a year to £120. His annual salary as a seaman had been just £24.

Alfred Cotgreave was not just becoming an experienced librarian, he had managed the entire set-up process for a significant and successful institution. It was only a matter of time before an even more important local authority sought his services. The moment came in 1880, when he moved to Richmond to oversee the establishment the first Free Library under the Libraries Acts to be opened in London, then the largest city in the world.[3]

Alfred had clearly impressed the local dignitaries because they had increased their initial estimate of his salary from £100 per year to £120, presumably to match what he was getting in Wednesbury. He would also get free accommodation in Richmond, but not until construction of the Library building was complete. Alfred promised 'constant attention to my duties and strict obedience to the wishes of the Committee'. He went on to establish a reputation for being 'experienced, capable and courteous'.

It was while he was at Richmond that Cotgreave began to dabble more seriously with designing and inventing useful appliances. A design survives from this time for a paperweight, but it was his furniture – shelves, step ladders, magazine racks and most of all his indicator – that really enthused him. He exhibited his inventions at the Library Association meeting, held that year in Dublin. On a much bigger scale, the International Health Exhibition not only displayed Alfred's contraptions to the world, it actually used some of them in operating the public library which formed part of the event. His first attempt to apply for a patent – for a type of bookshelves – did not result in a patent being granted, but over the subsequent two decades, Cotgreave would register numerous ideas for improvements in library and book-related apparatus. He would become known as a source of assistance and advice on communicating with the Patent Office and would form two companies to exploit his ingenuity, one called the Library Aids Company and another named Cotgreave's Indicators Ltd. Some of his inventions were popular, others less so, especially when he strayed from his area of expertise into things that had nothing to do with libraries. His attempt to secure a patent on a walking stick or umbrella with an integral matchbox and cigarette case failed at the first hurdle and so did his cork extractor. His combined book cover, bookmark and satchel, however, was deemed 'a most useful article'. His automatic step was celebrated in the journal *Invention* as 'of great utility'. When he left Richmond, the Chairman of the Library Committee gave him a testimonial that focused on his inventions. Soon after, his new

---

3   There had been a public library in Westminster since 1856, but its legal basis was different; Alfred Cotgreave himself described it as being 'in a very inadequate building in a back street'.

employers also recorded that they were impressed by Alfred's inventions and designs, especially the 'ingenious' indicator, which was coming to dominate his reputation for entrepreneurship.

When a committee of worthies was established in Wandsworth to put into effect a ratepayers' vote to found a free library, they needed some professional help. The Richmond Commissioners agreed that Alfred Cotgreave could assist, even giving him permission to take a regular half-day off on Friday afternoons to go to Wandsworth. But they lived to regret their generous decision a few months later, when their counterparts in Wandsworth offered Alfred a full time job. After a short negotiation, Cotgreave accepted the post on a salary of £180 per year, made even more lucrative because he was to receive free accommodation, coals and gas.

There was a great deal to do before the Library could open, but by now it was a well-worn path for Alfred. There was £106 worth of furniture to acquire and the Books Committee had to decide what volumes to buy. Cotgreave had to issue tenders for contracts to supply newspapers and for regular cleaning of the library. He had to draft 'various forms' for applications to borrow books, to authorise borrowing by people who were not automatically entitled to use the facilities as ratepayers, and so on. All these tasks were accomplished on time, and the doors were opened to the public in the spring of 1885; the official inauguration by the Lord Mayor of London took place on 1 October.

In the world of libraries, Alfred Cotgreave was now an established figure. However, for him it was not enough to have managed for the third time the successful establishment of a major public institution; he needed to prove just how successful it was. At Richmond, he had collated excruciatingly boring, precise and extensive data on the quotidian issue of books. But when the first annual report of the Wandsworth library was published in 1886, it contained a far more interesting and useful digest of who had borrowed which kinds of works. Darwin's *Origin of Species* was read by artists, builders, clerks and a whitesmith, Dante's *Divine Comedy* by a clerk, a law agent, musicians and a solicitor. Kingsley's *Westwood Ho!*, slightly lighter reading, was enjoyed by bricklayers, carpenters and gasfitters.

Despite his obvious success, at the end of the year, Cotgreave resigned his position at Wandsworth 'for reasons wholly apart from his duties as Librarian'. It is not clear what those reasons were, but they were possibly to do with his health, which seems never to have been robust. An announcement appeared that he was to be in charge at the new Wimbledon Free Library, but the report turned out to be false and someone else took the Wimbledon job. Whether the story was simply the result of an overactive rumour mill or whether Alfred had been in line for the appointment but some difficulty had arisen is not clear. In any case, Cotgreave was soon requesting references of his former employers as he sought a new challenge.

Throughout his career, Alfred Cotgreave would strive to make it easy for anyone to find the book they needed, even if they did not know which book that was. At Richmond, he had been officially 'instructed' to produce a catalogue, but only after he had made the suggestion himself, conscious that many readers lacked the courage to ask librarians for help. He became such an authority on cataloguing books that when he gave a lecture on the subject, he joked to his audience that they probably thought they would not get home until the early hours of the following morning. His libraries always issued catalogues and the one catalogue at Wandsworth was 200 pages covering everything from the Abbey Buildings at Westminster (look in the *Archaeological Journal*) to Zoologists (try Duncan's *Heroes of Science*). These were undoubtedly useful but Cotgreave realised that what was really needed was a more systematic index, one that would allow readers to locate material on whatever subject interested them, regardless of which publication it was to be found in.

So towards the end of 1887, Alfred Cotgreave was engaged by the proprietors of the Guille-Alles Library on Guernsey to catalogue their collection in a much more detailed way than had ever been tried for any library. The Guille-Alles had 40,000 books, a quarter of them in French. Cotgreave set to work in producing an 'encyclopaedic catalogue' of the whole collection, with the assistance of a francophone aide. It would take four years of reading, tabulating, indexing, describing and checking before the book would be published. It ran to a colossal 1,550 pages of tightly packed small print. It was so monumental that one of Cotgreave's critics satirically described it as being as large as the island of Guernsey itself. This scrupulous and comprehensive immersion in the printed word was what Alfred Cotgreave really wanted to do. It was later said of him that he was an 'omnivorous reader who takes a real interest in his work'. These qualities shine through in the encyclopaedic catalogue and there can be no doubt that the laborious work made Cotgreave happy. A decade and a half later, he would remember this as the happiest time of his life and would long to return to Guernsey to recapture those contented feelings. The pleasure clearly rubbed off on his colleagues because when he eventually left the Guille-Alles Library, they did not merely buy him a present (a pair of binoculars engraved with his name), they also printed an address which recalled the 'pleasant days we have spent together' and thanking him for his 'many past kindnesses'.

In his zeal to bring books and periodicals to the widest possible audience, Alfred Cotgreave was now among the most experienced people in the world. He had worked in six different libraries, and had been the founding organiser of three. He had personally created the most impressive library catalogue in the world. He was a leading light of the librarian's professional organisation and he had a successful company making and selling the useful devices that he had personally invented. He even had the seemingly perfect wife for a man of his interests – Maria Cotgreave was sufficiently interested in and proficient at librarianship that she was offered senior librarian jobs in her own right, but chose to remain dedicatedly by Alfred's side, assisting and promoting his career.

It was difficult to see what challenges remained. Despite his long list of achievements, Alfred Cotgreave was still only 45 when he left Guernsey to become the chief librarian of West Ham. Now indisputably part of London, West Ham was then a populous parish in Essex that had morphed into a suburban Borough. Alfred would stay here for 14 years, and even then would only retire because his health demanded it.

Two projects dominated Alfred Cotgreave's time at West Ham. Both were hugely important and influential elements of a drive to make it easier for everyone to access the benefits of reading. Although the specific results of his two big experiments were disappointing, nobody did more than Cotgreave to spearhead that drive.

The first project was to compile a universal index to the subject matter of English publications. Building on the experience of his previous attempts at catalogues, he wanted to produce a reasonably priced, accessible volume that would help readers find literally anything. It would take another ten years, but in 1900, Alfred Cotgreave's *Contents-Subject Index to English Periodical Literature* was published. The idea was that a searcher could start with any keyword and locate all the pertinent material even if it was hidden away in the middle of a huge book that was ostensibly about a different subject. In effect, Alfred Cotgreave had invented the search engine a century before Google. His misfortune was to have done it before the development of technology that would make it workable.

The *Subject Index* received some positive reviews but it was out of date before it even appeared on the bookshelves. Its value dwindled by the year and although he was employed for another five years and lived a further six in retirement, there is no evidence that Alfred attempted a new edition either on his own or by encouraging others. He believed that such a thing should exist, recognising that done properly and systematically, it would be a huge collaborative project and run to several new volumes a year. He came to believe that it could only succeed as a major state-funded public service. Others rightly thought it unrealistic, a 'counsel of perfections with a vengeance ... [a] stupendous plan' with little chance of finding a financial backer.

One of the reasons for his inability to take forward the idea of a continually updated universal index was that he had lost the argument in his second great project – to convert libraries to the use of an indicator system of management. His own device – the Cotgreave Indicator – was produced at his factory in Birmingham and had once been very popular. But indicators were becoming redundant in libraries where readers could browse the stock for themselves. 'Open Access' systems had originally been frowned on partly because of the obvious risk of theft but also, as Alfred never tired of pointing out, because they left people ignorant of any books that happened not to be on the shelves because they were on loan to someone else.

During the 1890s a battle raged in print between the proponents of open access and those who favoured indicator systems. Cotgreave was the cheerleader for indicators, while James Duff Brown, the librarian at Clerkenwell, led the cause of open access. The two sides kept their debate polite, but only just. Duff Brown took delight in pointing out that a library in Cornwall was using its Cotgreave Indicator as a notice board. There is more than a hint of personal jealousy from some of Cotgreave's detractors, who criticised his 'commercial sharpness' and the royalties he received on his inventions. There was childish name calling, with accusations that Cotgreave wanted to be the 'Czar' of indicators and even an attempt to link his name to the Number of the Beast in the Biblical Apocalypse.

Despite these attacks, Alfred never missed an opportunity to promote indicators and catalogues in general and his own versions in particular. He advertised everywhere, often giving lengthy lists of supportive testimonials – the inside of the back cover of one books included 24 extracts of reviews of his *Subject Index*. The *British and Colonial Printer* thought it 'welcome ... valuable ... serviceable' the *Irish Times* called it a 'monument of industry' of use to 'all who have to speak or write on public affairs,' and the *Westminster Gazette* described how it filled 'a pressing need'. Cotgreave pointed out that in New York, where public libraries were established on the open access system, some 5,496 volumes had been stolen in a single year. He listed all the public libraries that used his Indicator system, and he relentlessly picked flaws in his opponents' published opinions, even drawing attention to minor typographical errors. When he wrote that a diatribe against open access was not worth answering, he did so in the middle of a 1,000 diatribe answering it. Not content, he produced a further 800 words of follow-up material, claiming that he did not want to waste paper by going over old ground, when that was clearly exactly what he was doing.

As the war of words went on, Alfred Cotgreave was criticised for blatantly misusing for personal gain quotes that had supposedly been given on an anonymous basis. He in turn criticised a journal of which James Duff Brown was editor for being biased in favour of open access, although his comments were probably unjust given that he lambasted the first edition of *The Library World* without waiting to see if future issues presented the case for other systems. He was perhaps placated when he and his West Ham institution were extensively featured in the first of a series of significant articles on individual libraries and the leading characters who ran them.

Perhaps Brown published such a major piece about Cotgreave partly to placate his very public criticisms of open access. But he could only do so because, in the increasingly public and visible world of librarianship, Alfred Cotgreave was a towering figure. Added to his achievements in opening and organising major public libraries around the country, his published works, his contributions to the art of cataloguing and his inventions, there was his involvement in various library societies. He had been a Council member of the Library Association and was an elected Fellow of the Royal Historical Society. The Society of Public Librarians gave him an illuminated letter of appreciation for his 'conscientious devotion ... to the manifold and arduous duties appertaining to the high position you have held in the library world'. He was so proud of it that it took 'the most honoured position' in his home. He had given the inaugural annual lecture of the Library Assistants' Association, which had also named an essay prize after him. Library Assistants won a guinea for articles on subjects such as 'How best to popularise our Public Libraries'. He was said to be 'well known and thrice efficient,' to have the 'interest of his work thoroughly at heart' and to be a 'prominent' and 'distinguished' figure in English librarianship. Others went further; he was 'probably the highest authority on the subject of Public Libraries'.

For such a high achieving librarian, there was perhaps little left to aspire to during his time at West Ham. But he continued to develop and innovate the services to his readers. He opened new branches through the philanthropy of donors. He started a journal called *West Ham Library Notes* to bring knowledge of and debate about libraries to the widest possible audiences. He contributed to every important discussion and development, such as the attempt to encourage more collaboration among libraries so that readers registered at one could access the collections at others. He indefatigably put the case for more public libraries, better libraries with longer opening hours, more books of the widest possible range, and maximum access to them. When criticisms of the public library movement began to coalesce into coordinated pressure against them, it was to Alfred Cotgreave that librarians looked for a cheerleader. He wrote a lengthy article on free libraries for the *National Review*. Later, he grouped the allegations against free libraries under thirteen headings and 'effectively dispatched' them one by one. This was not enough for Alfred, who needed to ensure that the rebuttal was widely read, so he had it reprinted in several newspapers, he managed to get the *London Argus* and the *Daily News* to write reviews of the original article. He also gathered together comments praising public libraries from a variety of dignitaries including the Duke of Argyll, the Leader of the Opposition, the Prime Minister, the Lord Chief Justice and the Archbishop of Canterbury.

To those around him, his energy must have seemed endless but Cotgreave knew it had limits. Sometime around the end of 1904 or start of 1905, Alfred Cotgreave spoke to the Chair of the West Ham Public Library Committee to let him know that, owing to continual bad health, he was considering resigning. As long ago as 1896, the Society of Public Librarians had postponed consideration of one of his ideas for several months because illness prevented him attending meetings. In 1898, he had asked a friend to present one his papers at a meeting despite being present himself. For Alfred Cotgreave to forgo an opportunity to promote his own ideas, he must have been ill. In 1901, he claimed that one of his books had been long delayed by ill health. The root cause of his persistent illness is not clear; he joked about putting on weight but photographs show that while he filled out in middle age, he certainly was not obese. His colleagues bought him a 'smoker's cabinet' in 1895, so he must have been an enthusiastic tobacco user, and perhaps that contributed.

He worked on for a while, in part because he wanted to give his personal attention to the opening of a new branch library, and in part because the rapid expansion of the library network in the borough had caused financial problems for which he felt in part responsible. But at its meeting on 6 March 1905, the Committee finally accepted his resignation. As a sign of their thanks, the borough Councillors paid him an additional three months' salary, so that he could spend time recovering without any financial worries.

Having moved fairly frequently with work, Alfred and Maria Cotgreave do not seem to have considered any particular place their home, although he said that he would like to spend his 'last days amidst the lovely and peaceful scenery' of Guernsey. Alfred had unsuccessfully applied for the librarianship in his ancestral home of Chester in 1876 and he had visited the city when the Library Association had met nearby in 1899. But his parents and his half siblings were all long since dead and he had no remaining connection there. The couple had visited various places around the UK on annual summer holidays and Alfred had visited just about every town of note for the annual meeting of the Library Association. In the end, they moved from the bustle of London to the tranquillity of the coast at Great Yarmouth in Norfolk. The place was not chosen at random – they must have holidayed in the town during the summer of 1900 because on their return, Alfred had donated a *Guide to Yarmouth* and a booklet entitled *The Tollhouse, Great Yarmouth* to the stock of the library in West Ham.

When he retired, it was said that Alfred Cotgreave wanted to devote his time to his numerous inventions. By 1905, his name was on at least 25 patent applications, of which 12 had been granted. Although he would take out four new patents in the next three years, Cotgreave's health did not allow him to spend as much time as he wished on inventing. In 1906, when he was 60, he took a sudden turn for the worse and his situation was described as 'very serious'. He took to his bed and needed an operation. His doctors prescribed 'perfect quiet and freedom from anxiety of any kind'. In his lingering final illness, his correspondence was neglected. Whatever inventions he had intended to work on, he could not do so. He did not give up work altogether, corresponding with the publisher of a volume called *Best Books*, an indexed descriptive compendium covering 50,000 of the most useful and interesting publications across a vast range of subjects. But although the publisher's letters were headed 'Dear Sir,' they were addressed via Maria Cotgreave.[4] Alfred no longer had the energy to deal with his own correspondence.

Cotgreave lived for six years following his retirement from West Ham, but the documentary trail of his activities dried up. The papers and presentations for the Library Association and the Society of Public Librarians, the patent applications, the newspaper articles about his activities, thoughts and inventions were things of the past. Of his two commercial operations, the Library Aids Company effectively ceased to exist because it was a vehicle for the distribution and marketing of his

4   As if to prove Alfred's point that a comprehensive subject index would be a mammoth and perpetual task, the third edition of *Best Books* eventually took 25 years to produce between 1910 and 1935.

books and publications. Cotgreave's Indicators Ltd, however, was a registered company and it continued to function, under the supervision of Maria Cotgreave's nephew, Joseph Richardson Maconochie.

Alfred Cotgreave died at home in Great Yarmouth on 21 August 1911 after a serious illness. He was suffering from a chronic infection of the inner ear and 'epileptiform convulsions'. He had a cerebral infection, which could mean anything from bacterial meningitis to a tapeworm or other parasite in the brain. Eventually, he slipped into a coma from which he did not recover. Obituaries and death notices appeared throughout the world of library affairs and in the localities with which he had been associated. It was fitting that when the probate court asked Maria Cotgreave to nominate someone as her legal surety in administering Alfred's meagre personal effects, she named the local librarian.

Alfred Cotgreave and his devoted wife Maria had never had any children, but his books, inventions and company looked set to perpetuate his name. However, within a few years, Cotgreave's Indicators Ltd was in trouble, and by 1915 it went into liquidation, even though public libraries all over the country were still trading with the company. From Southend and Portsmouth on the south coast of England to Elgin in the far north of Scotland, from Oswestry in the Shropshire countryside and Alloa in the Lowlands to Kensington, Tottenham and Ealing in the capital. Bootle, Blackburn, Bolton, Bangor, Birmingham and Burton all used Cotgreave inventions. The people of Colwyn Bay, Walsall, Weston Super Mare, Hucknall Torkard, Dublin and Kilkenny, all had the benefit of one or more of Alfred Cotgreave's products in their libraries. East Kent Brewery, the Trimble Working Men's Club and the Columbia Laundry were all customers, because they had items (such as barrels) that needed to be tracked, just as libraries needed to track individual books. The volume of historic trade was sufficient that it took the liquidator six years to wind down the company fully. In his first set of accounts, he predicted that the process of wrapping up the finances would be completed within a year. As the months passed, the estimated time to final winding up remained stubbornly at a year away. It was not until 1921 that the book was finally closed.

The idea that Cotgreave's Indicators Ltd was inherently unsustainable is simply not borne out by the facts. But the force of Alfred Cotgreave's personality had been lost. The company could have continued to be successful, to innovate and invent new things, to market them aggressively and to demonstrate how they promoted reading among the population. But it could only do those things with Cotgreave's active input, and without it, there was little point in trying.

Alfred's personality had become crucial to the success of his ventures. Within the world he had inhabited, he became something of a celebrity. And there are hints that it started to go to his head. In the merchant navy, he had signed a declaration that his birthday was 2 June 1846. That is consistent with the facts that he had been baptised in April 1847 and his age had been recorded as 14 in the 1861 census. But in his mini-autobiography published in *Views and Memoranda,* he said that he had been born at Eccleston in Cheshire in 1849, and this date was repeated in other sources. For public consumption, the vain ageing man had shaved three years off his vintage.

Many people must have been bored by the relentless monotony of Alfred Cotgreave's comments about using indicators rather than open access systems. But most nevertheless liked and respected Alfred Cotgreave in equal measure. He had a sense of humour, joking in print that the serious criticism of his detractors should have made him a lesser man but the weighing scales proved he was becoming greater. When he left Guernsey, he was given not just a parting gift but also a scrolled address as a 'tangible memento and verbal expression of ... personal esteem'. At West Ham, there was apparently no special occasion needed for his staff to show their appreciation by presenting him with a polished oak smoker's cabinet as a mark of esteem and respect. His colleagues in the Society of Public Librarians also gave give an illuminated address as 'an expression of its esteem'.

Despite his cruel demolition of his critics and his boring obsessions, it is easy to see why Alfred Cotgreave was so well respected. Everything Cotgreave did was in the service of widening access to scholarship, learning and the enjoyment of reading. He opened his libraries on Sundays and late into the evenings to ensure that working people could use them and he was critical of their wealthy employers for not being more supportive. He refused to bow to the patronising bigwigs who complained that the lower orders should not be encouraged to read fiction. He was recognised for promoting 'good reading among young and old'. He supported his staff, lobbying for pay increases and testifying in court to give a character reference to an assistant. He ferociously defended the professional standards of trained librarians and library assistants. At Guernsey, his staff thanked him for generously sharing his professional experiences. In West Ham, 18 professional signatories recognised his 'uniform kindness and consideration'. Alfred Cotgreave always celebrated the efforts of colleagues as they advanced the cause of free libraries. Even his great rival James Duff Brown had his photograph reproduced in Alfred Cotgreave's wonderful book *Views and Memoranda of Public Libraries.*

Views and Memoranda proved just how much Alfred Cotgreave loved libraries, especially free public ones. He summed up his love of books by saying that if we met Shakespeare in the flesh, we would find him all too human. He might happen to be in a bad mood: 'touched with infirmity, or oppressed with weariness, or darkened by the shadow of a recent tragedy,' but if we took a volume of his works down from the shelf, we had access to his timeless 'best thoughts embalmed in the best words ... the golden fruit of wisdom ... the finest effluences of truth and beauty'.

In the end, it was not libraries or books that were important to Alfred. It was what they had the potential to achieve. Critics complained that drunken 'loafers' hung about in public libraries or that sitting reading books all day was causing people to neglect their work or reducing the amount of healthy exercise they took. Alfred Cotgreave replied: 'It would perhaps be better if public libraries were not expected so much to cure ills and abuses as to prevent them'. To him, libraries had the power to make the world a better place.

Alfred Cotgreave's books and inventions are no longer used; some of the publications are hard to come by in the second-hand market and most Cotgreave Indicators were destroyed decades ago. But the institutions he founded, the skills he taught, the innovations he introduced, persisted in promoting reading among the general populace. The first free public library in which he worked was at Birmingham. It grew to the point where it has become, in its own estimation, 'a major cultural destination, rewriting the book for 21st century libraries'. Whoever wrote those words did not know it, but the book they were rewriting had first been written by Alfred Cotgreave.

SECTION TWO

WAR AND CONFLICT

Conflict is an inevitable part of life, whether at the level of disputes between individuals, simmering family feuds or violent wars among nations.

The five lives in this section were all to some extent dominated and defined by conflict. They begin with a younger son who made a name for himself at the battle of Agincourt and end with an associate of Nelson whose adult experience was to be permanently at war. There are tales of two farmers, one from the fifteenth century who lived in a world where violence was always just below the surface, and one from the seventeenth century who used the court system to argue with everyone, in an attempt to recover what he believed was his family's former glory. In between is a Jacobean murderer who went on the run for several decades following a one-off act of inexplicable violence.

CHAPTER NINE

1415

Robert Cotegreve fights at Agincourt

Robert Cotegreve made the tiniest imprint on the written record. During his elder brother's lifetime, there are only four known pieces of paper or vellum that bear his name, and one of those is a mistake. By contrast his brother William is recorded hundreds of times. But while William Cotegreve's life record shows the daily administration of an elder son, well–off but bound tightly and repetitively to his plots of land, Robert's is characterised by the excitement of making a name for himself. Robert Cotegreve took part in the most famous military victory in English history – he fought at the battle of Agincourt.

Born sometime in the 1370s or 1380s, Robert Cotegreve was the second surviving son of a minor landowner in Cheshire.[1] His older brother William was not only in line to inherit their father Ranulph's estate but also inherited lands through their mother's family.[2]

Nothing is recorded about Robert Cotegreve until in 1415 his name appears on the list of soldiers contracted to serve with the Earl of Arundel as part of the large army that Henry V amassed to invade France. These men did not of course know that they were about to take part in a battle that would have a glorious reputation for centuries to come. But with military pay worth more than £18 a year for a man–at–arms, the rank in which Robert served, they knew that it had the potential to be financially advantageous. Cotegreve was earning as much in a month as some of his neighbours took home in a year. Military service in Cheshire had come to be dominated by younger sons and minor gentry, men who could afford

---

1   There is no record of his birth and no instances of his giving his age, but his older brother stated his age on several occasions, which put his birth in the first half of the 1370s, when their father was about 30.
2   See Chapter 21.

The earliest surviving example of the Cotgreave coat of arms. The original of this version dated from the lifetime of Robert Cotegreve who, as a veteran of Agincourt, had the right to embellish his heraldry [© The British Library Board (ADD MS 62541, f.78r)].

the equipment needed to kit themselves out, but who would struggle to thrive while their fathers and elder brothers were deriving the finite income from limited landholdings.

As part of a successful recruitment campaign, men were encouraged to join up at the Chester County Court, and a band of men joined Arundel's retinue. Robert Cotegreve would have known them all. William Brereton was a neighbour whose father had served as a tax collector with Robert's brother; Ranulph Brereton was his cousin. One of Ralph Venables' close relatives had acted as a court surety with Cotegreve's father. Hugh Cotton and Richard Taillard were Robert's kinsmen (Robert's mother was a Cotton and his great grandfather's sister had married a Taillard), Ughtred Dodd and John Done were from families that were involved in legal processes with the Cotegreves and Vaughan 'Chokelake' no doubt came from Shocklach, a few miles from Robert's home.

Robert was probably in his thirties when he and his colleagues travelled to Southampton during the summer of 1415. Here they joined up with the rest of the huge army, and on 11 August, they sailed across the Channel to invade the old enemy. As a man-at-arms, Robert Cotegreve may have taken four horses on his journey: a warhorse trained in dealing with the noise and physical stress of battle, a packhorse to carry his belongings, including his heavy armour, a palfrey or lighter horse for general transport especially when speed was important, and perhaps a rouncey or general-purpose nag. The whole set-up presupposes that he had some kind of servant or assistant.

The siege of Harfleur was an horrific and brutal event in which the hot weather, marshy surroundings and vast quantities of human and animal excrement all contributed to an outbreak of dysentery. It killed Cotegreve's colleague William Brereton and caused death or serious illness (enough to invalid them home) in about a quarter of the Earl of Arundel's men, including Arundel himself. On his deathbed back in England, the Earl arranged for his men to be paid, and they marched on to Agincourt under different commanders.

As they waited for the battle to start, many English soldiers expected to die. They had spent the last three weeks marching through hostile terrain and the weather was appalling. They were hungry and many were ill. Some archers actually cut their breeches and underclothes off because they were rancid and sticking to their flesh, but men-at-arms like Robert Cotegreve could not do that because they were trapped inside their armour. The French army far outnumbered the English. On the morning of 25 October 1415, each side waited for the other to attack, believing that the men who stood firm would beat those that charged first. Robert sat on his horse in a thick line of cavalry, wearing his coat of arms – Henry V had ordered that everyone entitled to heraldic dress should do so, to show that they were ready for battle. In the end, it was the English who broke first but not before every man had knelt in a semi-religious act, and eaten a tiny piece of soil from the field. What followed was hours of violence and blood in which miraculously, the larger, better-fed, healthier French were slaughtered. History tends to give the credit for the English victory largely to the skill and equipment of the archers, but the men-at-arms like Cotegreve played an important role. Early in the battle, they resisted the first charge of the French cavalry, reformed their ranks quickly and professionally and then pressed forward in hand-to-hand combat; this was a key element of the English success. If they had not been so professional, modern historians think there would have been 'disastrous consequences'.

At the end of the day, Robert Cotegreve and his colleagues were still hungry, still wet, still ill, and still a long way from home in a country that had just become even more hostile. Although English casualties were many fewer than the French, friends had been killed and wounded. But these men were the indisputable winners of one of the most remarkable victories in military history. The name of Agincourt would be remembered for all time.

When Robert Cotegreve returned home to Cheshire, he must have been held in exceptionally high regard. There had been spontaneous celebrations and cheering crowds as soon as news of the victory had reached England, but these were nothing compared to the junketing that followed when the army returned home in November. However, despite all the partying and backslapping, Robert was still the younger son of an ageing man (Ranulph de Cotegreve was 71 in 1415) who could not afford (or did not want) to divide his estates between Robert and his older brother. In 1416, the year after the battle, Robert Cotegreve was back in Chester, a war hero, and his name appears on a jury list at the Chester County Court. Someone thought he was important enough to be independently qualified for jury service. But it was a mistake – Robert did not meet the land ownership qualification and he did not in fact serve on the jury.[3]

Eight years after Agincourt, Robert Cotegreve must still have been living with his father or his brother and it was clear that the father, Ranulph, could not survive much longer; he was nearly 80 and had begun to retire from active public life. Then in 1423, the old man took a lease on a local cottage called Dicken's Croft. The property was to be held in Ranulph's name until he died, and then in Robert Cotegreve's own name for the rest of his life. Ranulph was buying his heroic son a house. At the age of about 40, Robert was getting his own home.

While William Cotegreve left so many traces in the record that it is possible to imagine something of his daily life, it was surely Robert – most of whose life is a complete mystery – who is responsible for one of the most beautiful artefacts arising from any of the stories that are told in this book – a splendid painting of his heraldic inheritance.

To honour the men who had fought at Agincourt, Henry V allowed those veterans who came from gentry families to alter or improve their heraldic symbols in ways that would have been illegal for anyone else. A special level of national chivalric distinction was being accorded to the men who had won the most glorious battle in English history.

---

3   A few years later, someone called Robert Cotegreve was a juror at a local inquisition but this may have been his nephew of the same name, who was by then an adult.

It is surely no coincidence that the earliest record of the Cotgreave coat of arms dates from the time of Robert Cotegreve. There is no doubt the family acquired its red shield with its ermine-tipped, zigzag band and images of three golden hunting horns much earlier, but it was not actually recorded in any of the surviving lists of arms from before the fifteenth century. In 1445, someone added the shield to a catalogue illustrating English armorial designs. The original has long been lost, but the surviving copy, which dates from a few decades later, is as vivid now as the day it was painted. The red background is brilliant and striking. The black symbols that define the zigzag as 'ermine' may be sketchily painted but they are elaborate and symmetrical. The gold-coloured images of cows' horns, shown hollowed out to make musical instruments, are heightened with intricate black edging and detailing.[4] The whole ensemble makes an arresting image.

In later centuries, the coat of arms appeared on the trappings of Hugh Cotgrave's horse, on Eleanor Cotgrave's portrait, in William Cotgreve's church and on Jonathan Cotgrave's tomb. It was carefully recorded in manuscripts and engraved in published books. It was used to make inferences that the earliest Cotgreaves may have been huntsmen and to make up false stories about grand ancestors.

And although its origins almost certainly predated him by at least 150 years, it was Robert Cotegreve, a soldier at Agincourt about whom almost nothing else is known, who wore the coat of arms into battle, who brought it to prominence, who ensured that it was recorded, and whose legacy was to raise its status. Men-at-arms probably did not carry shields during the fighting at Agincourt. They would have been overweight encumbrances for people already sporting heavy armour. But many of them did have decorative shields showing their family heraldry. Perhaps Robert Cotegreve brought one back from France and kept it in his cottage at Dicken's Croft to remind him of the one day in his life that made him stand out above the brother whose name was written down dozens of times more frequently than Robert's, but who is not recorded as having done a single really interesting thing.

Robert Cotegreve outlived his brother by twenty years. When William died in the 1430s, the Cotegreve lands passed to his son Randle, but it appears that his mother's Cotton estates became Robert's. His name started to appear in regular jury lists. In 1454, his appearances abruptly stopped, and Dicken's Croft was leased to someone else; it was described

---

4   In formal heraldic terms, the description is 'Gules, a fess dancette Ermine, between three bugles horns Or'.

as 'lately' inhabited by Robert Cotegreve. Since his lease lasted as long as he was alive, the inference is plainly that he had recently died. He was at least 70 at the time, and probably a little older.

Robert Cotegreve's life lasted for a minimum of 25,000 days. While his brother lived, his name was written down just four times, one of them a mistake. Even by the standards of the fifteenth century that is a sketchy record of a middle-class man's life, but the image of Cotegreve's coat of arms makes up for the deficiency. It is a lasting tribute worth more than countless written accounts.

CHAPTER TEN

1463

Richard Cotgreve avoids the noose

The fifteenth century was an aggressive time. Richard Cotgreve and the people he knew lived in a world that was comfortable with violence. They even wrote songs about it – the Ballad of Bewsey tells the story of a brutal premeditated killing by some of Cotgreve's circle of associates.[1] And this was not an isolated incident – Cotgreve's extended family included a man who openly made a good living as an independent mercenary for hire by the highest bidder.

One of the responses to this backdrop of brutality was for men to gather together under the protection of the great magnates, wear an identifying badge and make formal agreements to serve the interests of their leader and to protect one another. This system was repeatedly criticised and even outlawed, but the big landowners were prepared to pay their associates to protect their interests, and men felt safest in an organised group that could fight back against rival groups – what today might be called a gang.

One such magnate was Sir William Stanley, one of the most powerful men in the north west of England and North Wales. Stanley controlled a vast range of administrative and legal processes as Chamberlain of the Chester Exchequer, Sheriff of Cheshire and of Flintshire, Constable of Flint, and Steward of the Prince of Wales's household. He would also become Chief Justice of North Wales and the King's Chamberlain. In 1463, Richard and Robert Cotgreve were in a relaxed party with Stanley discussing family matters with their neighbours. Ralph Bostock (who was a relative of theirs) asked William Bostock and Sir William Stanley to be

---

1   Thomas Stanley and William Savage knew the Cotgreves well; the murder victim's grandson married Jane Cotgreve.

godfathers to his son, whom he would name William after them. Perhaps Stanley was also godfather to Richard Cotgreve's youngest son William, who would go on to marry Ralph Bostock's daughter. Having a powerful sponsor would certainly explain how the young provincial William Cotgreve secured an opening to train (as a draper) in one of London's livery companies, extremely valuable for a youth with two older brothers.

The Cotgreve brothers presumably wore the red and white jackets with the emblem of a deer's head that marked out William Stanley's retainers, and it is a reasonable bet that one or other of them was with him in some of the military battles where his large force of troops was decisive. The most famous was the Battle of Bosworth, where Stanley's last minute intervention won the Crown for Henry VII. Sadly, the names of the vast majority of his men are not recorded but a ballad that tells of how Stanley and his brother came to end up supporting Henry points strongly to the fact that the Cotgreves were amongst them. The main characters in the song are Humphrey Brereton and Sir John Savage who were closely associated with the Cotgreve family. The Breretons and Cotgreves knew each other well – Sir William Brereton and Richard Cotgreve were named together in a recognisance, and Richard's grandson was married to Humphrey Brereton's sister-in-law. Sir John Savage was related to the Cotgreves, and his family employed some of them – his grandson would marry Eleanor Cotgreve.[2]

Given Richard Cotgreve's close association with Sir William Stanley and with the main protagonists on his route to Bosworth, it seems certain that either he or his brother was present at the battle. On his way to the field in August 1485, Stanley collected a large group of Cheshire gentlemen at Nantwich, described as 'the flower of Cheshire'; Henry VII later acknowledged the importance of the role played by the men of Chester in his victory.

Being feted by the king for their victory in battle was a far cry from the Cotgreve brothers' brush with trouble in their youth. It was two decades earlier, in 1462, that Richard Cotgreve of Cotton Edmunds and his younger brother Robert had found themselves in dangerously severe trouble. The county sheriff convened a jury to decide who should be indicted for serious crimes, and the jurors said that the Cotgreve brothers were thieves, together with John Egerton, William Egerton, Thomas Egerton and William Rider. The group had allegedly stolen 16 shillings in money and goods worth a further two shillings from the home of John Tushingham in the village of Spurstow, about 11 miles from the Cotgreves'

2   See Chapter 2.

farm. Richard Cotgreve's uncle had recently died and Tushingham had married his widowed aunt Margaret. Perhaps Richard believed that through the marriage, John Tushingham had his hands on property that rightly belonged to the Cotgreve family. Whatever his motivation, having apparently dealt with the situation by ganging together with his associates and taking the law into his own hands, Cotgreve's problem now was that theft at this level constituted a felony, and if convicted, he and his associates would all suffer a mandatory death penalty.

The trial took the best part of a year to come before the court. In the meantime, Richard had to find sureties to ensure that he would turn up when the court was ready. His friend John Dutton agreed to support him in a device known as a mainprise, which in theory meant that if Richard broke the terms and absconded, it would be Dutton who faced trial and could even (in principle though not in practice) be executed. This was a clearly a serious business, but Richard Cotgreve was nevertheless treated as innocent until proven guilty; in October 1462, after his indictment but before the trial, his name is listed as one of the jurors sitting in judgment on their neighbours at the Chester County Court.

It was March 1463 before Richard Cotgreve was eventually allowed a trial, but by then he must have known that he would be acquitted, because his brother and the three Egertons had already been found not guilty in January. For some reason, William Rider had to wait until August for his trial, and when it came, the jury also found that he should not be hanged for felony.

The men had, however, clearly done something wrong. The charges may have been exaggerated, but they were not entirely fabricated. There was bad blood between Cotgreve and Tushingham and the dispute was rumbling on. In view of this, the court convicted the thieves of criminal trespass, a lesser crime than felony. So on the same day as his acquittal for the capital crime, Richard Cotgreve agreed to pay a fine.

To begin with neither Richard Cotgreve nor any of the accomplices actually paid the fine, possibly because the brothers were soon absent from the county fighting in the north of England. William Stanley was ordered to muster Cheshire forces in the early summer and although the names of only two of his soldiers are known, they are strongly suggestive that it was the Cotgreve's circle of acquaintances who responded to the call. One was Richard Cotton of Cotton Edmunds, the brothers' cousin and next door neighbour, and the other was Ralph Bostock, also a close relative of the Cotgreves and the man who had been in the group when godfathers were being chosen.

Once the dust had settled the following year, the court imposed the fine a second time and it must have been paid because the matter was never mentioned again. Nevertheless, Richard Cotgreve and the Egertons had an uneasy relationship with John Tushingham for years to come. A large number of bonds survive, showing that the men were legally bound to behave well towards one another on pain of serious fines. These documents give the impression of a finely balanced society in which the courts repeatedly threatened to impose severe financial penalties if arguments escalated out of control. John Egerton had to keep the peace to the Tushingham family; John Tushingham had to keep the peace to Egerton and Cotgreve. If the terms were broken, the fines would be ruinous – typically £40 or £100 in an age when £2 was enough for a workman to live on for a year.

Even five years after the trial, the Cotgreves and the Egertons were still being bound over to behave peaceably towards Tushingham. As late as 1470 – eight years after the original indictment – Tushingham was having to find sureties that he would be peaceable to Richard Cotgreve. In the end, however, the men seem to have realised they were stronger together. In 1470, the Cotgreves' friend Ralph Bostock started supporting John Tushingham and by 1484, Robert Cotgreve was himself standing as Tushingham's surety. Soon Richard Cotgreve and John Tushingham were acting together in support of a mutual friend. Some sense of how the men ganged together for protection is clear from a bond in which Cotgreve and a group of neighbours were bound over to ensure that Tushingham 'and all his adherents' behaved themselves. It reads as if Tushingham had a lot of hangers-on.

Although the dispute between Richard Cotgreve and John Tushingham was resolved, the endless list of peace bonds in which they were involved shines a light on how much violence was just below the surface of their society. The Cotgreves were sureties for Richard Bulkeley in a dispute with John Watson and for Thomas Bulkeley in one with a relative. Thomas Bulkeley, the Cotgreves and the Egertons had to keep the peace towards a family called Barton. Cotgreve supported Thomas Colstonoke in his dispute with Robert Fisher and backed up Nicholas Davenport 'and all his children and servants', who had to behave peaceably towards Thomas Legh. In the years following their trial, Robert and Richard Cotgreve were named in over 50 bonds relating to at least 36 different potentially violent disputes. It is plain that although the bonds may have been successful in forcing the men to keep a lid on the violence, they did not put an end to the underlying disputes, some of which lasted for decades. And during that time, shifting allegiances are clear: in 1476, Richard Cotgreve supported Thomas Crew in a fight with Thomas

Frodsham, but in 1490, both the Cotgreve brothers were sureties from Frodsham when he had to keep the peace to Crew. In the early 1470s, they backed the Smith family against William Stretton but then they switched sides; in 1475 and again in 1480 they supported Stretton against the Smiths.

The jury at Richard Cotgreve's trial had acquitted him and his friends even though it was perfectly obvious that something criminally violent had occurred. Perhaps they disliked the idea of the men hanging. Everyone knew that Richard and Robert Cotgreve were guilty of what was technically a felony, but since practically everyone was involved in potentially violent arguments of their own, nobody thought that hanging people was an attractive solution. The criminal trespass convictions were perhaps an agreed compromise or 'plea bargain'. Maybe the men were vulnerable while their friends and associates in William Stanley's circle were out of the county and their rivals tried to fit them up. Either way, they learned their lesson, and despite the ongoing disagreement with John Tushingham, they managed to avoid further violent entanglements with the law.

Their brush with crime seems to have given both Robert and Richard Cotgreve a taste for involvement with criminal law. In April 1465, Richard sat on the Grand Jury that indicted John Bridge for theft at Bramhall near Stockport. Five months later, he was again at Chester Castle to indict a Welshman called Richard of illegally occupying land at Kinnerton; then early the next year, he was one of the jurors that confirmed the indictment of Thurstan Witchell for violence against Reginald Done. He kept coming back, time and again. In the next 30 years, he sat on at least 74 panels that indicted people in the County Court. Robert Cotgreve did the same thing: he was also on over 70 indictment panels. The brothers had become an integral part of the process that led to men hanging. The Cotgreves were regular jurors in other courts and tribunals too. Perhaps it was merely that they lived very close to Chester and were often able to attend when the sheriff was looking for people to do their civic duty. But even allowing for this, the sheer volume of indictment juries on which Richard and Robert Cotgreve sat is astonishing. The Grand Jury was powerful, and by sitting on it, men could protect their own interests.

Whatever he felt about narrowly escaping the noose in his youth, Richard Cotgreve was only too keen to play a sustained part in prosecuting others for the acts of violence and criminality that were familiar to so much of fifteenth century society.

CHAPTER ELEVEN

1604

Robert Cotgrave commits murder
and goes on the run

Robert Cotgrave killed a man. The resulting paperwork amounts to tens of thousands of words, but the bundle of vellum sheets is not among the records of a criminal court. Rather, the documentary record is concerned solely with the monetary consequences of his violent outburst. There is no evidence that he ever faced a judge or jury, just a single paragraph on the rolls of a criminal court asserting him guilty of murder. But Cotgrave was not there for the hearing, it was not made until seven months after the event, and it does not even record who the witnesses were, let alone what evidence they gave. The Exchequer hearing into his finances, by contrast, took place within days of the victim's death and it reported verbatim what each witnesses said in answer to a host of very specific questions.

It is not clear why Robert Cotgrave was involved in a fight with Thomas Sefton in the first place. Cotgrave was a well-off landowner and at one time the Seftons had been tenants of his family. In 1597, Robert's cousins had complained to the courts about something Sefton's father had done, but a deal had been reached in which the Cotgraves kept the land that was unquestionably theirs but the Seftons had been entitled to the properly-quantified benefits of the investment they had made in drainage and repairs. Whether this legal dispute indicated an underlying tension between the families or whether it was unrelated to the fight that broke out seven years later is impossible to tell. But on 16 October 1604, Robert Cotgrave went to the suburb of Chester known as Great Boughton, looking for Thomas Sefton and carrying a rapier in his right hand (one of the few details about the incident to be recorded). When they met, Sefton received a serious wound, said to be an inch wide and as much as fourteen inches deep. There is no record of whether there was a scuffle, or whether Cotgrave just walked up to Sefton and stabbed him. We know nothing of whether Sefton was armed, whether anyone else was involved, or whether Cotgrave meant to kill him or just to scare him, or even if it was an accident.

Surprisingly, with such a deep stab wound, Thomas Sefton did not die immediately, but it was obvious that his injuries were life-threatening. He 'languished' immobile at Great Boughton after the attack. A few days later, he made his will, describing himself as 'wounded grievously' and 'grown into debility'. He was not quite at death's door, but things were not looking good. His decline was lengthy and a full ten weeks passed before, in the days following Christmas 1604, he finally died. He was buried two days later, on 30 December, in one of the churches in central Chester.

With Sefton dead from what had always been described as a mortal wound, Robert Cotgrave was in trouble. If the authorities could have laid hands on him, no doubt he would have been hanged for murder. But more than two months had passed since the altercation at Great Boughton, and Cotgrave had wisely taken the opportunity to run to London, where he could be lost in the teeming impersonal metropolitan conurbation. He had brothers there through whom he could be contacted, and he certainly involved one of them, Stephen Cotgrave, an embroiderer who lived in the City of London. When Robert wrote and asked his friends to collect rents from his tenants, he told them to do so in Stephen's name. His other London-based brother Randle was extremely well-connected, working for the Earl of Exeter, whose brother was the King's Secretary of State.[1] Randle's connections might easily have found Robert a way of escaping overseas.

Without knowing where he was, the worst the criminal courts could do was threaten to outlaw Robert Cotgrave if he did not show up to face trial for murder. Since he had already been found guilty and since the Exchequer had already taken control of the financial investigation, there was little incentive for him to appear. But while the state apparatus did not seem to care unduly that a killer was free, it took an extremely keen interest in his finances. Sefton had died of wounds inflicted by Cotgrave, and Cotgrave had fled. That meant that Robert Cotgrave's entire estate would be forfeited to the Crown. Everything he owned would be confiscated. To achieve this, the authorities would need a full and detailed account of his wealth and property.

The commission that investigated Cotgrave's financial affairs officially

1   See Chapter 3.

consisted of four local dignitaries. Robert Whitby had been sheriff of the city in 1607 and would be elected mayor within two years; his was an influential family and his son would become Chester's MP in 1613. Hugh Davenport's family name was a pervasive presence in Cheshire society – at the herald's visitation in 1580, no fewer than six separate branches had registered their right to use the ancient Davenport coat of arms. Like Whitby, Davenport would become an alderman of the city. Thomas Booth was a landowner whose moveable goods alone (let alone his real estate) were worth hundreds of pounds. Between them, these three men represented an extremely strong network of local influence and power. The fourth member appointed to the commission, Hugh Bromley, did not in the end take part.[2]

The three commissioners who were present had a prepared list of questions to ask each witness, designed to discover the state of Robert Cotgrave's finances on the day he had fatally wounded Thomas Sefton. Technically, there were nine questions, but the interrogations sought to establish three simple things: Did you owe Cotgrave any money, do you know if anyone else was in debt to him, and what valuable possessions did he own? Anything that Cotgrave had possessed and any money that was due to him on that fateful day would be forfeited.

While the questions were simple, Cotgrave's friends and relatives made sure the answers formed a convoluted and incomprehensible tangle of misdirection and obfuscation. Like many well-off people, Robert Cotgrave's financial affairs were genuinely complex. He owned some properties and leased others, some of which he sub-let to under-tenants. He had borrowed money from some people and lent money to others. In at least one case, he had borrowed from and lent to the same person in different forms. In three cases, he had transferred large sums to men who had agreed in return to pay him an annuity for the rest of his life. In some of these arrangements, his estate would expect to recover the original capital when he died, in others not. Some of his holdings were in the form of a 'lease for lives,' which meant that an ordered list of people held the tenancy in turn, with the lower-placed names taking over the lease if they outlived those higher up on the list.

So it was easy for witnesses to misdirect the commissioners. Unconvincingly, the Mayor of Chester was somewhat vague about whether the money he had borrowed was from Robert Cotgrave or from

---

2   Although he is listed on the record of proceedings, his signature is completely absent from the documents, whereas the other three each meticulously signed every page.

his brother George. He thought the paperwork might have named Robert but he was sure the cash must actually have come originally from George Cotgrave because it was to George that he had always paid the interest. Given that the mayor lived in the same town as Robert but 30 miles away from George, this must have seemed a little unlikely.[3] It was true, he said, that he had also accepted a large sum from Robert in return for which he was paying an annuity for the rest of Robert's life but although he had searched 'diligently' for a copy of the original agreement, he was sorry but he could not lay his hands on it. So he could not be precise about the terms. And actually, he thought Robert may have owed him money rather than the other way around.

The quantity of missing or dodgy documents is so astonishing as to be literally unbelievable. William Cotgrave, with whom Robert had left his trunk full of paperwork, testified that when he opened it, all it contained was history books 'and not anything else'.[4] William himself had borrowed £30 from his cousins without anyone bothering to write anything down; once Sefton's wound had started to look fatal, just to be on the safe side, Robert had made it clear that the money was George's. So William Cotgrave had signed a bond in George's name. People said that Randle Brereton owed Robert Cotgrave £40, or maybe it was £50 and maybe it was William Brereton rather than Randle, or perhaps a joint debt. So Randle Brereton was questioned, and admitted that he had signed a bond to Robert Cotgrave for £40, but it had been cancelled and converted into George Cotgrave's name because the money was really his, and anyway Brereton had sold the debt on to his son William.

William Gamull (who was related to Robert by marriage) knew that Robert had made a legal settlement of his affairs but he had no idea whether or not it pre-dated the fatal fight with Sefton. Christopher Hasselwell owed £3 and 15 shillings to Robert but it had actually been payable last September, so technically it was not still owing on 16 October, the day Cotgrave's rapier had gone fourteen inches into Sefton's side. The only reason it had not been paid was that Robert, evidently a paragon of generosity, had mercifully agreed to wait for his money (interest free).

Witness after witness threw dust in the faces of the investigators. Rich and titled men who had complex financial dealings with the Cotgraves, Robert's servant, his brother George and his cousin William, his aunt and

---

3 George is described in the documents and elsewhere as living in Sefton in Lancashire.

4 This was the son of William Cotgreve, See Chapter 31.

her hapless husband, who testified that he knew literally nothing.[5] The only thing everyone agreed on was that it was unthinkable that Robert Cotgrave could possibly have done anything that was prejudicial to the Crown's interests.

When it came to Robert Cotgrave's physical possessions, all he seems to have owned was his horse, described rather disparagingly as an 'ambling nag,' presumably to lower its estimated value (if he had ridden it to London, nobody could challenge the description). True, on the day of the fight, Robert had been to his aunt's house with almost £15 in gold and a gold ring, which she had passed on to his servant later the same evening, but nobody seems to have had the slightest idea where they were now. The history books in Robert's trunk were simply ignored among the tally of his things.

The commissioners were faced with obfuscation, dissembling, forget-fulness and a remarkable capacity for accidentally mislaying crucial documents. Far from being the patently rich man Cotgrave really was, a picture emerged of someone whose worldly goods comprised a few worthless books and a slightly less worthless horse. His brothers appeared to be remarkably generous, allowing him to treat vast quantities of their money as it were his own, without ever bothering to keep a record of any details. The commissioners may have been intensely frustrated, or perhaps they played along; they were after all neighbours of the Cotgraves, colleagues of the mayor and at the very least acquaintances of the other witnesses. Their families would have been unique if they did not have dealings with William Gamull, William Hurleston and Edward Dodd, three of the witnesses who came from long-established and important Chester clans.

However they felt personally, the commissioners could hardly go back to the Exchequer empty handed. There are signs in the evidence that here and there, either deliberately or by accident, the witnesses left loopholes so that relatively small amounts would be collected. Debts were owed by the Breretons and a man called Swanick, but some of the money had been repaid, allowing a chance that the rest could still be recovered for the Crown. There were four bonds from local farmers that had been payable in Robert's name and which had been transferred to George's account after the fight on 16 October. William Cotgrave testified that three of them really were George's money, leaving open the possibility that one

5   Owen Harris, a 36-year-old ironmonger 'neither knoweth nor hath heard any thing,' which was slightly surprising given that his wife testified that Robert had left £40 worth of gold at their house.

(by a remarkable coincidence the smallest amount) might genuinely have been Robert's. An obvious defect in the story emerged when one of the debtors admitted that while inducing him to transfer the debt from one name to another, George Cotgrave had offered him a six-month interest-free period on the loan.

Where the evidence was genuinely in Cotgrave's favour, witnesses who were otherwise vague about crucial details and lacked any written evidence could suddenly remember things with astonishing precision. Thomas Trafford's debt to Robert Cotgrave had definitely been discharged because William Cotgrave remembered giving him a receipt (by returning the cancelled bond) between one and two o'clock on the afternoon of 28 December. Given that William Cotgrave could not remember anything else (except for letting slip that Robert actually had two horses), this was a remarkable feat of memory. But although it may have frustrated Whitby, Davenport and Booth in their investigations, it made no difference to the outcome.

Robert Cotgrave had disappeared into thin air. Nobody was really looking for him because it was plain that he had none of the money with him and was too clever and too well connected ever to be caught with any of it. At some point the court was told that he had died, but it looks more like a convenient way of wrapping things up than an evidence-based statement. There is no record of a burial, no written evidence of any event that might have been associated with Robert Cotgrave's death. Perhaps his family told the commissioners that Robert had died in London, and it was simplest to pretend to believe them.

For 30 years, nothing was heard of Robert Cotgrave. He had vanished, his brothers and cousins had tied his assets up in such convoluted accounts that the authorities would never be able to recover the majority; his interests were best served by lying low. It was put about that he was dead and everyone either believed it or pretended to.

But he was not dead.

In 1598, Robert Cotgrave had bought twenty houses and an extensive acreage of arable, wood and scrubland in Childer Thornton on the Wirral, from a man who went by the name of William Baxter alias Mayo. The property formed part of Cotgrave's estate at the time of the inquiry in 1605, but it was kept out of the hands of the commissioners. At some point soon afterwards, some of the property was quietly transferred to a man called Richard Fletcher of Morley, a distant cousin. In January 1611, Fletcher sold one of the houses and gardens on, and the document recording the sale included a clause confirming that the vendor had good title to sell – that the buyer would not end up dealing with claims from previous owners. The previous owners were listed as 'Richard Bavand ... deceased, William Baxter alias Meyo ... tanner and Robert Cotgrave gentleman'. Two things are clear. First, while Bavand was listed as dead, Baxter and Cotgrave were still very much alive. Second, the list of former owners ended with Cotgrave, so Fletcher must have acquired the property directly from him, after the commissioners had supposedly sniffed out all of Cotgrave's assets.

Nearly 30 years later, when Robert Cotgrave would have been an ageing man, a family of Cotgraves sprang up suddenly in Staffordshire and at its head was a man called Robert Cotgrave. A younger man, also called Robert, presumably his son, was married and fathering children. They would spawn a huge family of Cotgraves throughout the English Midlands in Lichfield, Stoke-on-Trent, villages in Staffordshire, in Oldbury and Birmingham. There were carpenters and publicans, coalminers, tailors and shoemakers, and people who were good at cricket and football. By the middle of the nineteenth century, there were dozens of Cotgraves descended from the man named Robert Cotgrave, who appeared out of nowhere in the 1630s. He was perhaps a scion of the Cheshire family whose birth is unrecorded. Maybe Cotgrave was not his real name and he is nothing to do with other Cotgraves, although a genetic study certainly showed some similarities between his descendants and other branches of the family. But maybe, he was the same Robert Cotgrave who had vanished into thin air three decades before. By the time the ageing Robert Cotgrave appeared in Staffordshire, the main players from the events of 1604 were all dead. George Cotgrave had died in 1608, William Cotgrave in 1620, Stephen Cotgrave in 1626. Edward Dutton, the shifty Mayor of Chester, had passed away in 1617 and Randle Brereton in 1624. Of the commissioners who investigated Cotgrave's affairs, Hugh Davenport died in 1622 and Thomas Booth in 1624. Even Hugh Bromley, the commissioner who had not turned up for the hearings, was dead by 1628. A quarter of a century after the commission of inquiry, as the 1630s began, the last significant player left alive was commissioner Robert Whitby, and he passed away soon afterwards. Perhaps it is a coincidence that immediately afterwards the family of Robert Cotgrave came out of the shadows at Burslem in Staffordshire, or perhaps not.

With his pursuers all gone, Robert Cotgrave could come back from the dead.

CHAPTER TWELVE

1618

Ralph Cotgreave starts one of 100 court cases

Ralph Cotgreave was grumpy, proud, and not–infrequently stupid. He fell out with everyone, and it was generally his own fault.

It is not difficult to work out what might have upset him. His family had once been big shots in and around Chester, but by Ralph's generation, they were not what they once had been. One of his aunts was married to an MP and another was a Dame who knew the Queen.[1] He had an uncle who was a royal herald, another who was a City lawyer, and a third who had worked at court and had met Henry VIII.[2] His cousin sat in Parliament, and simultaneously held the posts of Recorder of Southampton, Alderman of Chester and a Bencher at the Inner Temple. Closer to home, his father had been a gentleman whose elder brothers had died young and unmarried, leaving him the fortuitous inheritor of a large amount of land. But the aunts' impressive marriages had required impressive dowries and his father had to sell land to pay for them. Worse still when his father died, Ralph's mother, sisters, brother and cousin were all heavily fined for defying the authorities by refusing to renounce their belief in Roman Catholicism.[3] To cap it all, he even blamed someone else that his wife was lame.

Ralph Cotgreave, who had once believed that he could be rich, important and well-connected, found himself less rich, unimportant and surrounded by expensive criminal associates. His high-flying legal

1   See Chapter 2.
2   See Chapters 14 and 22.
3   See Chapter 29.

Ralph Cotgreave disputed the ownership of these two pieces of land in
Christleton in the 1620s; 'How Hay' is now part of a larger pasture field,
and 'Badgers' is the site of houses known as Badgers Close.

relations and society cousins must have seemed a long way from his dwindling farm in Cheshire.

For four decades, Ralph Cotgreave used the legal system to take his frustration out on anyone and everyone. He must have spent so much time and money on disputes that what was left of his farm was neglected. Between 1597 and his death in 1636, the Cheshire courts listed well over 100 actions involving someone called Ralph Cotgreave, and although there were other men with the same name, the vast majority relate to the disgruntled farmer from the village of Christleton. To take 1610 as a typical year, he was involved in three cases in the Chester Exchequer and one in the Pentice Court of Chester. One of the cases lasted for more than a year and one of them was a procedural issue arising from a separate case in the national courts in London.

Ralph Cotgreave's knowledge of how to play the system became impressive. He knew the precise jurisdictions of the different courts and used this knowledge to the full. When John Walton sued him in the Court of Common Pleas in Westminster, Ralph went to the Chester Exchequer, arguing that the ancient privileges of the semi–independent county of Cheshire were very specific. Only its own Palatinate courts could try cases relating to matters within its boundaries. The ancient privileges of the county had been the same 'for all time whereof the memory of man is not to the contrary' and could not be over–ridden. The judge agreed and ordered a stop on the London proceedings. Although Walton thought (entirely credibly) that the London courts might ignore the provincial order, Ralph had it reissued. Walton gave up.

Delaying cases in distant metropolitan courts was one thing. Back at home, the name of the game was obfuscation. Cheshire had a bewildering array of different courts with overlapping jurisdictions and Ralph Cotgreave used them all. The mayor's court in Chester (known as the Portmote) and the sheriff's court (named the Pentice after the building it occupied), the Court of Great Sessions (equivalent to assizes in other counties), the Exchequer of Chester, two different sets of Quarter Sessions (one for the city and one for the county) and the local manorial courts. Cotgreave skilfully worked out when to convince the judges in one to interfere with the business of another. Sometimes it backfired, as in 1604, when Thomas Fisher sued Cotgreave for the price of a horse he had supplied. On the evidence of Ralph's wife Mary, the case was transferred from the Exchequer (which was concerned primarily with what was fair) to the assizes (which was more interested in the legal technicalities). Cotgreave presumably thought there might be a legal loophole. But it was a misjudgment, and he lost.

In one of his favourite tricks, Ralph Cotgreave would get creditors off his back by agreeing in court to pay them but then not doing so. When George Cowles sued him for £5 in October 1612, Cotgreave confessed that he did in fact owe the money; the court had nothing left to adjudicate, and its procedure naively assumed that penitent defendants would pay up. After five months, when the money had not appeared, Cowles went back and secured a court order to force payment. But it was completely ineffectual and the judges were still issuing fresh orders well over a year after the original case. Five years later, Cowles was still trying to extract the money, and the whole merry-go-round started again. Ralph Cotgreave again confessed, but failed to pay, and the judge issued yet another order. There is no evidence that he ever paid.

A knowledge of court procedure was essential, but it was also useful to understand the law. When Rachel Bradshaw prosecuted Ralph Cotgreave in 1623 to enforce a lease he had undoubtedly granted her, he claimed (with some success) that the Statute of Uses of 1535 and Act Against Fraudulent Conveyances of 1571 rendered the lease illegal. In doing so, he was shamelessly claiming that he had deliberately committed fraud seven years earlier. But the case was being heard in the Exchequer, which had no jurisdiction to punish him for fraud, and he knew that nobody would actually bring a criminal case.

Another certain way to hold things up was to lose the paperwork. Like many of his contemporaries, Ralph showed no shame in saying that crucial documents were 'casually lost' and when the going got tough, it turned out a crucial bond had unhelpfully been sent to a relative in Ireland in a trunk full of belongings.

Even when the authorities tired of Ralph Cotgreave's behaviour to the point of arresting and imprisoning him, he still knew how to work the system. He secured his own release from Chester gaol so that he could pursue one of his in-laws in one court in order to halt proceedings in another, even though it became clear the man in question had a genuine case and would certainly have won if it had ever been properly dealt with.

Just as he could spring himself from gaol, so he could melt into the background when things became too hot to hang about. At some point towards the beginning of the seventeenth century, he had disappeared to Ireland and in 1614 (while there were outstanding orders for him to pay at least £36 plus costs in three different cases) he moved temporarily to London. In the 1630s, he absconded for a while and nobody knew where he was, vaguely locating him in 'remote and obscure places'.

But despite his capacity for conveniently being a long way away, Ralph Cotgreave's sphere of interest was very definitely his home village of

Christleton. Many of the cases involve fields and cottages there where he claimed some exaggerated rights. The biggest mystery is why anyone ever believed him when he said he owned a house and tried to sell it or lease it to them. In at least some cases, the property had once belonged to his family and he presumably thought it still should.

Perhaps most ludicrous of all Ralph Cotgreave's attempts to recover his family's lost glory was his effort to repossess a local house called Dicken's Croft. It had first been acquired by the family in 1423 as a home for Robert Cotegreve, but it was held on a long lease and when Robert died in the 1450s, it reverted to the original owner.[4] Then a century later, two Cotgreave brothers, John and Raffe (father of the grumpy litigious Ralph Cotgreave), had leased it back as a joint investment. John Cotgreave had later bought his brother out, with his full ownership probably starting from the end of the 21-year lease that the two of them had first acquired. But in the late 1570s, when John was dead, and as part of a deal to settle the complicated affairs of the two brothers' estates, the property had been passed in its entirety to John Cotgreave's son Randle, who then sold it outright in 1598 to a family called Venables.[5] So when the younger Ralph Cotgreave began an action in the Chester Exchequer in 1624, claiming that he still owned the cottage, he was demonstrably wrong for at least three reasons. First, his father had only ever possessed half the rights to a lease that ended in the 1570s. Second, Raffe Cotgreave (the father) had given up all right to the title over 40 years earlier anyway. Third, the house had been sold to Thomas Venables over a quarter of a century ago. Moreover, this was all perfectly provable from the title deeds, which Venables could produce and which are still among his family's archives today.

This was just one in a series of cases that involved property in Christleton – fields called How Hay and Badgers, a cottage called the Lowe and another called Some Croft. And because they were local, the disputes were often with members of his own family. Ralph's cousin Richard Cotgreave was a particular antagonist; in 1605 Richard admitted not repaying a debt but said he was keeping the money 'in recompence of many wronges'. On one occasion, Cotgreave bizarrely claimed that while it was true that his mother had paid his uncle William Brock rent for a piece of land, she had never actually believed that Brock owned it – it really belonged to an estate the Cotgreaves rented from the church. The

4   See Chapter 9.
5   Randle operated under the name Richard Cotgreave, apparently (at least in part) to distance himself from his criminal past as a recusant, See Chapter 24.

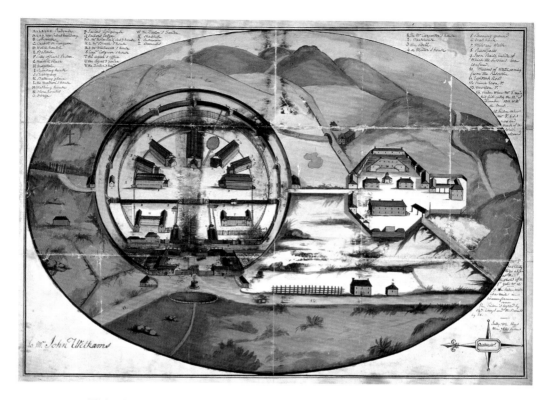

This plan of Dartmoor Prison from 1813 shows Isaac Cotgrave's house
as the governor, charged with incarcerating thousands of French,
Spanish, Danish and American prisoners of war [The National Archives
MFQ1/147(1)].

permanently at Portsmouth, where he spent more than two years on mundane assignments. The boredom must have been too much for him, and just after Christmas 1767, he used the authority of his patron Sir John Moore to get himself relieved of his duty. He wanted to go somewhere more exciting than the south coast of England

Not convinced that his future was in the navy, Isaac Cotgrave applied for a cadetship in the Indian Army, a route that proved successful for his elder brother John, who rose to the rank of Major and married an heiress.[2] Admittedly, John Cotgrave ended up being killed in battle, but when Isaac was looking for a new job that was still two decades away. Isaac Cotgrave's change of heart did not last (apparently he was too ill to travel to India at the right time), and he soon rejoined the Royal Navy, starting again as an able bodied seaman aboard HMS *Yarmouth*, but soon managing to get himself rated midshipman, and then master's mate, on a series of vessels. On one of these – HMS *Triumph* – he served with a 13-year-old sailor called Horatio Nelson. Within a few months, Cotgrave transferred from the *Triumph* to the *Glasgow*, again as a midshipman. With all this ship hopping and changes of mind, it was now more than ten years since Isaac had first stepped on board a ship as an officer, but he was still in the same low rank; any concession to his youth had long since passed. Moreover, his ship was still not going anywhere exciting – mostly it was not going anywhere at all. Isaac doubted once again whether the navy really was his future. On 28 November 1771, following a short period of shore leave at Spithead in Hampshire, he failed to come back on board at the appointed time. Initially, this might have been considered a technicality – there were all sorts of reasons why a man might be delayed on land. It soon became clear, however, that Cotgrave was deliberately staying away and his captain signed a certificate that the midshipman had absconded from the Royal Navy. Desertion was a serious matter, and if caught, the least the 23-year-old Isaac Cotgrave could expect was a flogging.

Isaac Cotgrave kept a low profile for the next few years, and by the late 1770s he had crossed the Atlantic to New York. There is a good chance he had been in America all the while because his brother Arthur had settled there. But Arthur Cotgrave was an officer in the army in North Carolina who fought for an independent USA against the British. If Isaac was associating with his brother, he would be compounding his crimes in the eyes of the British authorities. Running from your ship was one thing, running into the arms of the enemy was something altogether worse.

2   See photograph, p 185.

Many of Isaac Cotgrave's colleagues were killed in the raid on Boulogne in 1801, and he was only saved by his strong swimming skills, which he presumably learned in the River Dee as a child. Nelson said he had never seen 'more determined, persevering courage'. This picture by Louis-Philippe Crepin is called *Nelson fails against the flotilla near Boulogne* [Public Domain].

It might very well be punished by hanging. Even if Isaac was having nothing to do with Arthur, a sojourn in America would not look good when the time came to recover his reputation in Britain. That moment came in 1778 when in his early thirties, Isaac Cotgrave met and married in New York a young woman called Margaret Blake. Within a couple of years, she was pregnant with the first of at least 14 children.

Now a married man facing imminent fatherhood, Isaac Cotgrave needed to get his career back on track and the Royal Navy was the only profession he knew. He had more than enough service to meet the entry criteria for the next step – his lieutenant's examination – but he had to ensure that his dodgy past remained unnoticed during the process. He was a deserter who had spent time in America where his brother was fighting against the British. If the authorities knew any of this, he would not only fail to advance his career, he might be in very serious – life threatening – trouble. And while his time in the United States might just about be conveniently covered up, his desertion from the navy a decade earlier was a matter of obvious record and was known to officers who were still around. If anyone checked the records, they would link Isaac's name to his old patron Sir John Moore, and if consulted, the old admiral would surely let on that Cotgrave was a deserter. As luck would have it, Moore's health was poor and he died soon after Cotgrave's wedding.

A potentially more serious problem was that to attend his promotion interview, Isaac needed to list the ships in which he had experience, especially those where he had served as a midshipman or master's mate. But if he included his time on the *Glasgow*, and anybody checked the records, they would discover he was a deserter. Nor could he count his period on the *Triumph*, because that ship's muster book directly linked his name with his transfer to the *Glasgow*.

To qualify for the exam, Cotgrave had no choice but to scrape together various separate periods on different vessels – one month, three weeks and one day as a temporary midshipman on the *Yarmouth*, just over ten weeks as a master's mate on the *Bellona*. It was a messy hotch-potch of eight different bits and pieces of service, and it would probably put the panel in a sceptical frame of mind, especially since it was over ten years old. But it was verifiable and technically enough. So in November 1780, Isaac Cotgrave duly presented himself for a viva examination by three qualified sea captains, clutching his sea journals as a record of his navigation skills.

During the interview, Isaac must have given a credible account of what he had been doing for the last ten years. Either that or he still had enough contacts to rig the process. At any rate, he passed. Isaac Cotgrave now held the rank of lieutenant in the Royal Navy. He could be commissioned to serve in senior positions, even to command vessels. In due course, he might be eligible for promotion to post-Captain and even Admiral. But holding rank and having a job are different things and the first was no guarantee of the second. Some lieutenants never actually achieved a commission. Isaac's own brother Randle Cotgrave, who qualified in 1765, would continue to serve as a midshipman and even as a lowly able seaman for years, and he died without ever holding a paid lieutenancy. Isaac, despite his past and the death of his patron, somehow managed to secure his crucial first commission, although it took him nearly two years.

In 1782, he was appointed Second Lieutenant – third in rank after the Captain and First Lieutenant – of HMS *Alcmene*, a smallish, highly manoeuvrable warship that had been captured from the French three years earlier. Although Isaac Cotgrave was now progressing in his naval career, and potentially starting to make a slightly more impressive income, he appreciated the very substantial risks: from the ferocity of the sea, from the violence of the enemy and from the incomprehensible randomness of disease. So it was while serving on the *Alcmene* that he wrote his will, leaving everything to his wife Margaret, who spent months and even years alone at various addresses on the south coast of England.

A series of short term commissions followed, including six weeks as Lieutenant of the *Duke* and 14 months as Second Lieutenant of the *Director* before Cotgrave had his big break – lieutenant commanding the cutter HMS *Ranger.* Cutters were small, fast vessels, typically with a minimal complement of officers led by a lieutenant, who could use the opportunity to show skills in a variety of fields. Under Isaac Cotgrave's leadership, the *Ranger* (which had 14 cannons) was responsible for capturing much larger smuggling vessels, transporting men and supplies, successful reconnaissance missions around the coasts of France and Spain, and the recapture of French prisoners of war who had managed to escape aboard an American ship.

These were short missions, so the *Ranger* was in port frequently. Margaret Cotgrave and the growing family (she had borne three boys and four girls by 1793) may not have seen much of Isaac but most weeks they could at least expect news from his ship. So when in June 1794, the *Ranger* was missing for several days, it caused real concern. By the end of the month, Margaret knew that while off the French coast at Brest, HMS *Ranger* had been forced to fight off two French vessels and after 'a smart action,' the French had captured Isaac Cotgrave's cutter. They had forced him and his men to strip naked and bundled them into the hold. The next day the English were made to stand on deck all day, naked in the pouring rain, starved of any food. The French humiliated Isaac in front of his men by jumping on his officer's cockaded hat and boasting that they would do the same to King George III. Once into the harbour, two days later, things became worse. Taken to a prison at a place the English remembered as Pantezon, all of their goods and money were confiscated, and they slept on the hard floor with no covers in 'damp, filthy and nasty' conditions of 'closeness [and] stench'. They were insulted and assaulted, denied soap, tobacco or even a knife to cut up and share out the meagre food they were allowed. When Isaac requested a little wine for the sick, the guards said that only republicans should drink wine and treated the patients with 'absolute neglect'. Typhus was rife and men died in the stinking dungeon every day.

As if this was not enough, when the surviving men were released months later, Isaac Cotgrave was automatically subjected to trial by a court martial. He had, after all, been in command of a British naval vessel that had fallen into the hands of the enemy. The trial took place on board HMS *Cambridge* on 7 September 1795 and the evidence proved quite conclusively that Lieutenant Cotgrave was not guilty of any fault or neglect. He was honourably acquitted, and enjoyed a brief period on shore in Hertfordshire, where he obtained a licence to hunt game.

By the third week of November, he was on board ship again and a year later was promoted to the rank of Commander and given a larger vessel, HMS *Volcano*. The *Volcano* was a recently-acquired specialist warship and the Admiralty was keen to learn Cotgrave's views of its utility. But he was more concerned to get the ship properly manned. He had to pester the Admiralty to appoint a purser, while the boatswain still had not turned up two months after he had been appointed. Once ready, Isaac Cotgrave used the *Volcano* to good effect, destroying enemy ships off the coast of France. Promoted to a sloop called HMS *Gannet*, he was equally successful in capturing a French lugger called *La Vengeance*.

By the beginning of the nineteenth century, Isaac Cotgrave was an experienced naval leader, with time served in the North Sea, the English Channel, the coasts of France and Spain, the Mediterranean, the Atlantic and the Caribbean. He had known Admiral Nelson for a long time, so it was not surprising that when Nelson was looking for five crack leaders to stage a daring raid on the French fleet at Boulogne, Cotgrave was among them.[3] It was widely believed that the French ships amassing in the Channel port were preparing for an invasion of England, and the admiral thought that a pre-emptive strike could scupper Napoleon's plans by destroying or capturing a significant number of the vessels. After a couple of false starts, a well-prepared attack was planned for the night of 15/16 August 1801. Each of the five divisions consisted of a dozen or more boats including flat bottomed vessels that could get the British in among the anchored French fleet and a number of smaller rowing boats that could then be attached to French ships to tow them away as prizes. Because there was always a high risk that this kind of capture would fail, the British vessels were heavily armed so that as a back-up plan, they could bomb or burn the enemy ships.

At 11pm, the signal was given and the raid began. Cotgrave realised early on that the original plan for his division would not work; trying to keep his 15 boats all together in tight formation was slowing things down, eliminating any element of surprise. So he gallantly led the front vessel on its own, in among the French ships. French cannon hit the boat so

---

3   Nelson's comprehensive biographer described Cotgrave as 'one of Nelson's earliest naval acquaintances'.

many times that it rapidly sank and Cotgrave was only saved because of his 'dexterity at swimming'. Perhaps he had learned in the quieter waters of the River Dee when he was growing up in Chester. He and his men persisted as long as they could but with many of them killed and 'no prospect of success', Captain Cotgrave withdrew what remained of his boats between 2am and 3am on the morning of 16 August.

Isaac Cotgrave's experience in the dark and turbulent sea was not unique; each of the five divisions had failed in its mission and two of the five hand-picked leaders had died. In its own stated terms, the raid was a total disaster. Only one small French vessel was captured, none was destroyed, and hundreds of British sailors drowned. But Nelson, who always understood the power of public relations, did not let the failure stop him from burnishing the reputation of his colleagues. He had never seen 'greater zeal and ardent desire to … attack the enemy' or witnessed 'more determined, persevering courage'. Isaac Cotgrave was now not merely an experienced and able ship's officer, he had proof that the country's greatest naval hero considered him to be brave, committed, skilled and patriotic. His name became famous, as his report and Nelson's encomium were reprinted in newspapers up and down the country, from Carlisle to Ipswich, Hereford to York. When they appeared in the *Chester Chronicle* on 21 August, many readers would have recognised the name of a childhood friend. None of Isaac's ten brothers and sisters could boast about their brother's exploits, because all of them had by this date died. Now in his fifties, Isaac Cotgrave was no longer a young man.

Despite its ostensible failure, the raid on Boulogne was not entirely without value. It had at least proved that if Napoleon thought he could gather an unhindered armada in the Channel, he was sorely mistaken. The plan to invade England had never seemed so unrealistic, and soon afterwards, in March 1802, the Treaty of Amiens signified a (short-lived) peace between Britain and France. It was followed by a rapid increase in the rate of promotion of British naval officers, and one month later, Isaac Cotgrave was raised to the rank of post-Captain. In theory, this held out the prospect of eventually becoming an admiral, but Cotgrave knew that it had come too late. At 55, Isaac Cotgrave had no chance of outliving enough of the many more senior officers ahead of him in the queue. Moreover, peace meant that fewer combat vessels were needed, and fewer officers to command them. Cotgrave would never go to sea again.

Within a year, however, war with France resumed and one of the consequences was a huge and growing number of prisoners of war. They needed to be incarcerated, fed, recorded and controlled, and that required an able and willing staff of officers. So before long, Captain Isaac

Cotgrave was appointed Agent for Prisoners of War at Plymouth and was soon responsible for some 6,000 foreign servicemen, mostly held in prison ships.[4] It was unrealistic to keep them all closely confined, and many were released on parole. This involved dealing with the civilian authorities led by the Mayor of Plymouth, a prickly character who refused to help arrest Prussians straggling around the town, but expected the captain's help with violent Spaniards. The Spaniards seem to have been Isaac's main problem at the time, and he even had problems with French prisoners pretending to be Spanish because they thought they would get better treatment. He complained that the official interpreter appointed by the Spanish authorities, who could confirm whether or not someone was a genuine native speaker of the language, had gone home to Spain.

In the summer of 1808, a rumour emerged that Isaac Cotgrave was leaving his post at Plymouth; someone else applied for his job. The story turned out to be true and the 61-year-old captain was given a new and challenging role as governor of the newly-built Dartmoor prison. Famous now as a penal institution for hardened criminals, the remote gaol on the Devon moors was actually constructed to house the burgeoning number of French, American, Danish and other prisoners of the Napoleonic wars.

For six years, Isaac Cotgrave was responsible for keeping many thousands of hardened rank and file soldiers and sailors incarcerated. Later, accusations would emerge that he was a harsh and cruel gaoler, and history judged him 'a disciplinarian without the saving grace of humour'. But leaving aside the fact that Dartmoor was not meant to be a holiday camp, the evidence does not justify this assessment.

It is true that some inmates felt harshly treated and one American in particular considered that Cotgrave's 'cruelty exceeded murder' and that 'his feelings had become callous by continuing so long among the suffering of the French prisoners'. The prisoner believed that 'the name of Isaac Cotgrave ... of cruel memory, will ever be engraven in odious characters on the mind of every American'. But even this inmate had to admit that when the American authorities neglected their own countrymen, it was Isaac Cotgrave who ensured that the wretched men received (from the British government) the rations and supplies that their own government had undertaken to provide but failed to deliver. There was certainly no truth in the idea that Isaac lacked a sense of humour – he had trouble concealing his laughter when some French inmates made a joke of overpowering some of the guards.

---

4   In December 1806, he was responsible for 6,569 prisoners, mostly French and Spanish with 131 Prussians, housed in one prison on land and eight hulks.

When bored French prisoners gambled away their clothes and food, Cotgrave set up a system for trustworthy inmates to supervise their feckless compatriots to ensure that every man had his allocation each day. And when some of the inmates complained about conditions at Dartmoor, a government inquiry, far from agreeing with them, thought that if anything Captain Cotgrave was too nice. Even his harshest critics admitted that the cruelty they witnessed was largely a result of the orders Cotgrave had received from faraway London. The Danish prisoners at Dartmoor even thought him so kind that when they were released they clubbed together and asked their government representative to buy Cotgrave a gift of some kind of silver or gilt plate or cup.

So it was entirely fair, if predictable and formulaic, for the *Gentleman's Magazine* to conclude that, having 'devoted himself with integrity and zeal to the service of his king and country', his actions at Dartmoor demonstrated that 'his humanity and integrity were uniformly conspicuous'.

Managing the prisoners was not the only role expected of the Agent for Prisoners of War, and an important part of Cotgrave's job in running the prison was business acumen. He negotiated contracts for the supply of timber, food supplies and coal, and ran tenders to see which local farmer would pay most to remove the tons of human and animal excrement produced by the prison, to use as fertilizer on the poor Dartmoor soil.

The tiny isolated community into which the vast prison at Dartmoor had been planted had no place of worship, and as the civilian population grew to service its needs, a proper church was required. As the most senior official in the area, Isaac Cotgrave was asked how many people it should accommodate, and replied that it would need to be in the region of 500 to 600. It was January 1812 before authorisation to start work finally come through, and although the captain was heavily involved in overseeing the work, it would be two years before the building was completed, by which time he had retired.

While all of these things were occupying much of his time, the ageing man found time to continue an active personal life. His last daughter was not born until 1806, a quarter of a century after his first son. By about 1810, several of his older sons had joined the navy, some of them having begun their careers as junior officers on his own ships.[5] He entered 14-year-old George William Cotgrave into the Royal Naval Academy in February 1809. Later the same month, the Admiralty was confused when an officer called Cotgrave wrote from Dartmoor asking to be appointed to the command of a ship – civil servants were surprised that the old prison

5   One of his sons was Lieutenant Richard Cotgrave, See Chapter 5.

governor wanted to go back to sea. Isaac replied to explain that it was his son Lieutenant Edward Stone Cotgrave,[6] who was staying with him, who sought employment having recovered his health following an incident in the West Indies where he had lost an eye.

Isaac Cotgrave had a licence to hunt game on the moors and took a liking to Dartmoor's semi-wild ponies. Having seen one he particularly wanted, he took some helpers and chased it onto a precarious rocky outcrop, but as a younger, more nimble man climbed to secure it, Cotgrave looked on in 'infinite surprise' as the pony leapt over the man and escaped.

It was just before Christmas 1813 when Isaac Cotgrave finally decided that it was time to retire from the remote, harsh and demanding life at Dartmoor. He had first joined the Royal Navy more than half a century earlier. His youthful transgressions were long forgotten – if anybody now remembered that he had once been a deserter, it was never mentioned. But life had taken its toll and he looked older than his years; he was 66, but people believed him to be 72. Six months later he was dead.

Captain Isaac Cotgrave RN had lived a life of contradictions.

He came from a family that had occupied the same few square miles of Cheshire for half a millennium but he travelled thousands of miles around the globe. He lived most of his life at sea, but his reward was a job inland, where he could not even see the coast. He had a long and successful marriage to a woman with American heritage, but it was the Americans in his custody who were vitriolic in their hatred of him. His success as a ship's captain depended on getting a group of men working together as a team, but his job at Dartmoor was to do exactly the opposite. The sheer number of the inmates meant that if they had successfully made common cause, they would have become unmanageable. He had been treated contemptibly as a prisoner of war but by the judgment of his day, he was compassionate almost to a fault in his own treatment of the men he incarcerated.

The greatest contradiction of all came in 1806. Isaac Cotgrave had spent his lifetime trying to kill or capture Frenchmen, to stop Frenchmen killing or capturing him and his comrades, and in general treating the entire French nation as an incorrigible enemy. He had beaten the French at the Battle of the Glorious First of June in 1794 and then been beaten by the French at the raid on Boulogne in 1801. He had been locked up in a French dungeon and in turn had kept French prisoners locked up in British hulks and prisons. He had fought with Nelson, who became the

6   See Chapter 26.

nation's greatest hero by giving his life to the cause of proving Britain's supremacy over France. Nelson wrote that he had never witnessed such zeal in fighting the French as that shown by Isaac Cotgrave.

But when Nelson was buried, the code and custom of war meant that the French admiral whose navy had killed him was invited as an honoured guest to the funeral; Isaac Cotgrave was expected personally to honour him. Admiral Pierre-Charles-Jean-Baptiste-Silvestre de Villeneuve was technically a prisoner of war, which is why Cotgrave was involved, but he actually lived in comfort in a Berkshire inn. He attended Nelson's funeral in the autumn of 1805 and was then allowed home in April 1806.

As the French admiral embarked at the Pier Head in Plymouth, a crowd of spectators gathered to watch. Villeneuve was rowed with his escort out to the ship on which he would travel home. As he left, the admiral made one final gesture of respect to the nation against which he had fought all his life. For a brief moment, the pride of the whole of Britain was embodied in one man in a blue jacket and cocked hat, who had started life in Chester and was now standing in a rowing boat in Plymouth harbour.

Admiral Villeneuve 'bowed politely to Captain Cotgrave'.

FAMILY
AND
FRIENDS

It is inevitable that most people's life stories are heavily influenced by those closest to them – their family, neighbours and friends.

These seven lives include two women who fought to secure their family inheritance, one by shifty dissembling and one by the sheer force of a remarkable personality. They include family disagreements and examples of extraordinary love, including a Georgian knight whose family let him down, and his daughters who went out of their way to distance themselves from their relatives. These stories end with the bizarre tale of a woman whose eccentric father gave her nine forenames, but who rarely used any of them, and the long and productive life of a geriatric Victorian who counted one of the world's most famous statesmen among his friends.

CHAPTER FOURTEEN

1576

Hugh Cotgrave has his picture engraved

Hugh Cotgrave had a beard, was quite tall and was thinner than his colleagues. We know these things because one of the finest artists of his day engraved a picture of Cotgrave and his workmates in 1576.[1] It is also possible to say exactly where Cotgrave was on specific dates, and even times, and with whom. Even more unusually, there are records of what he was wearing and since there is a hand-coloured copy of the engraving, we know that he had auburn hair. Volumes of his writing have survived and it would be fairly easy to assemble a tableful of papers and books that he once held, and which might even retain a faint imprint of his inky fingers. For someone who died well over 400 years ago, rather a lot is known about him.

But it is hard to avoid the impression that this is not what he wanted. Throughout his life, he went nameless, or allowed others to get his name wrong, or made use of the fact that his job title would serve as a substitute for his real name. When he was promoted, the part of the ceremony where his name should have been read out was omitted, but a small crowd shouted out his job title. He either deliberately obscured where he lived or else lived somewhere so obscure that it cannot be identified. Most surprisingly of all, even though his job was to record people's family trees, his name is missing from every known contemporary copy of his own family's pedigree, including one very detailed version that he himself wrote and owned.

Hugh Cotgrave became a member of the College of Arms in 1553, in

---

1 Cotgrave is shown as being about ten per cent taller than the shortest figures, and none of the other men shown on the same sheet as him is taller. Some of the others are shown as considerably wider than he is. He is also the only one wearing a hat.

Hugh Cotgrave is shown taking part in the procession of the Order of the Garter in 1576 [Imaginary Composite Procession of the Order of the Garter at Windsor, engraved by Marcus Gheeraerts (1521–86) 1576 (coloured etching), English School, (16th century) /British Museum, London, UK/Bridgeman Images].

the junior rank of Rouge Croix Pursuivant, then in 1566 he was promoted to Richmond Herald, one of six heralds who were overseen by the Kings of Arms.

The work of regulating heraldry included visiting various parts of the country and registering the family trees of anyone claiming the right to use a coat of arms. Known as visitations, these events produced dozens of volumes of invaluable information about sixteenth-century England. In 1561, Hugh Cotgrave took part in the visitation of Essex, Suffolk and Norfolk, riding out of London with his boss and five servants, all dressed in the bright colours that typify armorial designs. By 1566, when he had been promoted to the rank of herald, he led the delegation that checked the credentials of the gentry in Huntingdonshire and Northamptonshire. He is best remembered for a document now known as *Cotgrave's Ordinary*. It is a catalogue of coats of arms which Hugh Cotgrave painstakingly compiled in the early 1560s.

Among his other roles, Cotgrave spent a high proportion of his time attending funerals of the gentry and aristocracy, regulating the ceremonial aspects, ensuring that the churches were properly adorned and recording the family histories of the deceased. Many of these events were routine, like the burials of Sir John Radcliffe and Mr John Skinner in London and Mrs Elizabeth Hopton in Surrey. Others were grander – the funerals of the Archbishop of Canterbury at Lambeth Palace, the late Lord Mayor at the chapel of the Mercers' Guild and Henry VII's granddaughter at Westminster Abbey. Attendance meant constantly being called at short notice to travel around the southern half of the country to burials at rural churches in Berkshire, Middlesex, Buckinghamshire, Suffolk, Norfolk, Sussex, Oxford, Worcestershire, Kent and even North Shropshire, 150 miles outside London. He was part of a large entourage at the burial of a former Lord Mayor's wife and accompanied Lady Neville's body from London to its burial place thirty miles away. He officiated at dozens of funerals for aldermen, judges, earls and countesses, knights, and government officials. Many were grand affairs, like the funerals of Lady Dudley in Oxford and the Countess of Westmorland in London, followed by a 'great dinner', and even the ceremonies that were held in London to mark the deaths of the King of France and the Holy Roman Emperor. One of the most ornate was the funeral of Lady Catherine Grey, the queen's cousin and possible heir, in Suffolk in 1568, for which Cotgrave had a special outfit made, and where he received more than £63 in fees, travelling expenses and costs for banners and painted shields. The events often involved trumpeters, elaborately dressed horses and 'a vast retinue'. At Lady Dudley's interment, Hugh was part of a mourning procession, wearing a black gown with his hood over his head, and at Sir Harry Grey's funeral he carried the dead man's armour helmet. When his colleague Lawrence Dalton died, Cotgrave headed the lengthy procession through the London streets, carrying Dalton's coat of arms on a flag, with two bellringers clearing the streets to make way for him. His role in Ann Barrett's funeral was so significant that she was said to have been 'buried by Hugh Cotgrave, Richmond Herald'.

Possibly the most elaborate of all these occasions was the three-month ceremonies after the death of the Bishop of Winchester, who was also Lord Chancellor, in 1555. At the original services in London, it was Cotgrave who enjoined everyone to pray: 'Of your charity, pray for the soul of the Reverend Father in God Stephen Gardiner,' reciting his offices and titles, before beginning the Lord's Prayer. Then 13 weeks later (when the weather had improved), the body was taken to Winchester, and he performed the same function – called 'bidding the bedes' – at each church where the cortege stopped on the journey.[2] Hugh Cotgrave's horse wore colourful trappings decorated with the bishop's coat of arms and he was watched by the clergy and parish clerks as the procession travelled through 29 parishes. When the cortege arrived in Winchester over a week later, he assisted the chief mourner at the funeral mass and guided the Mayor of Winchester in his role. He was paid two shillings and sixpence a day and received expenses for black cloth to dress the cathedral and other fabrics used to make the decorative cushions and drapes needed for such a solemn and important occasion.

Cotgrave and his fellow heralds were familiar around London, where they acted as conduits for government information. As a pursuivant in 1559, he accompanied the mayor and aldermen to announce to the citizenry of London that a three-way peace had been concluded between England, France and Scotland. He was decked out in his finery for the annual Garter Procession and was near the front of the 100-person pageant that accompanied the Duke and Duchess of Norfolk as they came into London from one of their country residences. He acquired four yards of black cloth to make suitable clothes for the funeral of Queen Mary in 1558 and another four of expensive scarlet for Queen Elizabeth's coronation shortly afterwards.

Not all of the work was glamorous and Cotgrave was required to be 'quiet, sober and discreet'. Some of his duties relied on careful diligence.

---

2   It was said to be at 'every parish till they came to Winchester' that there was a mass, although it was only actually three churches, but with several masses said in each.

Sometimes it actually mattered that the details of family trees were precisely recorded. At New College, Oxford, the rules allowed the dons to favour the relatives of their founder. Cotgrave recorded the pedigree but then changed his mind when he checked the details. His punctiliousness was clear when he happily paid his contribution to the coronation gift for Queen Elizabeth, but went to the trouble of obtaining a personal writ confirming that as a herald, he was actually exempt and need not have paid. Least glamorous of all was the basic administration of the College of Arms. The heralds maintained their own premises and when Cotgrave took his turn at running things, he had to pay a labourer to clean the gutters, arrange for 'a load of Rubbysh' to be removed from the courtyard, and buy a new door for the 'privy'.

Despite his very visible public role, Hugh Cotgrave's reticence makes it uncertain which part of the Cotgrave family he belonged to, but it is possible to make a good guess. Since he entered the service of a part of the Royal Household in the mid 1550s, it is a fair bet that he was introduced by one of the three Cotgrave siblings who had moved from Chester to be employed at court or to marry men who were – Robert Cotgrave, who had worked for Henry VIII's uncle, and his sisters Eleanor, whose husband was Master of the Royal Buckhounds, and Katherine, first married to one of the Sovereign's painters and afterwards to the Clerk of the Royal Stables. Hugh's first known employment, as servant to Garter King of Arms, appears to have involved painting shields of arms, so it seems very likely that he had some connection with Katherine Cotgrave's first husband, Anthony Totto, who created badges and insignia showing coats of arms to decorate buildings and tents.[3] Robert, Katherine and Eleanor Cotgrave's mother was buried in the London parish where Hugh Cotgrave based himself and one slightly later family tree suggests that the siblings had a relation called Hugh. It seems safe to assume that the herald known as Hugh Cotgrave was a close relative of the three Cotgrave courtiers from Chester.

When he first became a properly employed member of the College of Arms, Cotgrave was clearly known about town among some of the London citizenry but there was already vagueness about his surname. He was 'Huw, Master Garter's servant'. And much later, even when

---

3   Totto was married to Katherine Cotgrave; his receipts and accounts show him being paid for creating hatchments and badges for stables and for a celebratory tent in Hyde Park in 1551; one schedule lists 32 painters working under his supervision so it is easy to see how he could have been Hugh Cotgrave's first employer as an heraldic painter.

operating as a private individual, he was known by his title, not his name, selling property in Essex under the name of 'Mr Rychmond, the Harrald at Arms'. The house even went by the name of 'Richmonds'. Even the record of his burial calls him 'Mr Richmond, alias Hugh Cotgrave,' rather than the other way around.

The air of mystery extends to identifying where Hugh Cotgrave lived. He clearly operated in the City of London because it was essential to his job, and since he was summoned to funerals around the country, which could hardly be planned long in advance, he must have been readily contactable and not far away most of the time. There is no doubt that he had property in St Vedast's parish in the City because the taxman made a note of it and he was buried there, along with other members of his family. However, in the splendid set of heraldic records known as *Cotgrave's Ordinary*, he described himself as being from somewhere called 'Sermes'. But there is nowhere in Britain called Sermes, or any similar variant. Hugh Cotgrave claimed to live in a place that does not seem to exist.

None of the little details that make Hugh Cotgrave seem reticent about his identity is very significant in itself. It is not entirely surprising that a diarist should be unable to call to mind the surname of a young man who had only just been promoted to his first proper job, or that a formal but essentially private ceremony should be a little rushed and leave out one small part, and it was not at all unusual in Tudor England for people to refer to one another by their job titles rather than names; nor is Sermes the only place name that after this length of time is hard to identify. But overall, these individual niggles start to look like a pattern, especially when set against one of the documents that Hugh Cotgrave wrote and kept.

Cheshire, where the Cotgrave family was based, was visited by heralds twice during his tenure, in 1566 and 1580. Although Hugh was not himself involved in these particular events, he needed to keep copies of all sorts of genealogical records and it happens that one of only two surviving copies of the 1566 visitation of Cheshire was written by Cotgrave for his own use. There can be no doubt about this, because the handwriting is identical to other documents he wrote and on its impressive leather-bound cover is written in large and very clear contemporary handwriting the name he used for his work – Richmond Herald. The pedigree of his family in this manuscript contains unique information that is not recorded in other surviving documents. However, nowhere does it indicate Hugh Cotgrave's existence – he does not feature anywhere in his own copy of his own family's pedigree. Nor is he mentioned in copies of a family tree that was extensively researched in 1572 or in any of the documents associated with the 1580 visitation, when he was still very much alive and active.

If Hugh Cotgrave set out to be mysterious, he succeeded in one regard. It is a complete enigma why, studied with 400 years of hindsight, it looks as if he was deliberately trying to be opaque about his genetic identity and distance himself from his family.

Perhaps the most obvious explanation might be that he was shy about admitting his connections because he was illegitimate. If that were his reason, he could have used a different surname, and it would not have stopped his family from registering their connection with him at the visitations. In any case, he had on occasion used a version of the family's coat of arms, apparently without the normal marks that identified illegitimacy.

Maybe Cotgrave had fallen out with some of the other members of his family, but there is no evidence of such a disagreement, and if the argument was serious, there would almost certainly have been some. His relatives were not at all shy about pursuing their differences in court. But Hugh Cotgrave's name is not mentioned in any of the 130 court cases involving his family that are known between the date when he became a pursuivant and the day he died.

Religion was certainly a reason to keep your head down in Tudor England. When Cotgrave was first appointed, the devoutly Catholic Mary I had been on the throne for a matter of weeks after the death of her decidedly Protestant brother. The coming years would see a battle for the religious heart of the nation that involved executions and persecution in which Cotgrave's family would eventually get caught up. But his reticence was not caused by his faith. He was a religious chameleon, flexible enough to read the prayers at the funeral of a very Catholic bishop during the reign of a very Catholic monarch in 1555 and then in 1568 to officiate at the Protestant funeral of the Protestant heir of a Protestant queen. Cotgrave cannot have been very religious anyway because he was fined, along with two colleagues, for not attending supposedly compulsory Whitsun services for the heralds.

There is one other remote possibility. In 1535, a man called Thomas Cotgrave from Barrow near Chester was imprisoned in the Tower of London for making counterfeit coins, a treasonable crime. The evidence against him was at least credible, and his name does not appear in any subsequent records, so he presumably suffered the consequences and was executed, or else he died in custody with the stigma hanging over him. Maybe Hugh Cotgrave was his son, and sought to divert attention away from his connection with a convicted traitor. Thomas Cotgrave appears to have been the uncle of the Robert, Katherine and Eleanor Cotgrave[4] who later succeeded at court, so it is entirely possible that if he had a young son at the time of his execution, the child might have been brought up with his cousins and later benefited from their contacts.

In the engraving made by Marcus Gheeraerts in the 1570s, Hugh Cotgrave is smiling as he and his colleagues process in a very public ceremony, dressed in eye-catching clothes. It represents everything about his official life – visibly and expensively travelling from county to county, sometimes in a large entourage, with a gaggle of liveried servants, riding garishly decorated horses, decking out churches in colourful drapery, having bells rung to announce his arrival, interviewing local magnates about their families, and giving public performances of prayers and proclamations to large crowds. But alone among the people who are illustrated in Gheeraerts' image of the procession, Hugh Cotgrave is not looking forward into the crowd, or gazing at the monarch, or talking to a colleague; uniquely, he is looking away, as if he does not want the publicity.

A very small percentage of people in the sixteenth century were as noticeable as Hugh Cotgrave in his role as Richmond Herald-of-Arms. Yet for some mysterious reason, he obscured his name whenever he could, gave an address that nobody can identify, and left himself out of the family trees he was paid to produce.

He had something to hide, and he hid it well.

4   See Chapters 2 and 22.

CHAPTER FIFTEEN

1579

Eleanor Cotgreve secures an inheritance

Eleanor Cotgreve was different. Most records of the women from her time define them solely by reference to their male relations, but that did not happen to Eleanor. In a family tree drawn in 1566, she is straightforwardly and in her own right 'Eleanor Welsh of Overpool,' (her maiden name) while two of her relatives are called 'Maud bastard daughter of Piers Dutton,' or simply 'a daughter, wife to Richard Aldersey'.

The pedigree includes a minor mistake in her name – her original surname was almost certainly Welshman, suggesting that at some point in the preceding centuries, her forebears had come from over the border in North Wales to settle on the Mersey estuary.[1] By Eleanor's time, they seem to have been respectable but of limited means and it is unlikely that Richard Cotgreve, a gentleman with a coat of arms and his own farm and lands, had any great economic considerations in mind when he married her. His grandmother was the daughter of a knight, his aunt belonged to a major landowning family in Lancashire and his great aunt's family were barons. But his wife Eleanor was the daughter of a lowly farmer. There was clearly something about Eleanor Welshman's character that meant she was a person in her own right rather than merely one man's daughter or another man's wife. Richard astutely recognised in her the qualities that would serve his family's posterity in a far more important way than a fancy pedigree ever could.

Richard Cotgreve himself was born sometime around 1530, and Eleanor was probably younger, although there are no records to confirm her age. They were married by the early 1550s and rapidly had three

---

1   In 1569, she was associated with a man called Robert Welshman in her home parish, where there were also men called Thomas and John Welshman; in 1605, her son was co-owner of property with John Welshman.

children. There were two sons, called William (a name that could be traced back in the family to the twelfth century) and Peter (a more recent addition – Richard's father had been the first ever Peter Cotgreve). The daughter was called Alice, which was not particularly a Cotgreve family favourite and it is tempting to believe that the little girl was named after one of the Welshmans.

Richard Cotgreve died young. So in 1558, when Eleanor Cotgreve cannot have been much older than 25, she was left a widow with three children under the age of five. Most women in the period would have remarried very quickly, but Eleanor was different.

It appears that members of her own family were supportive of Eleanor, and although she kept the lands her husband had left at Foulkstapleford, she did not initially live there, but moved back to her home parish, about ten miles away. In 1569, when Richard had already been dead for a decade, her name appears in a fascinating court case where she and two male relatives were accused of forcibly occupying a house and 55 acres of land that was said to belong to a local dignitary. The statute used for the prosecution related specifically to occasions when someone used force to hold on to land wrongly even though they had originally entered it peaceably and legally. So the most likely explanation is that Eleanor and the men had rented the property and were refusing to leave when it was alleged that their lease was up. When the accused were listed in the court record, Eleanor was repeatedly named first, as if she were the prime mover. It is plain that there was something about this young woman (she can only have been in her thirties) that meant she was treated differently from others. Ten years later, in another court case, she would reveal what that something special was – the steel and determination she successfully showed in a fight against powerful men.

In the intervening years, Eleanor Cotgreve moved back to Foulkstapleford and in 1574, she was again in dispute with a male neighbour. On this occasion, she succeeded in obtaining a court order that he must keep the peace towards her and her children. It required the troublemaker to behave well towards the young Alice Cotgreve, who was now a teenager, so perhaps he was pressurising the family to arrange a financially advantageous marriage. If so, Eleanor was having none of it and wanted to protect her vulnerable daughter.

In 1576, apparently as soon as he came of age, Eleanor's elder son William Cotgreve sold the property his father had left as the family's inheritance and went off to Ireland. But he had no right to sell, at least not immediately, because under the terms of his father's bequest, his mother was entitled to live in the house and use the land as long as she lived.

Eleanor found herself faced with irate new owners who had bought in good faith, and having to rely on arguments about her son's recklessness when he was not even in the country to answer. People who knew them said that there was a love and 'motherly zeal' between them. To some, this suggested (wrongly) that Eleanor and William were in cahoots to achieve some dodgy objective. In fact, whatever their relationship had been in the past, William had now exposed his mother to substantial risks and problems.

Worse was to come because after a slightly opaque process, the new owner turned out to be another man called William Cotgreve, who was a cousin of Eleanor's late husband. He was a powerful member of the Chester community; very soon he would be sheriff of the city, he would go on to become mayor, he personally knew the lords and magnates who controlled many people's lives and he himself owned plenty of property and land in the area.[2] Moreover, he was friends with the local manorial lord, Sir William Brereton, who had an historic interest in the Cotgreve estate, and who collected an annual ground rent from the property. So Eleanor was in a very difficult situation. She was a widow who lacked powerful male relatives of her own, the person who had caused the problem was her own son and he was not around, while the individual she might have turned to for help, an influential member of her late husband's family, was the very man who was now causing her the greatest difficulty.

If ever Eleanor Cotgreve needed to show the qualities that made her special, now was the time. And she did. The Exchequer of Chester operated as a court of equity, supposedly ensuring that neighbours dealt fairly with one another, without particular reference to the minutiae of the law. Eleanor Cotgreve set out to make it do its job. She brought an action aimed at forcing her late husband's cousin, the city dignitary William Cotgreve, to back down and recognise that the farm was hers for as long as she lived. But William Cotgreve was a seasoned litigant, and he succeeded in dragging the case out, with various stages listed in the court books time after time. Eleanor knew she was right, however, and she would not give up even in the face of her late husband's combative cousin. Alone she battled. And in the end she won.

On 5 October 1579, the court ordered that as long as she lived, Eleanor Cotgreve, the widow of the late Richard Cotgreve, was the rightful occupier of her mansion house, barn, oven house, orchard, fruit gardens, meadows, herbage, wood and fields. Moreover, she only had to pay half of the ground rent to the manorial lord. Since William Cotgreve had a

2   See Chapter 31.

fact, Margaret Cotgreave's relatives had been surprised at the time to find out that she had married the Reverend Charles Aldcroft.

None of this was fatal to Margaret's case. Cotgreave and Johnson were interested in the outcome, but that did not prove they were lying. It would be a big step to accuse John Cotgreave of perjury just because he was a little vague about the precise order of events at a busy time almost a decade and a half earlier.

However, there seemed to be hard proof that the clergyman who had performed the service was lying. For a start, it was odd that the wedding had supposedly happened at Backford. Margaret Cotgreave had lived all her life in the parish of St Mary-on-the-Hill in Chester, where Charles Aldcroft worked as curate, in addition to his duties in Wallasey. The city of Chester would have been the obvious place for them to have been married. Margaret also owned property in the nearby parish of Eastham so it would not have looked out of place if the ceremony had taken place there. Neither of them, however, ever claimed to have any other connection to Backford except that, apparently randomly, they had chosen it for their secret wedding.

Because neither Margaret Cotgreave nor Charles Aldcroft was resident at Backford in 1734, it had not been possible to read the banns there. A written licence was needed for the wedding service, and the entry in the parish register recorded that it had been produced at the time. But when the diocesan records were checked, there was no evidence that such a document had ever been issued. There was a ledger enumerating every instance of licences being granted; the Aldcrofts' wedding in Backford was not listed. The clerk who was supposed to have issued the licence was tracked down and, remarkably given the passage of 14 years, said that he remembered writing one out, although he was adamant that Backford was not among the eligible parishes it had named. The priest was equally clear that the licence did really exist, but he admitted that it did look as if the word Backford had been added later. He even claimed that he still had the paper, although it never seems to have made its way into court.

The whole issue of the licence looked suspect, especially when the parish register itself was subjected to further scrutiny. The handwriting recording the marriage of Charles and Margaret looked different from the other entries on the page, as if it had been written by someone different or perhaps at a different time with different ink. Although they had not attended the ceremony, John Cotgreave and John Johnson were alleged to have made a special trip to Backford later, with a hint that they may have intended to forge the records. But again, nothing could be proved, and the handwriting certainly did not belong to either of them. In the end, it was agreed that it was the local vicar's writing. It was impossible to say when he wrote it, however, and Charles Aldcroft's family still maintained that the entry had been recently falsified. The officiating priest explained the appearance of tampering by saying that Charles Aldcroft himself may have tried to hide the original entry to keep his marriage secret, and that it had been re-written after his death.

Then a crucial piece of evidence turned up that had previously been overlooked. Each year, parishes had to copy out a duplicate of the annual records onto a loose sheet and send it to the registry in the cathedral. So in theory, the bishop's registrar had a contemporary copy of every register. These copies were filed away at diocesan headquarters, and it was not possible to tamper with them in the way it was with the original register lying around in the church. When the bishop's copy of Backford's register for 1734 was examined it was tidy, entirely credible and apparently complete. No parts were ripped, the handwriting was consistent and the letters had not faded.

But the suspect marriage was not there.

If an administrative oversight explained why the marriage licence had not been recorded in its proper place in the ledger, and if the passage of time could explain minor discrepancies in poorly-remembered dates, it was hard to find an excuse for the complete absence of any record of the marriage in the bishop's transcripts.

Moreover, it was well known that Charles Aldcroft and Margaret Cotgreave had not lived together as man and wife in 1734 and early 1735, or apparently for some time afterwards. If they were married why had they been pretending otherwise? That could easily be explained, said Margaret. Her brother had used her house as a base for his responsibilities as Mayor of Chester, because it was near the city centre, whereas his own home was a little distance away. It was not sensible for Aldcroft to move in while all those civic functions and other mayoral business meetings were going on. But Margaret distinctly remembered taking her new husband his meals using food 'from the mayor's table'. It was the sort of detail that might have had a ring of truth, but it was still deeply suspicious that nobody noticed at the time that the pair were married. In any case, the story could not be entirely true because of the demonstrable dating of events – John Cotgreave's term as mayor started in the autumn of 1735, not 1734 as Margaret and her brother seemed to think. But Margaret had another reason why she and Charles had pretended not to be married. She was continuing to trade as a skinner, her first husband's occupation. The restrictive practices of the city guilds only allowed her to do this as a skinner's widow. If she admitted she was married to someone else, she would have had to close down her (profitable) business. This even explained why she had not gone into mourning when Charles Aldcroft died. Neither she, nor her brother or son had even attended Aldcroft's funeral.

Margaret Aldcroft and John Cotgreave now came under more pressure. Specific dates and events were probed to prove that he had always accepted her legal name to be Johnson, not Aldcroft. For example, when their mother died and Cotgreave had administered her estate, he had allegedly accepted a receipt from his sister for her share, signed 'Margaret Johnson'. But Cotgreave denied this – no receipt had been needed from his own sister for a few household items, which was all their mother had owned. But this picture of relaxed family harmony was at odds with his own admission that whatever he said now, John and Margaret had fallen out over her relationship with Aldcroft, and had not spoken to one another for several years after the end of his mayoralty.

Evidence was stacking up for a clumsy attempt to forge the record of a wedding that had never really happened. Misremembering the date of her brother's big year, Margaret had arranged for the priest of Backford to slip a false entry into the register, made up a story that might just have been believable if she had recalled the date correctly, and then used John Cotgreave's status to try and bluff her way out of a situation that was acutely embarrassing and financially problematic. Either she had lived in sin with a man – and a clergyman at that – for years and was now fraudulently trying to get her hands on his money, or she had deliberately pretended not to be married to defraud the city corporation's rules, with the active connivance of her brother who had been head of that very corporation. But the stakes were large enough to risk the reputational damage – an inventory proved that the estate was worth about £1,000.[1]

Remarkably, even in the face of what looked like an overwhelming body of circumstantial evidence of fraud, all was not lost and Margaret continued to be recognised as Charles Aldcroft's widow. The law was on her side. It was obvious to an impartial observer that Margaret's story was dodgy, but admitting it would mean accusing a well-known alderman, an honourable tradesman and a respected clergyman of outright lying and forgery. There was just enough evidence to support their case for the verdict to have a touch of credibility. Witnesses were found who had seen Margaret and Charles Aldcroft behaving as man and wife, even that

---

1   The total comes to around £942, but no estimate was included for a number of items, including almost 100 books and the interest on some debts that were owing at the time of Rev Charles Aldcroft's death.

she had been in his bedroom early in the morning wearing nothing but a shift. Even now, one witness questioned what this proved; they could have been 'married or worse'.

At the time of Margaret's alleged wedding, there was no legal need for witnesses. The only living people who could claim to know what had happened were her and the vicar, and they both implacably insisted that on 3 December 1734, she and Charles Aldcroft had been married in Backford parish church. The missing licence, doubts over the chronology of Cotgreave's mayoralty, the witnesses' blatant conflicts of interests, and the discrepancy between the original register and the bishop's copy all looked highly dubious, but they were not in the end relevant.

Margaret Aldcroft, as she continued to call herself, lived for another 16 years after the infamous court case. The evidence had centred not so much on the people as on her house. It was noticeable that Charles Aldcroft had moved into her home, not the other way around. John Cotgreave had used her house as his mayoral headquarters, not his own. Numerous witnesses had spoken in detail not just about what they had seen in general but what they had seen in Margaret's house in particular; they even described whether they had been upstairs or downstairs at the time. Several of them were at pains to point out where the house was – near the bridge over the River Dee at the bottom of Bridge Street. Even Charles Aldcroft's son from a previous marriage, who stood to lose everything if the case went against him, testified that he had been a welcome guest in the house, released by the master of his apprenticeship to stay there at weekends. More than anything else, it was this house that was the centre of the case. The reason was at the heart of Margaret's motivation throughout. Just as the whole case was about her securing the Aldcroft wealth, and her deception had been about continuing the lucrative skinner's trade, so her obsession with her house by the bridge was financially motivated. Everyone who passed her home to cross the bridge out of Chester had to pay a toll, and it was Margaret who profited. She had been granted the right to collect (and keep) the tolls in 1734, for an annual fee of £20, renewing an arrangement that her first husband had put in place in 1716.

As a result of her efforts, the property by the river stayed in Margaret's family; half a century later, her grandson Sir John Cotgreave would own it.[2] And when she died, the burial register at Saint Mary's Church for 16 April 1765 made two clear points – Margaret had been married to the late Mr Aldcroft and she had belonged right there in that house by the riverside. It reads 'Mrs Margaret Aldcroft Widow Near ye Bridge'.

2   See Chapter 17.

CHAPTER SEVENTEEN

1795

John Cotgreave chooses a motto

Sir John Cotgreave was an insecure man. He felt the need to exaggerate his late father's importance and to add an ornamental top to his family tree. He added a spurious branch to his genealogy so that he could claim important people were his cousins while simultaneously ensuring that he took precedence over them. He gave his children old and impressive-sounding names to lend his familial claims an air of truth. For good measure, he fabricated evidence about how long his forebears had owned land and property, added irrelevant facts to his own story, gave his fictional ancestors impressive jobs, and used heraldic symbols that were not rightly his. He pressed the message home by adopting a motto that emphasised his family's antiquity, seemingly the principal focus of his insecurity.

None of it was necessary. Cotgreave's family was truly ancient, the important people really were his cousins and he could legitimately have used interesting and impressive heraldry to bolster his image. Whether or not his particular lands had been in his family for half a millennium as he claimed was irrelevant, given that he owned so much property, some of it genuinely old, that he was by any standards rich.

Most importantly, John Cotgreave was obviously popular with just about everyone for reasons that were nothing to do with his genetic heritage. He was a caring, likeable and talented human being. He was also lucky. The reason he was knighted was that he happened to serve as Mayor of Chester at a time when a group of provincial dignitaries went to London for a royal wedding, and a representative selection of four of them received honours. The chosen four happen to have been one from the westernmost reaches of South Wales, one from the far northeast of Scotland, and two from cities in the South East and North

An officer's commission in the militia, personally signed by King George III, was one of the signs that John Cotgreave had entered the upper echelons of society.

West of England. It looks suspiciously like Sir John acquired his title by geographical accident.

It is easy to see why John Cotgreave lacked confidence in his place in society. In a status conscious world it had not always been certain that his popularity and luck would lead to renown, wealth or happiness. For a start, he was born plain John Johnson, the son of a small-scale cloth manufacturer.[1] His parents both died when he was two, and he was put into the care of an elderly uncle. Not exactly poverty, but it was hardly gravitating him towards his rich, unmarried, ageing cousins, the people who might help him recover something of what he believed were his family's former glories. The Johnsons were well-established but they

1   See Chapter 20.

John Cotgreave
registered an
updated and
more elaborate
version of his
family's heraldic
emblems in 1795
[College of Arms
MS 7 D.14 p.260,
reproduced by
kind permission of
the Kings, Heralds
and Pursuivants of
Arms].

were mostly tradesmen who got their hands dirty. John's grandmother, however, had been a Cotgreave, and what the little John Johnson saw as he was growing up was that Thomas and John Cotgreave, his grandmother's nephews, lived in opulent style, were already well past the age when they were likely to get married, and had no closer relations to whom they could leave their money. Their sister had married well and she had no children. The Johnsons were the only proper heirs the Cotgreave brothers had.

In the race to inherit the money, the problem with the Johnsons was that there were so many of them. Thomas Cotgreave's will mentions William Johnson, Joseph Johnson, Elizabeth Johnson, two different John Johnsons, the Reverend Jonathan Johnson and Charles Johnson, plus their children.[2] Despite the family competition, as he grew to adulthood, the young John Johnson had high hopes. They were justified, and in

2   See Chapter 32.

1795, he accepted the terms of the bequest and changed his surname to Cotgreave.

As John Cotgreave, his fortune was made and his place in society was set. Even before he had officially changed his name, he had been made a freeman of the city of Chester on the basis of inheritance. He now rapidly became a member of the vestry of leading parishioners at St Mary's Church, the owner of a licence to hunt game (his sporting rights extended over 300 acres) and an officer in the volunteer forces. He joined the local lodge of freemasons and was rapidly promoted through its ranks. Within a few years, he was an elected official of the Chester Corporation and of his own parish, and became a regular member of the Grand Jury at Chester Castle, sometimes its foreman. In 1800, he served as one of the two city sheriffs, which was a good route to eventually serving as mayor, an office that came with the added job of chief magistrate. Parliament appointed him as a commissioner for implementing the Act for enclosing lands in and around Chester.

Cotgreave was also a significant property owner. As well as houses in various parts of Chester, he had fields, woods and lands in the surrounding area and a significant farm in North Wales. He managed to swap individual fields with Earl Grosvenor to bring his holdings together into a consolidated block and in one of his properties near the River Dee, there was a suite of rooms reserved for the Earl of Shrewsbury. By the early years of the nineteenth century, John Cotgreave was looking to expand his own living accommodation, and he extended what was described as a 'beautiful cottage' just outside the city into an impressive Georgian mansion. While digging the foundations, his workmen uncovered burial urns, one of which was lifted intact, containing the cremated remains of a Roman inhabitant of Chester. The home he created, Netherlegh House, was set in nine acres of grounds including gardens and orchards, and was furnished with 'superior' mahogany tables and chairs, 'elegant beds, superb window curtains, costly and magnificent vases' and a host of other finery that constituted 'every other article requisite in a gentleman's house'.

A member of the city Council, John Cotgreave clearly knew how to cultivate different constituencies. It was a blatantly populist move when he threatened to name and shame those bakers who were defrauding citizens by using adulterated flour, and it is noticeable that he took part in services not just in his parish church but also at other local churches and nonconformist chapels. He did not, however, try to be all things to all people, and was overtly against giving Roman Catholics greater influence. He took a hardline stance on crime and disorder as a member of two

When he published his coat of arms in Joseph Hemingway's *History of the City of Chester* in 1831, Sir John Cotgreave fraudulently claimed associations with various other families.

different associations for the prosecution of felons. Immediately on taking office as mayor, he delivered on a pre-election promise to crack down on city-centre hooligans, and the local newspapers commented on how the streets were 'free from riot and disorder'. His swearing-in ceremony was accompanied by lengthy cheering as he promised to direct all his energies to the general welfare of the city.

Sir John made a point of mixing not just with the great and good, but with the 'respectable tradesmen,' with whom he shared an evening of excellent food and gleeful singing in a tavern during the same week that he attended a more staid grand dinner with civic dignitaries. Chester had a sizeable Welsh community, and Sir John was obviously its friend, ordering hymns to be sung in Welsh at his inaugural banquet as mayor, and subscribing to books about the history of the nearby town of Hawarden in Flintshire and even a geography book written in Welsh. He patronised the annual Venison Feast of which he was President, a local music festival in Chester, the King and Constitution Club, Chester Racecourse and the River Dee Regatta, where a toast was drunk to him at the celebratory dinner. When the proprietors of a local hall had a celebratory feast they toasted that 'he may long enjoy the distinguished honour' of his knighthood. He espoused popular causes such as infrastructure development – agitating for an application to Parliament for a new bridge across the River Dee – and citizens' freedoms when Parliament suspended the Habeas Corpus Act. Under his patronage the local theatre put on comedies and farces and gave new talent a chance to perform.

But Cotgreave's popular touch was not just political expediency. Perhaps his early days had taught him something about the value of money, because he had a genuine concern for the needy. The major theme of his inaugural speech as mayor was the need to ignore the 'distinctions of persons' but to look equally to address the grievances of both rich and poor. He set up a committee at the beginning of winter to make sure that adequate provision was made to help the poor and another to inquire into the inequity of the property tax system. He would take on the great and good, arguing with a marquis in public about the merits of proposed legislation and prosecuting Earl Grosvenor's gamekeeper even though he strongly supported two of the Earl's family members as Parliamentary candidates, entertained the Earl to dinner, and did various land deals with him. Cotgreave was one of the two leading patrons of the Beneficial Societies in Chester, and was also one of the largest donors to funds for the relief of the poor and a financial backer of Sunday schools. He was the organiser of more than one benefit event, for example on behalf of a local man 'and his helpless family' and the widow and children of a tradesman who had died after a long illness. 'To those who know the anxious feelings of a parent's heart,' John Cotgreave believed 'argument on this occasion will be needless ... the voice of real distress is never raised in vain'. He was not just interested in handouts to the needy, but wanted to give them chances to help themselves – he advocated better banking facilities so ordinary people could build up savings.

His approach certainly paid off in terms of civic appeal. When the newly knighted Sir John Cotgreave rode back into the city from London, his extraordinary popularity was plain. The cathedral bells were pealing and a cannon salute was fired from the castle walls. When his year of office ended, the citizens gave serious consideration to electing him for an immediate second term, something that had not occurred for well over a century. It would be, they said 'a reward for his meritorious services and active exertions'. Years later, he was still a popular choice in the annual election of aldermen and celebrated at civic dinners.

Amid all this, John Cotgreave seems genuinely to have been interested in gardening. He proudly boasted that he had Provence roses, gilliflowers and polyanthus in flower out of season and that he could grow unusually large strawberries and pineapples. A prize-winning variety of red-fruited gooseberry was named 'Sir John Cotgrave' after he (or more likely his gardener) bred the original examples.

Despite his unquestioned financial, political, social and personal success, Sir John Cotgreave never quite felt that the establishment had accepted him. When he was admitted to the freedom of the city of Chester, he claimed that his father was a Fustian Manufacturer, making him sound like a factory owner, when during his lifetime John Johnson senior had been described by the rather less grand title of chapman. When he changed his name to Cotgreave, he registered a pedigree at the College of Arms that entitled him to a fancy and ancient coat of arms. He chose as his motto *Antiquam obtinens,* which means 'possessing antiquity,' in an attempt to bolster his claim to be descended from an ancient Cheshire family. He did not in fact know his family tree very well – key dates are left blank in the College of Arms pedigree, and it only goes back to the eighteenth century. But when Burke's *Landed Gentry* was published later in his life, he included a fictional family tree taking his Cotgreave ancestry back to 1384 and including a ludicrous amount of specific detail that he could not possibly have known. He even added a dash of verisimilitude by including a man who really had been sheriff of Chester and another who had been mayor. In two different publications, he inserted a branch of the Cotgreave family that made it seem as if he was a distant cousin to

Thomas Cotgreave, the Lord of the Manor of Tarvin near Chester, but pointedly claiming that documents in his possession showed that his own branch was the senior.[3] In fact, they really were related, and rather more closely than the specific way that Sir John claimed. He even made up an elaborate pedigree for his mother and his first wife (who were both called Catherine Cross).

Several times, his humble origins were brought up, when he was referred to as 'Mr Johnson Cotgreave' or 'John Johnson Cotgreave,' but he was clear that this was not his name. When a court case was brought against the city dignitaries and he was listed as 'Johnson Cotgrave,' his formal reply said that the issue and it was nothing to do with him, but he was more concerned in the first line to describe himself as 'John Cotgreave Esquire ... by mistake called Johnson Cotgreave'. His own lawyers went through their account books crossing out the occasions on which they had recorded Cotgreave as having the middle name Johnson.

Sir John and his two wives gave several of their children middle names that strengthened the impression of being related to important Cheshire families. Francis Gamull Cotgreave was supposedly related to Sir Francis Gamull, an MP who had entertained Charles I during the Civil War, Alice Holme Cotgreave was named after a mythical ancestor of the Home family of Tranmere (which produced the three great antiquaries all called Randle Holme) and Frances Brerewood Cotgreave was fictitiously connected to a sister of Sir Robert Brerewood, an MP and distinguished judge of the seventeenth century. Sir John claimed that his coat of arms was entitled to include the family designs of the Holmes, Gamulls, Crosses, Johnsons and Spences, even though in some cases, he was not even related to people with those names, and in others, only to people who had no right to armorial designs. He allowed people to think he was called Sir John because he was an hereditary baronet, not merely a knight. In the list of property that he included in the book of *Landed Gentry*, he correctly reported that his great grandfather had bought the Manor of Netherlegh in the mid–eighteenth century (he proudly called his new house Netherlegh House), but he also said his ancestors had continuously owned some property since 1435, although he was sufficiently vague about where it was that nobody would ever catch him out.

The overall impression he sought to create was that his title, lands and position were his by birthright as a member of one of Cheshire's oldest families. It seems rather sad that he was downplaying the merits of his own personality and abilities, which in reality must have been more

3   See Chapter 34.

important factors in the hearts of the many people who clearly liked and respected him.

After his death, Sir John Cotgreave's family let him down. Within a few years, his widow was bankrupt and his children were at war over the inheritance. His eldest legitimate son took too seriously the business of drinking with the local tradesmen and was a laughing stock when a drunken 'well-known character' said he had taken a drink with 'Thomas Cotgreave, Esq,' who later died of liver cirrhosis.[4] Perhaps the most telling sign of Sir John's posthumous fall was the story that was told about him in court, where his son was wriggling out of debts by technically accurate but morally dubious means. Contemporary records prove that John Cotgreave was knighted at Carlton House after presenting a congratulatory document to the Prince Regent, while wearing his official finery as mayor and surrounded by colleagues from the Chester Corporation, local Parliamentarians and noblemen. But in Chester castle a few years after his death, in front of the Chief Justice, it was joked that he had knelt at the foot of the king to congratulate him on recovering from a fit of gout; the court erupted in hilarity.

John Cotgreave's relatively humble origins might have rendered him inappropriate for public distinction had the force of his personality not cancelled them out. For all his efforts, his feckless wife and children made him the figure of fun that he had worked so hard to avoid becoming, and which he did not deserve to be. Despite the way he was celebrated in his lifetime, there is no statue to his memory, no portrait in the Town Hall or even a plaque in his parish church.

Sir John Cotgreave had known that this would happen. He had not been afraid to acknowledge the intransient and insignificant nature of his own importance. He was happy to be associated with a sermon based on a text from the 103rd psalm, comparing a person with a flower that briefly blossoms before being blown over by the wind: 'and the place thereof shall know it no more'. His reputation was blown over by the ill wind of his family's behaviour, and his place – Chester – knew him no more.

4   See Chapter 35.

CHAPTER EIGHTEEN

1858

Mary and Catherine Cotgreave get their mother's name wrong

Apart from her last will and testament, not a single verifiable word survives that was said or written by Mary Cotgreave. Even the will was written by a lawyer based on his understanding of her wishes rather than recording her actual words. It is impossible to know what she herself thought or felt about anything. But the defining feature of her life was surely the contrast between Mary Cotgreave's secure childhood in a settled family tied to a particular town, and the isolation of her later years. She became so removed from her former self that she longed to return to a mythical former idyll, and her old friends took no notice when she died. She and her twin sister either genuinely forgot their own mother's name or else separated themselves psychologically so completely from their previous existence that they came to believe that she – and by implication they – were not who everyone thought they were.

Mary and Catherine Cotgreave were born in Chester in June 1796 and Mary was probably the older twin; there may have been some concern for one or both of their lives because they were baptised immediately. Had they been born a year earlier, their surname would have been Johnson, but their father had changed his name as a condition of inheriting a fortune from cousins called Cotgreave.[1] It was only when the second of his two unmarried cousins died in 1795 that he discovered just how rich he had become. His wife, the twins' mother, was called Catherine Cross, and it was later claimed that she was a descendent of an ancient and noble family from a place called Cross Hall. This may have been true, but equally it may not – John was not averse to publishing flagrantly false pedigrees.

1 See Chapter 21.

The two sisters were brought up in comfort in the city of Chester, learning the pursuits considered proper for girls at the time. Mary seems to have enjoyed her musical studies, with her harp and piano becoming two of her most treasured possessions. The girls' father was a leading member of the local gentry but he never lost the popular touch. He remained conscious of his less illustrious background, and of the need to assert his place. He chose as his motto *Antiquam Obtinens*, meaning 'Possessing Antiquity', to demonstrate that even though the Johnsons might have been nobodies, the Cotgreaves from whom he was descended formed a very long established local family.

In 1811, the twins' older brother died at the age of 20 after a long and debilitating illness. There were no other siblings, which meant that their father was now without a male heir. Their mother was 50 and had not had any children since the girls had been born 15 years earlier. There was no hope of her providing a new heir. Mary and Catherine were now set to become rich. Their long dead and enlightened cousins had made specific provision for daughters to inherit if John Cotgreave died without sons, so their father could not stop them from doing so even had he wanted to.

As time progressed, John Cotgreave became ever more important and he was knighted when he went to London to represent Chester at a royal wedding in 1816. He had a mistress and three illegitimate children, including two girls who may also have been twins, and a boy called John. No doubt Sir John Cotgreave, as he now was, was delighted with his new son and perhaps he favoured his second family over his teenage daughters. But it made no difference to Mary and Catherine's financial prospects because a bastard could not inherit under the terms of the family settlement. In 1822, however, Mary and Catherine's mother died and Sir John Cotgreave soon married his mistress, a dressmaker called Harriet Spence, who was already five months pregnant with Cotgreave's next child. The baby was a healthy boy whom they named Thomas, and his existence changed the twins' lives forever. He may have been conceived in sin but he was born in the sacred state of his parents' marriage, and so there was now a legitimate male heir to the Cotgreave fortune. Barring any special provisions Sir John could make for them, Mary and Catherine might ultimately be dependent on the charity of a half brother who was nearly 30 years their junior.

Sir John Cotgreave realised the difficult situation in which his daughters might find themselves, and in the weeks before his marriage to Harriet Spence, he had gone some way towards bolstering their financial independence. First, he conveyed some lands into a trust so that the rent – £100 a year – could be used by the trustee for the benefit of the two young women. Second, he changed the terms of a deed that arose from his original inheritance. It permitted him to raise £2,000 for his children by borrowing against the value his property, and he arranged that the twins were to get three quarters of the total, with the remaining £500 to be split between any legitimate children he had with Harriet (they eventually had seven more legitimate children, of whom five survived to adulthood). Mary and Catherine Cotgreave thus received £750 apiece, while the children of Sir John's second marriage would each get about £100. Sir John continued to make sure the girls had resources deriving from their Cheshire property. As late as 1832, he acquired a lease in favour of Catherine, while Mary owned a share of an inn in Chester and nine cottages in nearby Frodsham. Moreover, Sir John ensured that the property portfolio was as profitable as he could make it, arguing with his advisers about how much rent it was appropriate to demand for one of Mary's properties. 'Your Father wants £150 per annum instead of £120, which is the present rent' her trustee told Mary in 1827.

By then, the two sisters were not living in Chester. They had remained in touch with their mother's family, having received a legacy from their uncle William Cross, and were apparently living in Bath with (or near) a relative called Mrs Cross. In 1829, Catherine was married at Walcot, a suburb of Bath, to the Rev. Stephen Cragg, the vicar of a parish in Essex.

The next few years formed the one period of their lives when the twin sisters are known to have lived apart, with Catherine following her husband when he was appointed to a parish in Coventry and Mary staying, at least for a while, with a Gloucestershire lawyer called Henry Rogers and his sister.

Things back in Chester did not go entirely well for the twins' stepmother and half siblings. Thomas was involved in court cases about money he allegedly owed and Lady Cotgreave was declared bankrupt in 1842.[2] Mary and Catherine were unaffected, although Thomas Cotgreave must have been paying interest on the money they had received from their father's estate, which was secured against the value of his property. At a typical rate of five per cent, the £1,500 that the girls had received between them would cost Thomas Cotgreave £75 a year in interest unless he could pay it off outright.[3]

The twins were still receiving the income on their own Cheshire investments, and in the 1851 census, Mary was described as a 'landed proprietor'. In Catherine's case, it was now her husband who was the formal beneficiary. The interest on a £950 investment that Sir John Cotgreave

2 See Chapter 35.
3 In perspective, it was perfectly possible to live on £50 a year.

had made in the Turnpike Trust between Chester and Whitchurch was paid to 'the Rev S Cragg [and] Miss Mary Cotgreave'.

Financially, things were now very different from how they seemed a few years earlier. Their father's efforts and their own prudence meant that Mary Cotgreave and Catherine Cragg were comfortably off. But reckless stupidity had left their stepmother and half brother in trouble. In an attempt to claw something back from his sisters, Thomas Cotgreave allied with his other siblings and tried to overturn their late father's wishes. It had been illegal, they argued, for Sir John Cotgreave to distribute the £2,000 he had charged to the property in such an uneven way, with Mary and Catherine getting so much more than the others. It was the clear intent of the old cousin's original bequest that every child should have the same – something short of £300 apiece. But the twins fought the case in the Court of Chancery and won, with the judge ruling that Sir John had been free to distribute the money in any shares he chose.

If they had not already done so, Mary and Catherine must now have broken all ties with their Cotgreave relatives in Chester. Everything about their earlier days – the people, the places, the sense of belonging, even the money worries – were gone. Mary lived out her days at her sister's house in Coventry, where Rev Cragg had been posted in 1846. She developed stomach tumours in 1856 and died in 1858; she was buried in the municipal cemetery at Coventry. Her twin sister Catherine lived until 1874 to be buried in the same grave.

It was only after their deaths that the degree of the sisters' isolation became apparent. Mary's will mentioned Cheshire only because she owned property there; she had little choice but to appoint a local solicitor as one of her executors. But nothing in the will was left to her Cheshire family or any old friends from the county; everything went to Catherine's family. Later, Catherine's daughter chose to publish some lines of poetry that had been written while Catherine and Mary had been walking around Stivichall churchyard south of Coventry some years earlier; the words were attributed to 'the late Mrs Cragg' but they had expressly been written 'when walking with her sister Mary Cotgreave'. Both women were represented in the verse. The poem idealises the simple rural life of the 'peasant' who is tied to the land, and lives in a cottage that is the 'pride of the grove,' just as the Cotgreave sisters' family had been tied to the land of Cheshire for six hundred years before they had been cast out by the circumstances of their father's second marriage. Great delight is to be found in 'the return ... homeward,' something the twins would never achieve. Even the setting of the poem, a delightful semi-rural churchyard (the word 'green' is used three times in three short verses) contrasts with the impersonal municipal burial ground in which Mary and Catherine eventually rested.

Stivichall churchyard, where Mary and Catherine Cotgreave wrote a poem about a rural idyll to remind them of their childhood in Chester, is now in the built-up area of Coventry, but it still has a glade of bluebells under mature trees.

Back in Cheshire, the deaths of the sisters went completely unnoticed. In 1887, decades after both were dead, the Deputy Chairman of the Chester Quarter Sessions found it necessary to propose that £82, 1 shilling and 8 pence be repaid to the Earl of Shrewsbury. The money was rent that the local council had received for a piece of land next to the castle in Chester. Lord Shrewsbury held the freehold but his great-grandfather had let it to Sir John Cotgreave and his daughters nearly six decades earlier. The council had bought up the lease from the family, but the term had to remain the same – the lifetimes of the Cotgreaves. When Catherine Cragg died in 1874, the arrangement should have come to an end, the council should have given the property back to the Earl and he should have received the rent that accrued over the next 13 years. The local newspaper reported, however, that the council had gone on receiving the rents 'in happy ignorance' of the Cotgreaves' deaths. When the Deputy Chairman explained, the court broke out in laughter. This was the council over which Sir John Cotgreave had once presided so brilliantly that the citizens had wanted to give him an unprecedented second term. But it had not even acknowledged that his daughter was dead, did not know that the lease was anything to do with her, and found it funny when the truth became apparent. This was a plot of land in the heart of their home city, just metres away from their childhood home; it had been leased for the term of their lives, but it had forgotten who they were.

However, the clearest indication that the twins were separated from their former lives came when, having been distanced from their father's family, Mary and Catherine Cotgreave tried to associate themselves with their mother's relatives. They managed instead to show just how distant they had become from their roots. For most of her adult life, Catherine had used a middle name, calling herself Catherine Crewe Cotgreave until her marriage, and then Catherine Crewe Cragg; the name persisted and continued to be used as a middle name in the Cragg family. At her christening, Catherine had in fact been given the middle name Crue, an old spelling of Crew or Crewe. It is not clear why, but Sir John gave several of his children middle names that were blatant attempts to link his family with illustrious Chester lineages – William Gamull Cotgreave, Frances Brerewood Cotgreave and Alice Holme Cotgreave were named after a former mayor, a parliamentary representative and an important antiquary. Perhaps he called his daughter Catherine Crewe because the local manors of Christleton and Rowton, the ancient homes of the Cotgreaves and still the residence of one of Sir John Cotgreave's wealthy cousins, were owned by a family that descended from an aristocrat called the Honourable Catherine Crewe.

But it appears that Catherine and Mary chose to believe that the name was a link with their mother. It seems inconceivable that the sisters had in fact recorded their own mother's name incorrectly. They had not exactly been too young to remember her when she died – they were 26 at the time. They had lived in Bath with a Mrs Cross, who was presumably a relation, and they had received an inheritance from their uncle, William Cross, when they were about 12 years old. Their father, who did not die until 1836, made no mistake and his first wife's surname of Cross (spelled Crosse) was recorded by him in *Burke's Landed Gentry*. The twins, who were 40 when it was published, must have seen this book.

But there is no doubt that the sisters did make a mistake. When Mary died, her obituary, for which the information was surely provided by Catherine, and which was repeated in a number of publications, stated explicitly that their mother had been called Catherine Crewe. The mistake cannot be dismissed as a typographical error – when Catherine died, her own obituary described her as 'twin daughter of the late Sir John Cotgreave, of Netherleigh, Chester, and of Catherine Crewe, his first wife'. Either the two sisters were so far isolated from their family and their upbringing that they genuinely made a mistake about their own mother's name, or somehow, through some bizarre psychological need to divorce themselves from the past, they got her name subtly but unquestionably wrong. In alienating themselves from their father's Cotgreave family, and misidentifying their mother, the sisters had redefined themselves.

CHAPTER NINETEEN

1869

Tilley Cotgreave is given nine forenames

Hannah Maria Matilda Sophia Juliana Georgina Lucretia Cinderella Martave Cotgreave almost never used any of her nine forenames. She generally called herself Tilley, an abbreviated form of her third name. Sometimes she was known as Anna or Annie. She used her boyfriend's surname before they were married and then changed back to her maiden name after the wedding. She confused the records so comprehensively that it is impossible now to locate her death certificate, even though she did not die until the well-documented twentieth century.

Wherever her parents got her names from, it was not the family. Her mother was called Mary Ann and her grandmothers were Catherine and Sarah. Between them, her parents had at least six sisters, none of whom shared any of Tilley Cotgreave's nine names. Even the familiar names in the list were alien in her family – there is no record of any other Sophia Cotgreaves before her birth, and there had not been any Matildas for 400 years.

Nor do her parents seem to have been especially interested in their other children's names before Tilley was born. Her five older siblings were all called boring things like Frank and Harriet and only one of them had a middle name. The penchant for strings of bizarre monikers lasted until her next sister was given five even more ridiculous forenames – Cecilina Dodeonia Frosterino Malgarina Disraelo – but she was only ever known as Cissy.[1] Then for the baby of the family, born eight years after Tilley, the parents returned to convention and called him Charles Henry.

So whatever had motivated her unusual nomenclature, the novelty

---

1   Although all the names are given on her birth certificate, only the first is included in the record of her baptism and there is no evidence that she or anyone else ever referred to any of her middle names for the rest of her life.

soon wore off. Even by the time she was baptised at the age of 13 weeks, three of the names had been dropped – Julia, Lucretia and Martave – and one had been changed: Hannah was given in the church register as Anna.

Five of the names on her birth certificate were (and still are) reasonably commonplace, the others were (and are) not. Out of about four and half million girls registered in England and Wales in the five years either side of Tilley's birth, there were tens of thousands of Hannahs, Marias and Sophias and over 9,000 Georginas, but only a few hundred Lucretias and Julianas. Even when obscure spellings are included, there were only 26 Cinderellas and no other Martaves. In fact, from the beginning of civil registration in 1837 until the end of the nineteenth century, there was not a single girl whose birth certificate gave Martave as her first name. Lucretia would at least have been well known as a name to anyone who had studied either ancient Rome (the original Lucretia's story was pivotal in the creation of the Republic) or mediaeval history (Lucrezia Borgia and her family were the original Machiavellians). Cinderella was a character made famous by the Brothers Grimm in 1812. But Martave remains a mystery that even the wonders of Google cannot solve, a century and a half after Henry and Mary Ann Cotgreave chose it as the ninth name of their sixth child. Tilley at least fared better than Cissy, all four of whose middle names were unique, although they were not all made up by her parents – Malgarina is a real historical Italian name.

Henry Cotgreave was clearly something of a character, unlike most of his rather stolid brothers, who worked diligently as clerks and railway officials.[2] He had more in common with his older brother Charles, who was addicted to horseracing.[3] Henry kept a donkey that he entered into fun races, and failed to stick at any job for long. In the 1840s, he worked as a carpenter's apprentice, in the 1850s a bootmaker, in the 1860s, he called himself an 'agent' and by 1901, he was a clerk. Perhaps it was this slightly chaotic existence that caused Tilley Cotgreave and her sisters to go off the rails.

In 1889, when the Cheshire magistrates heard evidence about the illegal and immoral goings on at the Wilbraham Arms Pub in Chester, they were shocked by what they learned. The Police had turned up at 11.30pm on the night of 20 September and hammered on the door for three hours before they finally got in by scaling the wall with a ladder and climbing in through a window. They found a known prostitute in a

---

2   Including William Cotgreave, see photograph, p. x, and Thomas Richardson Cotgreave, See Chapter 20.
3   See Chapter 7.

room with a client, and Tilley Cotgreave in bed with a young man called Vernon Arthur Green.

At the trial of the pub's owners a few days later, Tilley was branded a prostitute in open court. She freely admitted to sleeping with Green, but claimed that they had been a couple for the past four years – since she was 16 – and had been living together for six months. She had been going home to her parents' house for meals, and staying mostly with Green at an address that was home to another family called Cotgreave (although they were not closely related). They had taken lodgings at the pub a few days before the police raid, claiming to be Mr and Mrs Green.

Green was unemployed at the time, having recently been demobilized from the army, and he was the son of a well-to-do professional who had been Managing Director of the River Dee Company. But Tilley's boyfriend was not like his own father, he was just like hers, and in the coming years would be described as a railway porter, a coachman and a 'canvassor for all kinds of adverts'. For the next few years, the couple stayed together, moving to Birkenhead, where Tilley was known as Annie. Then in 1895, some ten years into their relationship, they were finally married in Liverpool. For the wedding, she used the name Matilda.

There is no indication of why the couple felt moved to tie the knot at last, but the wedding was the death knell for their relationship. Within a few years, Annie Green had become Tilley Cotgreave again, and was living at home in Chester, with her parents and two of her sisters. Despite using her maiden name, she did not pretend to be single. It is not clear when the couple split up, but in 1911, Vernon Green claimed to have been with his new partner (they pretended to be married) for 16 years, which if true would mean they got together straight after his wedding to Tilley, or even before it.

Either Tilley Cotgreave was a bad influence on her two unmarried sisters, or they all fell foul of the same ill-disciplined environment created by their chaotic father; both went on to have illegitimate children. By 1901, all three of the sisters were living with their parents Henry and Mary Ann Cotgreave, supposedly working as dressmakers from the family home.

When her parents died, within a few days of each other in 1910, the deaths were officially registered by Tilley's brother and eldest sister. Neither of them lived in the family home any more, but both had been present at the deaths. The sister lived in Leicester, 100 miles away, and must have come to Chester to help nurse her mother, who was wasting away with severe pneumonia. The following year, one of Tilley's unmarried sisters was still living at the parents' old address and the other sister, who was now blind, had moved in with the brother and his family. Tilley was not there. To all appearances, she had just disappeared in her thirties, sometime in the decade after the 1901 census. There is no recorded death certificate, or bigamous marriage, for anyone called Tilley or Matilda or Anna Maria or Annie Cotgreave or any of the other names that she might have used. All the likely entries for people called Green can be identified as someone else. Perhaps the most probable explanation is that she took up with another man and used his surname.

Nine forenames and two surnames were not enough for Hannah Maria Matilda Sophia Juliana Georgina Lucretia Cinderella Martave Cotgreave.

She had gone from improbable uniqueness to bland anonymity. At the end, she had become someone else.

CHAPTER TWENTY

1894

Thomas Cotgreave lunches with Gladstone

Thomas Richardson Cotgreave was used to special meals. He presided over dinners for the assembled tenantry of large estates, entertained parties of lawyers at his home and attended the wedding feasts and wakes of upper and middle class friends and clients. The most noteworthy meal of all, however, was a much smaller affair. At the end of November 1894, as a treat for his 84th birthday, he sat down to lunch with an 'An Old Friend' – William Ewart Gladstone. Gladstone, who was a year older than Cotgreave, had resigned earlier in the year, the oldest person ever to serve as Prime Minister.

The men had known one another for decades. Thomas Cotgreave had worked for Gladstone's lawyers since he was a very young man, and had been involved in the running of the politician's Hawarden Estate throughout that time. Cotgreave did not share the MP's politics (his family were staunch Conservatives) but the Liberal statesman nevertheless valued the old clerk's company and his opinion and so it was that the two old men reminisced together over lunch at Hawarden Castle.

Unfortunately, just a few weeks before the meeting, Gladstone decided that after seventy years of assiduously keeping a diary, he would no longer subject himself to the 'grind of the Daily Journal'. So there is no record of what the two men discussed. There was certainly no need for William Gladstone to recount his life story because he was one of the most famous men in the world. And likewise, there was no need for Cotgreave to recite his, because Gladstone knew that he had been a law clerk in Chester all his adult life. Perhaps the old statesman asked Thomas Cotgreave if he was related to a young valet called Alfred Cotgreave whom Gladstone had met when visiting his political rival Disraeli, or to another Thomas Cotgreave, a neighbour with a nearby estate who was known personally to Gladstone. Most likely, since the occasion had explicitly been arranged to celebrate Cotgreave's long service with the same company, the conversation centred on the things he had seen and experienced in six decades of dealing with the affairs of the wealthiest families in North Wales and the northwest of England.

The eldest son of a Chester shoemaker who knew the value of education, Thomas Richardson Cotgreave had acquired his middle name from his mother's family, farmers who had lived at Tarporley for generations.[1] He had first entered the service of a law firm with offices in Shropshire and worked for a short while in Shrewsbury. There he met a young woman who needed her father's permission to get married because she was legally a minor. By the age of 21, however, Thomas had joined a Chester company known at the time as Barker and Porter. Although the name of the firm would change several times as its partners died, retired or were replaced, there was always a Barker involved, and when Cotgreave died at the age of 85, he was still working in 'the same service' for a firm that by then was known as Barker and Rogerson.

More than 60 years in one company was a remarkable feat, and must have provided great variety. Indeed, he did so many different things that people were never quite sure of Thomas Cotgreave's job title. Early in his career he had been quite simply a 'clerk,' and sometimes 'attorney's clerk' or 'solicitor's clerk,' hardly more informative. But as he progressed in the company, he took on more and more responsibilities, and these were reflected in how people described him. 'Confidential clerk' suggests that he dealt with some of most important and sensitive business. 'Cashier' and 'accountant' make it plain that he was trusted with money and suggest that he came to oversee the company's finances. In 1875, he was called the 'manager' and Cotgreave nearly always referred to himself as 'managing clerk,' because he was running the office. He was what today would be called the chief executive of a law firm.

No doubt many of Cotgreave's duties were similar to those of a modern company director but others were not. There was commercial business, including managing the sale of an artist's company and acting as an agent for an insurance corporation. It was not necessary to be a lawyer to have rights of audience in the plethora of lesser courts and he regularly made appearances on behalf of clients. In 1853, Thomas Cotgreave appeared at Birkenhead Police Court to enforce a claim on behalf of the trustees of a turnpike trust, and he appeared for the prosecution in minor criminal matters and for the proprietor of a pub at the magistrates' licensing court.

---

1   His younger brothers included William Cotgreave, see photograph, p. x, and Henry Cotgreave, See Chapter 19.

Apparently the largest volume of work was for private clients, running the agricultural, industrial and family interests of rich local families. He chaired manorial courts, which had some real business, such as deciding cases about stray cattle, but which also had a large social element for the tenantry of local magnates. He presided at annual celebratory dinners in place of the landowner, following these meetings of manor courts, and also after auctions and even on one occasion the wedding of his client's son. He turned up at sales to bid on property for his clients, buying a row of cottages for a local magnate called John Leche.

Thomas Cotgreave was apparently the exclusive point of contact for the clients with whom he dealt – it was he alone, for example, who 'conducted the affairs' of John Brock Wood, a wealthy landowner. That is how Thomas Richardson Cotgreave, a provincial official in a law office, became friends with William Ewart Gladstone, an international statesman. Nor were the Gladstones the only family of clients who became friends with Cotgreave. Presiding over the wedding feast of John Leche was perhaps the most extreme example of his involvement in family affairs, but Cotgreave and his wife Jane were also present at the wedding of Gladstone's son William H. Gladstone MP, and of several other clients' marriages. Moreover, they bought expensive presents – for example, a silver salver. Funerals were another occupational necessity. Gladstone's politician son died young and Cotgreave was one of the mourners. It was a sad year in 1877, when the company he worked for went by the name of Barker and Hignett, and Thomas Cotgreave travelled in one of the front coaches of mourners at the funeral of Horace Hignett on 12 December and of Richard Barker six days later.

Of course, with a well-paid job and rich friends, the expectation was that Thomas Cotgreave would fulfil the roles expected of the class of person he had become. He was a Visitor at the Bluecoat School in Chester, a property-owner on small scale, a generous donor to a fund for the relief of famine in India and a subscriber towards a testimonial portrait of the grandest local grandee of all, the Marquis of Westminster. He was a well-known and respected figure around the city.

What he was most well-known for was the sheer length of his career at one of the city's most prestigious and established companies. He was still working at the Barker family firm into his 80s, although he may have scaled back the level of his commitment. In every decadal census since 1851, he had called himself a 'solicitor's managing clerk' but in 1891, when he was 81, he opted for the more modest 'solicitor's clerk'; he was no longer managing the office.

Thomas Richardson Cotgreave died on 28 December 1895, the year after his birthday lunch at Hawarden Castle with one of the most famous people of the nineteenth century. The cause was certified as 'senectus', a fancy word for old age. By coincidence, another long-serving colleague at Barker and Rogerson passed away on exactly the same day. Thomas Garner was not as old as Cotgreave, but he too had experienced what by any normal standards was a long career in the same firm.

Perhaps it was because the end of the century was in sight, or because the long-reigning Queen was old and could not last forever, or perhaps both. But for some reason, the inexorable stability of Thomas Richardson Cotgreave's 60-year career, in the same office, struck a chord with the people of Chester. In 1878, after half a century of service at the same firm, he was given a silver plate, gold watch and other presents as a token of esteem, and he reciprocated by entertaining the partners and fellow clerks to a party at his home. Even a report of his Golden Wedding celebration with his wife Jane, which should surely have been about their life together, could not help focusing on how Thomas had been with the same firm for 'upwards of sixty years'.

Two years after Thomas Richardson Cotgreave died, Queen Victoria celebrated her Diamond Jubilee, and the *Cheshire Observer* published a summary of the most noteworthy local events for each of the past 60 years. For all his fame, Gladstone gets just a handful of mentions. But for 1895, the most memorable events included the simultaneous 'deaths of ... two old citizens and fellow clerks, who worked at the same desk' and the fact that 'Mr Cotgreave had been for sixty-seven years ... in the same employment'.

CHURCH AND STATE

Public and religious authorities have always sought to control aspects of people's lives, with varying degrees of success.

These five stories begin with a mediaeval farmer who had to decide where his loyalties lay between the powerful elite and the powerless poor. A Tudor businessman and his son learned that there was a balance between the benefits of official patronage and the dangers of being on the wrong side when policy changed. Where church and state interacted, a lifelong monk had to make his own way in a world when the monastic life was abolished, while in the seventeenth century, a poor woman and her family had to find a course that was true to their religious conscience without courting financial disaster. From the nineteenth century is the story of a man who just wanted to exercise his right to vote but came up against the complexities of the electoral franchise.

CHAPTER TWENTY ONE

1381

Ranulph de Cotegreve judges the peasants

Not long before Ranulph de Cotegreve was born, a huge swathe of southern Cheshire changed hands twice. On each occasion, his father, William, a landowner and leading tenant in the area, registered his claim to rights and privileges in the Barony of Malpas. A century earlier, the Cotegreves had been among the pre-eminent landowners in the area, close relatives of the baron himself. But as each successive generation passed and the inheritance was further divided, William de Cotegreve would prove to be the last of his family to make grandiose baronial claims. At the end of his long life, his son Ranulph's real estate transactions were on a far smaller scale – a lease on a cottage so his younger son could have a home.

Born in 1344 or 1345, Ranulph de Cotegreve was a teenager when his father died in the early 1360s, which meant that he automatically became a ward of the Earl of Chester, who at the time was Edward Prince of Wales. Edward later tried to atone for the rapacity with which he taxed Cheshire, but when the young Cotegreve's property came into his hands, the Prince's officials welcomed the extra income. They readily banked the 60 shillings a year that was generated by Ranulph's share of a salt works in Wych.

By the time Ranulph had become free of his guardian, and emerged as a fully functioning member of the county community, it was a decade and half since his father had died, and the clerks who recorded official business did not even remember his family – the first time he turned up for jury service in Chester, his surname was spelled Kodegreve. But many appearances would follow, and throughout his long life, Ranulph de Cotegreve became one of the most ubiquitous attenders at the various courts and gatherings that administered his area. He was so well known, he even had a nickname – 'Honkin'.[1]

For more than half a century, from the mid-1370s to the 1420s, the name of Ranulph de Cotegreve appeared again and again as a juror and surety in the county court, the sheriff's courts, coroner's inquests and the county exchequer. He indicted many men, collected a great deal of tax, convicted many wrongdoers and kept numerous friends and associates out of trouble by backing them with both his influence and his money.

In 1381, in the wake of the trouble caused by workers in the south east who were tied to their employers – the Peasants' Revolt – sporadic violence broke out around the country. Ranulph de Cotegreve and his colleagues testified that on the last Tuesday, Saturday and Sunday in July, the King's proclamation demanding peaceful behaviour had been read out in the county court at Chester Castle, where many adult men from all over the county would be gathered. It had then been declaimed at other sites in Chester and in parish churches in the surrounding villages, specifically at Eastham at the southern end of the Wirral. But on the following Monday, a group of villeins who were legally bound to work for the Abbot of Chester had been involved in an armed protest that had terrorised the population, starting at Backford, the parish immediately neighbouring Eastham. In the light of the publicity given to the proclamation, it was inconceivable that the troublemakers did not know about it. Indeed, it seems as if the public readings of the King's letter may actually have sparked the riot; the disturbance certainly looked like a deliberate act of defiance against the authorities. However, although the rioters were captured, they were not really punished. They had to produce sureties for their future good behaviour but that was apparently easily done, and no further action appears to have been taken. Ranulph de Cotegreve and his fellow local landowners wanted a line drawn under the whole episode and clearly thought that heavy handed central government would only make things worse.

The whole episode emphasised Cotegreve's status. He was a landowner, eligible for jury service, but he was not a magnate with hordes of villeins at his command to keep in check, and did not feel particularly threatened by their aspirations. While his father had made baronial claims, his son would be described as a gentleman. He stood at the turning point between grandness and ordinariness for his family. While he fully understood that

---

1   Derived from 'Rankin,' a diminutive of Ranulph, with a guttural pronunciation of the letter R, just as Hopkin is a version of Robkin as a nickname for people called Robert.

the revolting peasants needed to be brought to some kind of order, he could nevertheless sympathise with the unfair circumstances that had caused them to protest in the first place.

When he sat on indictment juries, as he did with slightly alarming frequency, Cotegreve took decisions not just about the villages in his immediate locality but also about what was happening on the streets of Chester, the castle and the abbey, as well as places throughout the county. Merely by living for a long time, Ranulph de Cotegreve became influential. He was on such a large number of juries over a 40-year period that his influence in county affairs must have been pervasive. Just about every family in a large swathe of Cheshire was in some way touched by a decision that he helped to make.

But his landed interests were not like those of his ancestors – he did not own whole manors and his share of the salt works at Wych was just one sixteenth. His property was not trivial, and he had claims to land in villages across the southwestern quarter of the county – in Chowley and Aldersey on the Welsh border, in Cotton Edmonds near to Chester and in Kelsall near Tarporley as well as in the parish of Malpas 20 miles away. He served as bailiff of both Broxton Hundred and Eddisbury Hundred, which gave him official authority over 300 square miles from the Shropshire border via an enclave in Wales to the banks of the River Mersey and the Cheshire plain, nearer to Staffordshire than to Chester. The reach of his decisions as a juror was even wider, from the tip of the Wirral to the border of Derbyshire.

But while Ranulph de Cotegreve looks from the records like a descendent of a rich and powerful dynasty, his offspring look much more like the progenitors of a middle-class family. His younger son Robert fought at Agincourt, which brought a certain special respect, but Robert Cotegreve did not even acquire his own home until he was over 40, and even then it was a modest cottage held in Ranulph's name.[2] The elder son William was unquestionably a gentleman, and the senior lines of his descendants would continue to own land for centuries to come, but by the standards of the gentry, he was fairly ordinary, and his interests seem to have been limited to small tracts of land and individual houses within the boundaries of Broxton Hundred.

Nowhere is the sense of change more subtly but distinctly observed than in the record of indictments made at the county court in Chester Castle on 10 April 1404. Ranulph and his son William were both on the same Grand Jury but their surnames were listed differently. Ranulph was

2   See Chapter 9.

'Ranulph de Cotegreve,' he was 'of' Cotegreve, specifically associated with an ancestral manor. His son was simply 'William Cotegreve' – it was merely a name that distinguished him from other men called William, and carried no association with past greatness. The records would waver for another half century about whether the 'de' was necessary, but this roll of jury lists marked the beginning of its end.

When Ranulph de Cotegreve died in the mid-1420s, he was no doubt mourned as a significant local character whose long life and wide territorial interests within his county meant that his life had touched a great many others. He was probably buried at Christleton, a parish where he owned land because of who his wife was rather than because of who his own family had once been. Cotegrave, the place after which he was named, had faded into nothing – it had not been referred to in the records for over a century, and had seemingly disappeared forever. But when Victorian surveyors turned up to make tithe maps half a millennium later, they had to plot out every square foot of every parish. They made an invaluable record of the names by which fields had been known locally for centuries, many otherwise unrecorded. When in 1838 they came to the part of Cheshire where Ranulph de Cotegreve had been born, the parish that had once had a manor called Cotegrave, they discovered that a couple of fields, nothing but 12 acres of grass and a small pond, were still known to the locals as Near Cotgreaves and Far Cotgreaves.[3]

3   See photograph, p. 3.

CHAPTER TWENTY TWO

1520

John Cotgreve is admitted to the Freedom of Chester

John Cotgreve was born within months of Henry VIII and died a few weeks after the king. Cotgreve's life tells the story of Henry's reign as it was experienced by a member of the provincial middle classes. The key moments in John Cotgreve's life – choosing a career, acquiring land, an accusation of treason, and establishing his family's posterity – all owed something to the way the country was governed by the powerful Tudor monarchy.

Born in the early 1490s, John Cotgreve was the son of a landowner with a moderate estate, whose family had lived off its farms in Cheshire for hundreds of years. Although his father was a second son, he appears to have been bequeathed some of the ancient Cotgreve inheritance, possibly because his older brother had acquired new and equally valuable lands by marrying a local heiress. As a teenager, John Cotgreve was betrothed to Alice Fletcher, the 12-year-old daughter of another smallish landowner with a set of locally distinguished ancestors.

If the marriage was based on family finances and legal documentation, it nevertheless proved persistently harmonious. The number of children they had, the strong relationships that John forged with Alice's relatives, and their success at using family contacts to secure jobs for their sons and marriages for their daughters all suggest that they came to love one another, or at any rate that mutual respect allowed them to collaborate successfully. Alice outlived John by decades, and was buried hundreds of miles away from their family church. But her family must have known this was not what she really wanted, and 40 years after her death, her daughter eventually had Alice's remains returned to lie with John's.

The defining moment of John Cotgreve's career came just after his betrothal to Alice Fletcher.[1] It was the decision to apprentice him to a trade. He did not expect to inherit the family farm because he had an older brother, although in the end that brother would die young and John would be his father's heir. The culmination of his training was admission as a freeman of the city of Chester, and John was now recognised as a specialist draper, trading in textiles, wool and other cloth. There is no record of whom he trained under, but it is a reasonable bet that his uncle, William Cotgreve, was involved because 30 years earlier, William had trained with one of London's master drapers. When he returned to Cheshire, William retained his interest in the cloth trade and either he or his son was described as a tailor. The Cotgreves had clearly settled on the cloth trade as the route to financial success because John's younger brother Thomas also served an apprenticeship in the industry, starting his education just as John qualified. Presumably Thomas was his older brother's first pupil.

Within a few years of beginning his independent life as a draper, John Cotgreve's skills were in demand when the sheriffs were presiding over a civil law case and needed to know how much a ship's sail was worth; they turned to John Cotgreve for advice. Again and again, over the coming years, his expertise was employed by the authorities, valuing clothes and pieces of cloth: a garment trimmed with fox fur, gowns, a tunic, a sheet, and something called in Latin a *tabula pannea*, which was probably a table cloth. His wisdom was valued in wider realms than his own specialism and he also helped to value crockery, jewellery, a silver cup, and even the hull of a ship.

Just after his father died in 1527, Cotgreve began a long career of using the sheriff's court in Chester, where the business centred around recovering relatively small debts. Perhaps he started out trying to settle his father's affairs, but he was soon in the swing of things and his name appears regularly among the court's records for the next two decades. At the same time, Cotgreve was taking on a more prominent role in civic duty, acting on behalf of the drapers' guild and sitting on local juries that fined violent criminals, customs dodgers and citizens who broke the bye-laws and ordinances of Chester's mayor and corporation. He was one of 14 men who enquired into the regulations regarding the payment of customs charges when ships unloaded on the banks of the River Dee, certifying that while iron and wine were subject to national taxes, other

---

1   Since he finished his training in 1520 and the process typically took seven years, John presumably started his apprenticeship in 1513.

commodities, such as cloth, honey and soap were the business of the local sheriffs.

By the 1530s, John Cotgreve was in a position to extend his landholdings, engaging in land deals with his cousin Peter Cotgreve and buying houses in the centre of Chester as an investment. Together with his uncle William, he took advantage of Henry VIII's policy of dissolving the monasteries, which flooded the market with land; they acquired fields at fixed annual rents, which meant that as inflation put up the general costs of living, the yearly expense of holding the land became relatively cheap. Meanwhile, there was steady growth in the real terms income from the food, wood, peat and other materials that the land produced. John Cotgreve also made use of his connections in the church. As churchwarden of Holy Trinity church in Chester (now the Guildhall on Watergate Street), he acquired a garden that was sufficiently valuable for others to try to squat there and forcibly retain it for their own use.

John Cotgreve was undoubtedly successful at a local level, but the route to significant advancement in Henry VIII's England was patronage. It was essential to be on friendly terms with the rich and powerful. Cotgreve had the skill – or luck – to pick the right side in a violent feud, allying with a man who was able to put opportunity in the way of his children.

William Brereton was related to John Cotgreve,[2] and their families had connections forged over centuries. Brereton was Chamberlain of Cheshire, a post that gave him sweeping powers across the county and in North Wales. He was also one of the king's Grooms of the Privy Chamber, which meant that he spent long periods alone with Henry VIII. Here he could judge the right moment to plug a friend's cause or criticise a rival. With these advantages, Brereton's powerful position in Cheshire was almost unchallenged. But not quite everyone thought that he should be in charge of everything. The sheriff, Sir Piers Dutton, fought for supremacy and the tactics were rough. Brereton managed to have an innocent opponent hanged even though a court had acquitted him, showing just how dangerous he could be.

John Cotgreve was firmly on his cousin William Brereton's side in the long-running and acrimonious dispute. In a dirty tricks campaign, Dutton bribed a witness to implicate Cotgreve in a serious crime. Called Peter Feldy, the man was a career criminal engaged in making counterfeit

---

2   Everyone was related to everyone in sixteenth century Cheshire; one of Brereton's cousins had married one of Cotgreve's, and his stepson would later marry Cotgreve's daughter.

coins. Dutton offered him a pardon if he would claim that various of Brereton's associates had been involved. John Cotgreve's name was casually included in Feldy's testimony, as if to give it the ring of truth, and Cotgreve was in serious danger.

The scheme eventually fell apart, possibly because Feldy realised that Sir Piers Dutton could not be trusted but would in the end let him hang as an inconvenience who knew too much. On the scaffold, Feldy reiterated that his evidence had been perjured. He apologised to the men he had tried to implicate and the families of those who had already died because of his testimony. The whole episode would have seen Cotgreve executed if Dutton and Feldy had been more competent, coherent and convincing. The situation was made worse because Cotgreve's brother really was involved in the counterfeiting operation. Thomas Cotgreve was imprisoned in the Tower of London and was never heard of again, presumably hanged.

It was around this time that Cotgreve's family was rewarded for his loyalty to Brereton. It was almost certainly William Brereton who secured Cotgreve's eldest son – known as Robert Cotgrave – a job with Arthur Plantagenet, Lord Lisle. Plantagenet was an illegitimate son of the king's late grandfather, Edward IV, and a prominent figure at court. He also happened to be Governor of Calais. Robert would work there for the next few years in the English Crown's last foothold on the French mainland. This foot on the ladder of royal service was the start of a new chapter for the Cotgreves, as one by one, John's sons and daughters began to see the rewards.

It may be that Robert was first advanced because of skills he had gained in his father's drapery business because his first recorded task was to choose new livery uniforms that had been produced for Plantagenet's servants. Robert was to discuss the clothes with the tailors who had made them, and he had the final say on whether or not his master's money should be used to buy them at the price offered. But his duties must have been much wider and he was one of a party that went to London when Lady Lisle sent Henry VIII two hampers of fresh peas as part of the system of flattery and gift-giving necessary to stay in his favour; it was Cotgrave who presented the vegetables to the king, who liked them so much that he rewarded Robert with a gift of ten shillings.

But life in the ambit of the court was precarious, and Cotgrave must have panicked very soon after he started work for Lord Lisle, when William Brereton very rapidly fell from favour in 1536. His downfall was spectacular – he was one of a group of men accused of sleeping with the queen (Anne Boleyn), all of whom were found guilty and executed. Most of the charges were rigged, and in Brereton's case, there appears to have been literally no evidence whatsoever. It was merely convenient for his enemies at court, and perhaps for the king, to see Brereton out of the way. His high handed and lawless administration of Cheshire and North Wales had become embarrassing and dangerous, and the problem needed permanently removing. Implicating Brereton in a high-profile case of treason was a simple and effective way of obliterating him.

Robert Cotgrave had lost his patron.

As it happened, he went unscathed for the time being; luckily he was out of the way in Calais, working for his new boss Lord Lisle. But he had seen the ruthless way in which the king's employees could be treated when their usefulness was over. That experience would prove formative if something similar were to happen again. At the Tudor court, it was only a matter of time before it did.

On 19 May 1540, four years after Brereton's death, Lord Lisle was suddenly and unexpectedly arrested as a part of pre-emptive move against the enemies of the King's chief minister, Thomas Cromwell. Lisle was shipped back to England and sent to the Tower of London, where he spent two years, before dying from the shock of being told that he was considered innocent after all.

But by then, Lisle's staff had long since been disbanded. Robert Cotgrave had lost his job on the day Lisle had been arrested. He had at least been paid off. As part of the retinue at Calais, Cotgrave was given 14 shillings and fourpence. What Robert Cotgrave did next is a mystery. Although he was certainly still alive seven years later, when his father mentioned him in his will, he must have died soon afterwards. One of his younger brothers became their father's heir. Whatever he was doing in the intervening years, he had sown the seeds for his family to find further opportunities in the system of patronage, friendship and nepotism that surrounded the court.

Robert's father, John Cotgreve, whose life had once been in danger because he was involved in a dangerous dispute between two magnates, would have been content that he made the right choice – the first job that Robert Cotgrave had obtained, checking the quality of some clothes, had led to royal connections that echoed in his family's fortunes for decades into the future. Robert's sister Katherine married one of the King's painters, an Italian known in English as Antony Totto, and when he died, her second husband was William Le Gris, who ran the royal mews, served as an MP and enjoyed the backing of the powerful Earl of Essex. Another sister Eleanor married the Master of the Royal Buckhounds and died a titled, rich and powerful landowner.[3] Hugh Cotgrave, probably their brother or their cousin, obtained a lucrative job as one of the monarch's heralds.[4]

Unlike Robert's father, his mother Alice, who had once been the 12-year-old subject of an arranged marriage, lived well into the reign of Elizabeth I. Despite seeing her children's success, she purported – rather unconvincingly – to be poor!

3   See Chapter 2.
4   See Chapter 14.

CHAPTER TWENTY THREE

1535

Randle Cotgreyve is thrown out of Chester Abbey

When Randle Cotgreyve was born in 1512, Henry VIII had been king for three years, having inherited the Crown seamlessly after his father's 24-year reign. Henry was a healthy young man with a healthy young wife and there was every possibility that he would reign for at least as long as his father had done. It must have seemed a model of stability to Randle's elderly relatives, who had lived through what we now call the Wars of the Roses, decades of baffling to-and-fro as power passed from one nobleman to another and back again.[1]

Randle was destined to enter a monastery as a youngster, a secure life for a junior son of a modest but secure family. He could not have known that the obstetric history of Henry's wives and his need to produce an heir would lead to his eliminating not just the traditional roles of monasteries but the institutions themselves. Randle, who always called himself Cotgreyve, and his brother John, who preferred Cotgreve, would be put out of the cloisters and into the real world. They would each embrace utterly different aspects of that profane and secular life.

Almost nothing is recorded of the brothers' early life, but they must have received as good an education as it was possible for someone of their rank to acquire.[2] Randle Cotgreyve certainly learned the art of exquisite handwriting and, later in life, people thought he would be interested in inheriting their books. He also rose through the ranks of the church hierarchy more adeptly than John. When it was clear that monasteries

1 See Chapter 10.
2 John is known to have been a pupil at Malpas grammar school before entering the monastery.

When Chester Abbey closed, the monk Randle Cotgreyve continued to serve as a canon in the cathedral; he lived in the cathedral precincts, somewhere near where the gatehouse still stands.

would not survive, it was the 26-year-old Randle who was a member of the abbey's governing body. He was among those who signed the leases that the abbot awarded to local farmers as a way of keeping the church's property out of the king's hands for as long as possible. In a first sign of how Randle would turn the abbey's dissolution to his family's advantage, his elder brother William was one of the peasant farmers who benefited from a long-term, fixed-rent tenancy.

Randle Cotgreyve immediately adapted to the changed circumstances. He became a canon of what was now Chester cathedral and used family connections to get himself appointed as rector of St Peter's church, the most central of the city's parishes and the one most closely associated with civic power. He also retained accommodation in the cathedral precincts – what had previously been his home in the abbey.

John Cotgreve on the other hand failed to secure any such advantages. He was probably a lay brother of the monastery rather than a monk[3] and there is no evidence he acquired any offices or employment, although he helped his brother fulfil some of his responsibilities at St Peter's. The fact that John lived in the parish suggests that he may have been occupying the rector's accommodation which his brother, comfortably housed around the corner in the cathedral complex, did not need.

As the years passed, the two brothers' lives became ever more different. Freed from any monastic concept of perpetual personal poverty, Randle effectively became a normal member of his middle ranking family. He acted as a surety for his older brother, sued his neighbours for debts, and received bequests in the wills of his colleagues. In fact, it is sometimes difficult to distinguish his name in documentary references from those of his secular nephew and cousins who were also called Randle. He continued to accumulate paid offices in the church, working as the cathedral Chapter's receiver, as a steward of the canons and as the sacrist, responsible for the fabric of the church. In 1547, he was taxed on moveable goods worth £10, equivalent to twice the annual salary of a skilled craftsman.

Randle Cotgreyve knew there was no point in rocking the religious boat and retained the rectory of St Peter's under the changing catholic and protestant policies of Edward VI, Mary I and Elizabeth I. He happily signed what the authorities deemed to be the latest compulsory versions of proper religious doctrine and he testified that everything was fine when the Dean and Chapter undertook a survey of the clergy. He acquired

---

3   His cousin asserted that John had, like Randle, been a monk, so he must have been part of the cloistered community, but he denied having actually been a monk.

his own interests in lands that had belonged to the church and appears either to have used his contacts to help his family secure benefits from the established church. William Cotgrave became rector of a church in Northamptonshire not far from former ecclesiastical lands that Randle partly owned, and Randle's nephew was appointed to the lucrative post of diocesan registrar when others thought they had better claims. In fact, he was a popular and trusted family member who was appointed a trustee and executor of the estate of his cousin John Cotgreve[4] and who later spoke of knowing and visiting four generations of his family at their farm in a village just outside the city.

None of this worldly existence meant that Randle Cotgreyve lacked religious conviction, scholarship or Christian charity. He owned both classical and religious books, including a life of St Bridget, a copy of Josephus's first century history of Rome and John Foxe's *Acts and Monuments*, which stressed the suffering of protestant martyrs. He was well respected by other senior churchmen, who were apt to leave him ecclesiastical vestments in their wills, and by civic dignitaries and landowners, who saw in him a trustworthy witness to legal documents.

His brother John Cotgreve achieved none of these things. When Chester abbey was dissolved, he must have shared some of his brother's theoretical potential for success. He used the same connections that Randle had exploited and had himself rapidly ordained into secular religious orders, becoming in turn an acolyte, subdeacon, deacon and priest. But beyond assisting his brother there is no evidence that he employed his clerical status or was employed because of it. Indeed, by the 1550s, he stopped appearing in the periodically updated lists of diocesan clergy. Everyone was behaving as if his priestly status was no longer relevant.

The reason is obvious in a string of incidents involving women. As early as 1540, John Cotgreve was involved in sexually inappropriate activity. He tricked a woman named Alice Gidlowe into having sex with him by giving her an apparently unbreakable oath that they would marry, which he promptly broke. Part of a group walking home after they had 'made merry' at a midsummer fair in Chester, John had asked Alice to go into a barn alone with him. She refused unless he agreed to marry her. The couple made formal-sounding statements of 'trothplight' in the presence of three of their inebriated friends. The rest of the group sauntered on towards Saltney, where Alice lived, leaving the pair of them kissing. John later admitted that on many subsequent occasions, the

4   See Chapter 22.

couple 'had carnal copulation'. He never fulfilled his promise to hold a wedding, however, and when on one occasion he happened to be out of the county, Alice got fed up of waiting and married someone else.

John Cotgreve and a woman called Alice were presented at the bishop's court in 1555 for some form of inappropriate behaviour. He may have been back with Alice Gidlowe, but Alice was a common name. It is just as likely that another unfortunate young woman had fallen for the inexplicably irresistible charms of an unemployed former member of the monastic community in his 40s.

John happily moved on and soon afterwards had two illegitimate children with a woman called Jane Dodd. They took their mother's surname.

In 1548, John Cotgreve, described as a chaplain, was ordered to keep the peace towards a woman called Beatrice Lebington, and although no details survive, it contrasts completely with his brother's court appearances, which were as a surety, a creditor and a helpful witness. Given his history, it is difficult to avoid the conclusion that John was sexually harassing Beatrice.

The most detailed account of all John Cotgreve's misbehaviour comes from 1562. A poor unmarried servant called Margaret Monelay reckoned that of the men she had slept with, her best chance of securing a decent future for her bastard child would be if John Cotgreve accepted that he was the father. Cotgreve vigorously denied that this was possible, saying that all his dealings were her had been standing up. But he was eventually forced to admit that although this was true, he had once had sex with her up against the back of a door. She testified that this had been at Christmas, so it was probably at the drunken end of a party, just as John's liaison with Alice Gidlowe had taken place on the evening of alcohol-fuelled midsummer revelries. But it became clear that Margaret Monelay had been sleeping regularly with another man, sneaking out of her bed and into his room when they were both employed in the same house. A midwife swore that at the height of the pain of childbirth, when nobody could possibly think clearly enough to lie, Monelay had still insisted that Cotgreve was the father. However, the midwife was portrayed as an unreliable gossip and in any case, the baby's date of birth was inconsistent with a Christmas conception.

The most poignant part of the record is that nowhere among the reams of evidence is there any real mention of the child – we do not even know whether it was a boy or a girl, let alone its name. Nor do we know whether it survived infancy.

This was the last of the problems recorded about John Cotgreve's behaviour towards women. He died in 1566, aged about 45, and was buried in one of the churches in the centre of Chester. Randle would live for a further 22 years, and was almost 80 when he died in 1588. In later life, the old priest continued to live in the precincts of Chester Cathedral, the building that had once been his monastic home. He had been born when England was a faithful member of the Catholic church and the pope granted Henry VIII the title of Defender of the Faith. He had lived through the fierce Protestantism of Edward VI, the equally fierce reversion to Catholicism of Queen Mary, the initial attempts by Elizabeth I to leave 'men's souls' alone and the subsequent realisation that religious beliefs were too powerful to ignore when they conflicted with government policy. People had been killed and persecuted on both sides, but Randle Cotgreyve had managed to thrive whatever the prevailing orthodoxy.

Randle and his brother had gone to the abbey in the first place because the alternative was not far from poverty; at best they could have hoped to perform manual work on their elder brother's farm. In the end, Randle had secured the economic benefits of joining the abbey but was freed from the restrictions that a monastic lifetime would have forced him to endure. His was the only generation in history for which this was possible, and it is to be hoped that, as he adapted like a chameleon to the slippery religious doctrines of his times, he never forgot to thank his own personal God for his many blessings.

CHAPTER TWENTY FOUR

1590

Elizabeth Cotgrave refuses to go to church

For 30 years, the English government hounded Elizabeth Cotgrave as a dangerous criminal. She was prosecuted on more than 20 separate occasions in five different courts for the same crime. She did not go to church.

It was not that she lacked religious conviction and she certainly attended religious services. Nor was there any realistic suggestion that her crimes were actually harmful to anyone. Since she was poor, her religious and political associations were hardly powerful. But the state had decided that Roman Catholics were disloyal to the Crown in a Protestant country threatened by Catholic powers – Spain, the papacy and France.

The problem began after Elizabeth's father, Raffe Cotgrave, died in 1588. He was a leading parishioner at Christleton, just outside Chester, who owned various pieces of land in and around the village. There was never the slightest hint of religious dissent while Raffe was alive; indeed, he had been chosen as one of a handful of the most reliable of men sworn on oath to tell the archbishop what was going on in the village. However, soon after Raffe's demise, his widow, his daughters and two of his sons not only stopped attending the parish church, but began hosting illegal Catholic masses in their homes.

The first hint of trouble came when the Archbishop of York sent a commission around the northern half of England in the summer of 1590, checking up on his flock. Margery Cotgrave – Raffe's widow – and their children Thomas and Elizabeth were all refusing to attend the parish church, together with Margery's former sister-in-law Elizabeth Williamson and Elizabeth's son by her first marriage, Randle Cotgrave. One of Margery's other sons, John Cotgrave, was operating as an illegal, unlicensed schoolteacher in the home of a known Catholic and was also a non-attender at the parish church in the village where he was living. Refusal to take attend services in the established church was officially called 'recusancy' and the family were accused of having been recusants for two years. Their crimes had started straight after Raffe Cotgrave had died.

The archbishop's court was relatively tame and nothing really happened as a result of his official visitation, but within months Margery, Thomas and Elizabeth Cotgrave were in more serious trouble. They were prosecuted at the Quarter Sessions before the local magistrates and a year later at the county sessions in Chester Castle in front of professional judges. The pattern of prosecution continued. First, the Mayor of Chester interrogated Randle Cotgrave, who told how the family had attended a Catholic mass in his aunt's house. Then the local bishop became involved, again finding Margery, Thomas and Elizabeth guilty of recusancy.

The archbishop, the bishop, the mayor, the magistrates and judges had all found different subsets of the Cotgrave family guilty at different times, but two individuals were always involved – the matriarch Margery and her daughter Elizabeth. The men were perhaps more cautious – John Cotgrave, for example, had only been mentioned once, Randle just twice. If the full power of economic sanctions were to be brought to bear, they had more to lose. Thomas, although a landowner who was generally described as a yeoman, had contrived to be recorded by the justices as a poor labourer, perhaps in an attempt to prevent them from fining him heavily. If so, the tactic did not work.

In April 1593, Margery, Thomas, John and Elizabeth Cotgrave were each fined £960, a colossal sum that it would take 200 years for a skilled artisan to earn. There was no prospect of anything like the full amount being paid and the only record of any money being recovered was when the sheriff of Cheshire came to Christleton and seized £11 worth of goods, just one quarter of one percent of the nominal total amount. Nevertheless, it frightened the Cotgraves and they began to transfer property into the name of Elizabeth's brother Ralph, who was attending church sufficiently regularly to keep out of trouble.[1] So when the Privy Council received a report on recusants in Cheshire, it recorded that Elizabeth Cotgrave was poor, had no possessions, and lived in a house that belonged to Ralph Cotgrave.

Nevertheless, the prosecutions persisted. The archbishop was involved again in 1595 and the Bishop of Chester prosecuted Margery and

1   See Chapter 12.

Elizabeth in 1598, together with Elizabeth's sister Ann, who had not been in trouble before – perhaps she had only just reached adulthood. Thomas Cotgrave was by now dead, and his cousin Randle realised that he needed at the very least to appear to conform if he was to avoid ruin. He escaped a further fine by telling the bishop that he would, on reflection, go to church occasionally, and he even changed his name (to Richard) perhaps to suggest a fresh start and to disassociate himself from his troublesome past.

In 1599, Elizabeth Cotgrave was assessed for yet another fine – this time of £240 – the bishop was after her again in 1601 and she was up before the judges once more in 1604, twice in 1605 and again in 1607. It had become a pointless ritual. Bishops, magistrates and judges knew they had to go through the motions, Elizabeth knew she had to accept the stigma of repeated conviction, but everyone knew that she was not a dangerous subversive and that whatever fines were imposed, she was never going to pay them. Randle slipped back into his old ways and was presented to the bishop with Margery, Elizabeth and Ann Cotgrave in 1606, but he capitulated and took the Oath of Allegiance (under the name of Richard) and once again avoided real trouble. It did not really work. He moved away from Cheshire temporarily, and a few years later would be prosecuted for recusancy in Sussex.

So when Margery Cotgrave died in 1608, it was only her unmarried daughters who were left to bother the Cheshire authorities. Yet another sibling, Alice, now joined the list of criminals, and Elizabeth and her two sisters moved out of their brother's house and lived a few miles away at Peckforton in the parish of Bunbury. How they subsisted is not clear, but all three were in trouble with the justices several times in 1610. Pointless prosecution after pointless prosecution was costing the authorities money and effort, making no difference to the women's behaviour and bringing in no income for the state because the there was never the slightest probability of any of the fines actually being paid.

Elizabeth must have been at least in her mid forties, possibly as old as 60, when, for the first time in 30 years, she was missing from the list of Cotgraves prosecuted for obstinate non-attendance at parish services. In September 1616, her sisters Anne and Alice made their tediously familiar appearance on the roll of cases, as the professional lawyers sat in judgment at Chester Castle. But Elizabeth's name was not on the list. There is no direct evidence of why Elizabeth was not within the sightline of the prosecutors, but it is unthinkable that she had given in to the pressure. After decades of what had become ritualistic prosecutions, she was hardly going to cave in now. The only realistic possibility is that she was somewhere else, perhaps with her cousin Randle, who went to Ireland after his brush with the Sussex authorities.

In any case, Elizabeth reappeared soon after, but she was no longer living with Ann and Alice. They were still in Bunbury parish, where they had lived continuously since the death of their mother a decade earlier. Elizabeth, however, was back in Christleton, presumably staying with her brother Ralph. Something was going on – Elizabeth had travelled out of the area, moved out of the home she had shared with her sisters for a decade or more, and was not staying with them when she came back.

The only thing that appears to be certain is that when she was away, she was moving around alone in areas where she was not known. In June 1621, the parish priest at Wimbledon in Surrey buried a woman who had died there unexpectedly. Her name was Elizabeth Cotgrave and she was described as 'a stranger' who had come there from Kingston-upon-Thames. But she was not a resident at Kingston, it was just the last place she had been before turning up on his patch. It is impossible to prove that the woman who died in Surrey was the same one who had spent decades ignoring the religious authorities in Cheshire, but two things certainly point in that direction. First, she must have been going somewhere on the occasions when she was missing from the prosecution lists. Second, after the burial in Surrey, the Cheshire woman is never heard of again in the records. Her sisters continued to be prosecuted. Alice seems to have died soon after Elizabeth, but Anne was named in court twice in 1624, and again in 1626 and 1628; she last appears on a list of recusants from 1629.

So what did Elizabeth start doing in late middle age? Given her lifelong devotion to the Catholic cause, perhaps she was a subversive after all; perhaps she was doing something more active to help the cause. After passively putting up with the persecution for years, perhaps the persecution itself had had the opposite effect on Elizabeth Cotgrave to that intended by the government.

CHAPTER TWENTY FIVE

1820

John Cotgreave tries to vote

Parliamentary elections in the early nineteenth century were rowdy affairs, and the citizens of Chester had a reputation for taking things a bit too far. In 1820, one candidate's carriage was tipped over a bridge into the River Dee and he had to be rescued from drowning by an alderman. The city's mayor later claimed that the rioting was so bad he had feared for his life, but he had a particular reason to be frightened. He was in an acrimonious dispute with John Cotgreave and a group of other young men who were being refused the right to vote. The mayor survived the fracas, but came to regret ever being involved.

The electorate for the parliamentary constituency of Chester was defined as all of the city's freemen, so long as they had lived in the city for a year and were not so poor as to need alms. In a few cases, people bought the status of a freeman or were granted it as an honour, but in general a freeman gained his place in one of two ways. He either earned it by serving a seven year apprenticeship with a tradesman or he simply inherited it if his father was already among the ranks of the privileged free citizens.

The intangible advantages of the city's freedom were hardly great on an average day, so there were always plenty of tradesmen who had finished their training but not got round to claiming their status, and a large pool of young men who were eligible by birth but did not feel the need to demand admission straight after their twenty first birthday. As soon as an election was called, however, there was suddenly a real benefit to joining the ranks of the free, and there was a swift rush of claimants wanting to vote. Parliamentary polls took place over several days – the 1820 election started on 8 March and finished ten days later. So as new freemen were enrolled, the registered electorate increased between the time the first vote was cast and the day the result was declared.

The procedure for admission as a freeman involved appearing before the mayor, who typically confirmed candidates' credentials by taking evidence from the masters of graduated apprentices or from the parents of young men claiming hereditary rights. Although the mayor had the sole right to perform the ceremony, he had no discretion to refuse a legitimate claimant; it was his 'bounden duty' to allow the privilege to anyone who was properly qualified. The procedure could take place anywhere – some men were visited by the mayor in their own homes for the purpose – but it was generally necessary for the mayor to operate from a convenient public base. In Chester, this might be the Exchange (or marketplace), the Pentice (a public building that served as a courthouse), the Town Hall, or the mayor might open up his own parlour. When Alderman John Cotgreave had been mayor in 1735, he commandeered his sister's house for such official business because she lived nearer the centre of town than he did.

Previous mayors had held special sessions to get through the backlog of admissions that suddenly arose at election times. They interviewed employers and family members, and checked apprenticeship indentures in the presence of the town clerk, who could advise if any questions arose. During the 1812 poll, the mayor had sat for four hours every day to make sure that every entitled person could have his name entered on the electoral roll in time to vote.

So on 14 March 1820, while a hotly-fought election was taking place for the Member of Parliament to represent the city of Chester, a 22-year-old shoemaker called John Cotgreave visited the mayor and asked to exercise his right to become a freeman. He was accompanied by his father Ralph, who had been a freeman for more than 35 years, and a group of friends who were also eligible to claim the city's freedom.

Ralph Cotgreave's rights had descended from his great grandfather, John Cotgreave, who had been admitted to Chester's civic honour in January 1711, having trained as a shoemaker. What John Cotgreave could not have appreciated was that he was founding a shoemaking dynasty in the city. For 150 years, the citizens of Chester would buy shoes made by John Cotgreave's direct descendants, members of the Cordwainers' Guild and freemen of the city.

In 1820, his great-great-grandson turned up with his friends, seeking their freedom and the rights that came with it. However, the mayor, a carpenter called John Williamson, point blank refused to allow the young men to become freemen during the election period. He claimed that he needed adequate notice before performing the ceremony and that it was not possible just to deal with people who turned up at his house.

Since the poll lasted ten days, there would have been plenty of time to address any questions, and in any case an attorney had in fact given the mayor advance details of the candidates. Moreover, everyone agreed that previous mayors had never demanded prior warning, and this looked like a weak excuse.

Williamson was a partisan in the election – a supporter of General Grosvenor's candidacy – and everyone knew that Cotgreave and the other young men whose were being disfranchised supported the other candidate, Sir John Egerton. It seemed obvious to everyone that the mayor was corruptly rigging the election by preventing some of Egerton's legitimate supporters from registering to vote.

When voting finally closed, General Grosvenor had won, but by a slender margin of just 18 votes out of almost 1,400. It turned out 44 young men had tried unsuccessfully to get their names on the electoral role wanting to vote for Egerton. Only seven of the disfranchised had expressed a desire to support Grosvenor. If John Williamson had admitted Cotgreave and his friends as freemen, the result would have been reversed and Egerton would have been sitting in Parliament instead of the General.

Outraged at the mayor's behaviour, the young men, their families and Egerton's supporters decided that something must be done. Williamson could not be allowed to get away with subverting the democratic process. So they began criminal proceedings in the Court of King's Bench, which ordered that John Williamson should be tried for electoral corruption. Williamson complained that he was now so hated in Chester that he would not get a fair trial, and the proceedings were moved to Shrewsbury. This would increase the sense of drama, as coachloads of witnesses made the 40-mile journey, and the prospect loomed of messengers dashing back to tell the people of Chester the outcome as soon as the jury came to a decision.

It was the autumn of 1821 before the trial took place, some 18 months after the General Election, but time had not dimmed the sense of injustice. The judge was William Garrow, a brilliant lawyer who was 'cogent and luminous'. With Garrow on the bench, John Williamson was in for a tough trial but a fair one.

The prosecution case against Williamson was damning. Elderly freemen testified that mayors had always performed admission ceremonies during elections and had never demanded advance notice. John Cotgreave stood in the witness box and described how he had tried in vain to obtain the ancient privilege that was rightfully his. A bank clerk's evidence proved that the mayor knew the ballot would be close and that his actions might affect the result. Servants of one of the mayor's friends described how he had deliberately gone into hiding, eating his meals in a private bedroom and even bribing them to say he was not there.

Williamson's team pointed out that the town clerk, a lawyer called John Finchett, had given legal advice not to admit freemen. But Finchett was the Grosvenor family's attorney. In the witness box, he dissembled uncomfortably and had to be pressed for a 'direct answer' about what he had advised the mayor to do. He was, in the words of the judge 'the last person' the defendant ought to have consulted. Alderman Evans testified that he had suggested to the mayor that he could absolve himself of blame for the decision, by convening a meeting of the aldermen and getting them to determine whether or not he should admit freemen during the poll. Williamson had at first agreed but had then gone back on his word as he went into hiding. John Williamson's legal team even resorted to painting a picture of a simple craftsman, who was 'rather illiterate,' not educated or prepared to cope with the complex legal issues of ancient customs and elections to the legislature of the British Empire. With all the evidence in, there was never any doubt what the jury would decide – Mayor John Williamson was criminally guilty of deliberately fixing the vote by rigging the electoral register.

The trial had taken all day, starting just after 9am and not finishing until 8pm. At that hour, it was not possible to communicate the good news to the citizens of Chester. Early the next day, three unnamed men climbed into a post-chaise (the fastest kind of coach available) and by 9.30am, they were home and the first Cestrians were beginning their tentative celebrations.[1] People wanted to wait for the witnesses before the partying really began and it was another two hours before John Cotgreave and the others started arriving on the regular coach services from Shrewsbury. They had presumably spent the night at an inn but there was no time now to nurse their hangovers. The city erupted. The crowds packed the streets, and the churches rang their bells in jubilation but they could hardly be heard above the 'shouts of the multitude,' whose 'expression of exultation was universal'.

The jubilant celebrations rapidly died down, and John Cotgreave went back to his ordinary life as a shoemaker. Ironically, John Williamson had by now admitted Cotgreave to the freedom of Chester. John Cotgreave

---

1   Regular scheduled stagecoaches took between 5 and 7 hours to travel between Shrewsbury and Chester. A post-chaise that did not need to make intermediate stops would have been quicker, but to have arrived by 9.30 would nevertheless have required a very early start.

had also become a member of the Cordwainers' Company and was now considered a 'master' of his trade, although his business was small and he did not actually employ anyone else to be the master of. He continued to use the constitutional rights and duties that came with being a freeman. He voted in the election for the city of Chester's sheriff in 1824 and the general elections of 1826 and 1859. Nor was his interest in politics merely passive – in the 1850s, he was one of a group of men that petitioned a local dignitary to stand as their MP (which he did, successfully).

John Cotgreave's son and grandsons followed in his footsteps and were granted the freedom of the city, claiming their right by birth, but not as cordwainers as their ancestors had done – John Cotgreave was the last of the shoemaking dynasty that had been founded in 1711. By the time his son became a freeman, the law had been changed by the Great Reform Act of 1832, and the right to vote in general elections was more standardised, based on the value of a man's home. But anyone who had the franchise as a freeman in 1832 kept it for the rest of his life, whether or not he met the new criteria as a householder. So did anyone who did not become a freeman until after 1832, so long as he obtained the status either by inheritance or by serving an apprenticeship. So John Cotgreave's son (also called John), who was admitted to the freedom in 1845 and also owned a house, could choose. He could exercise the ancient inherited rights as a free citizen, for which his father had fought, or he could vote under the modern rules as a householder. He chose the former.

John Cotgreave senior died aged 69, after a long and debilitating illness. His kidneys had been failing for a full year, and his body wasted away – the official diagnosis was cachexia, a persistent weight loss that cannot be reversed through nutrition.

As the century progressed, Cotgreave's noble fight for his ancient democratic rights was tainted. By 1859, it was clear that members of his family were abusing their privileges. His cousin William Cotgreave voted as a freeman in that year, claiming to be a shoemaker living in Commonhall Street in Chester. But although he had grown up there, he had moved 20 miles away to take a job on the new railway system, and he was not legitimately eligible.[2] But that was nothing compared to what came to light after John Cotgreave died.

It was clear to everyone that the Parliamentary election in Chester in 1880 was riddled with corruption. So there was a trial presided over by a high court judge, and then a Royal Commission to 'Inquire into the Existence of Corrupt Practices in the City of Chester'. At the trial,

2   See photograph, p. x.

William Cotgreave freely confessed that although he lived in the village of Gobowen, which was in another county and which he himself estimated to be 24 miles from Chester, he had nevertheless travelled to the city and voted. He admitted having been sent an encouraging letter from the local Conservatives, and subsequently admitted canvassing for the party. But he was adamant that he had not been bribed or received any other benefits for his vote, and was unambiguous in stating to the judge that he had paid his own train fare to attend the election. But once the Royal Commission was under way, he was forced to admit that he had subsequently been given 12 shillings for his trouble (his ticket had cost less than five). The sums were not great, but in the final report, William Cotgreave's name appeared in the list of voters who had been bribed.

The main finding of the Commission was summed up in the House of Commons: 'With respect to Chester ... the great weapon of Parliamentary warfare there was beer ... the Party who secured the most public-houses usually secured a majority of votes.' Most of the electorate, it was said, refused to go to the polls at all unless they were 'treated'.

And when the Commissioners inquired into who was responsible for the corruption, the name of one solicitor's clerk was prominent – Philip Cotgreave. Witness after witness mentioned his role, his employer spoke of Cotgreave handling sums as large as £20, and he himself admitted paying a variety of people, although when offered the opportunity to 'unburden' his conscience, he denied any knowledge of anything illegal. Unlike his cousin William, Philip Cotgreave was genuinely entitled to vote (he was both an hereditary freeman and a householder), but he was not entitled either to receive money for his vote or to pay and treat others to buy theirs.

Philip was the grandson of John Cotgreave, who had fought so clearly for the democratic rights of voters 60 years before. It would surely have pained John to see in the Royal Commissioners' final report, that the name of Philip Cotgreave had the distinction of appearing on two lists – the 'bribers' and 'those who received bribes'.

OVERSEAS ADVENTURES

Foreign lands have always provided exciting opportunities and unknown risks.

These accounts cover the spread of family members from Cheshire to four corners of the world, including daring adventures in the Andaman Islands, Australia and the Mediterranean. Two of the journeys are astonishing stories of women crossing the world to protect the interests of their children. Another describes the harsh reality of life in the fledgling United States of the early nineteenth century.

CHAPTER TWENTY SIX

1792

Jonathan Cotgrave loses his job

On 10 January 1845, the body of Dr Jonathan Cotgrave was delivered back to the city of his birth. He had died in Oxfordshire on Boxing Day. Arriving in Chester, the coffin spent the night at the Royal Hotel. The next morning, a truly impressive array of local dignitaries amassed in the coffee-room of the hotel to pay their respects: the mayor, the magistrates, the town councillors, the pre-eminent surgeons and medical men from the area, and the leading clergy. They were joined by a large number of the ordinary citizenry, and at 9am, the group walked through the city, following Cotgrave's remains on a horse-drawn hearse. A detachment of policemen headed the procession. The only member of Jonathan Cotgrave's family to attend was his cousin Captain Edward Stone Cotgrave of the Royal Navy. Immediately after the burial – which took place in front of the communion table of the city's most central and civically important church – Captain Cotgrave made his excuses and left. As he hurried away, he pressed into the mayor's hands a letter of thanks for 'the totally unexpected regard shown by the citizens of Chester to the remains of his esteemed relative'.

It is easy to see why Edward Cotgrave was so surprised at the turnout; he himself had been born 200 miles away, did not know the city and had probably never met any of the funeral party before. Moreover, the dead man had not lived in Chester since he was a young man well over 50 years earlier, and all of his eight brothers and sisters had died years before – it was a quarter of a century since any of them had lived in Chester. The only people at Jonathan Cotgrave's funeral who stood any chance of remembering what he looked like were elderly lifelong inhabitants of the city.

On the other hand, it would have been churlish of the authorities not to put on a bit of a show when Dr Cotgrave had bequeathed £2,000 to the local hospital. There was more to it than that, however. Captain

This monument in St Peter's Church in Chester commemorates
Dr Jonathan Cotgrave, who left the city in his early 20s and spent most
of the rest of his life overseas before being buried in his family's vault in
1845. The wings and head of the carved peacock, an ancient symbol of the
family, have long since broken off.

Cotgrave may not have cared much for his family's ancestral homeland but Dr Jonathan Cotgrave had. His bequest had been 'stimulated by his attachment to a city with which his ancestors had been for a long period connected'. He considered himself to be the 'head of the Cotgreave branch of the ancient Cheshire family of de Malpas'. Most significantly, as an army surgeon, he had spent half his life in uncomfortable, far flung, unbearably hot parts of the Mediterranean, soaked in blood and surrounded by screaming, broken soldiers whose unsaveable limbs he was hacking off as swiftly and cleanly as he could. Coming back to rest in the aisle of the church in which he had been baptised 76 years earlier, must have been a long-held hope, and the citizens of his native town seem to have appreciated it.

Dr Cotgrave's father had been a well-to-do dancing teacher who owned property in the city and in the surrounding countryside. With several sons to provide for, Thomas Cotgrave had called in favours and obtained an apprenticeship for Jonathan to train in the medical profession. Jonathan's grandfather, also called Jonathan Cotgrave, had been one of the leading doctors of his generation in the city of Chester, serving as surgeon at the local infirmary.

So at the age of 22, the young Jonathan Cotgrave, having trained under a local doctor called Charles Morrall, was following in distin-guished footsteps when he became an assistant in the dispensary at Chester infirmary, where his late grandfather's skills had so often been displayed. When the senior apothecary fell ill, Jonathan took sole charge of the busy practice, dispensing 200 prescriptions each week to the hospi-tal's patients, the sick of the workhouse and gaol, and out-patients all over the city. He also spent time shadowing a number of other doctors, training in various branches of medicine. According to his boss he showed 'utmost assiduity' and according to himself 'unremitting attention' to his duties. So when the dispensary's apothecary retired, Jonathan Cotgrave seemed the natural candidate for the job. He was not the only applicant, however, and although he had wide support and was patently well qualified, his youth was held against him. In the end, rather than force a split among the Governors who ran the infirmary, Cotgrave withdrew his candidacy. He was praised for the 'very handsome manner' in which he had behaved, but this did not change the fact that he now had no job.

Failing to obtain the post at a provincial hospital changed Jonathan Cotgrave's life; it widened his horizons and set him on a course that would make him rich enough 50 years later to leave a huge bequest to the infirmary that had rejected him. If his youth was the underlying problem, all he had to do was kill time until he was less youthful, but

Eliza Cotgrave's father John was a major in the British army in India. He was said to have 'gained the greatest honour by the presence of mind and firmness and gallantry' but his death in battle left his children nearly destitute [© The British Library Board (Tanner Collection Photo 143(29))].

the East India Company's hardship fund secured them a maintenance grant. Elizabeth, who was about ten, was presumably in India and must subsequently have been brought up by relatives. Her father's sister, whose husband (Richard Mathews) was the Commander in Chief of the British Army in India, was almost certainly involved because Elizabeth and her cousin Cotsford Mathews were educated together.

Nothing else appears to have been recorded about Eliza (as she was known) until she married a young merchant called William Ashburner in March 1790. He died eight years later, leaving Elizabeth as a pregnant widow in her mid 20s with three infants, the eldest of whom was seven.

Within 18 months, Elizabeth was married again, to another up and coming young merchant called Charles Forbes. He belonged to a family firm, Forbes & Company, that imported Indian calico and other luxury goods into Britain.[1] The company and the family flourished. By the early

1   The company is still a major enterprise in India, where it now specialises in infrastructure and real estate, although the Forbes family is no longer involved.

ELIZABETH LADY FORBES. 1800.

Reputedly painted in 1800, this portrait shows Eliza Cotgrave with one of her children, possibly her daughter Mary, who in 1810 was kidnapped and taken to America [Reproduced by kind permission of Rosemary Walker].

1810s, the couple were wealthy and had five Forbes children in addition to the brood of young Ashburners.

Many well-to-do members of the British community in India sent their children to be raised and educated at home in Britain. Eliza herself had been partly educated in England after her father's death, and was all too aware of the frightening uncertainty of a child suddenly finding itself alone in the colonies. Charles was no doubt keen to have his children properly educated in the UK. But the couple did not want to be separated from their children. The outcome of these competing pressures was that at any one time, some of the Ashburner and Forbes children were with their mother in India while others were at home in England or Scotland. In 1810, Mary Ashburner, who was about 15, had been staying in England for some years with an American governess called Mrs Morgan. John and Charles Forbes, aged nine and seven, were at school in London. Elizabeth Ashburner, and George and Katherine Forbes (aged 12, four and two) were with their parents in Mumbai. Communication between London and India took months, so from week to week, Charles and Elizabeth Forbes had little idea of what the UK-based children were doing and how they were faring.

Mrs Morgan had been recommended by a friend of William Ashburner's brother and although she had been in 'straitened circumstances,' there was no reason to suppose she was anything other than honest and reputable. But she was not.

The Forbeses received a terrible shock in March 1810, when a letter arrived telling them that Mrs Morgan had colluded in allowing someone (it is not clear who) to take Mary Ashburner to America without their permission and manifestly against their wishes. There was an ill-thought-through plan to marry the girl off to one of the governess's relatives, in the hope that some of the Forbes wealth would eventually find its way into the impoverished Morgan family. Utterly distraught, Elizabeth immediately set out to rescue her kidnapped daughter. But travel was time-consuming – the letter had taken seven months to arrive, much longer than it took to cross the Atlantic – so the girl had already been in the USA for many weeks and it would another six or seven months before Eliza could reach London, let alone America. Elizabeth Forbes rapidly packed and boarded the *Charles Grant*, but it took 143 days to travel to England, and although she had her other children (as well as her sister and her family) with her, the journey must have been uncomfortable and impossibly fretful. In the Indian Ocean the weather turned nasty; the ship's captain recorded strong gales, hard squalls and heavy rain. All the while, Charles Forbes was desperately worried and alone in Mumbai. 'God alone knows the trial of my feelings,' he wrote as he missed George, 'a fine honest boy' and Kitty, 'a most lovely little prattling girl … admired by all who see her'.

When Elizabeth Cotgrave disembarked at Portsmouth on 5 September 1810, it was well over a year since her daughter Mary Ashburner had been taken. Eliza had yet to get to America, let alone find Mary once she did so. Hearing that their sister-in-law's ship was due, two of Charles Forbes' brothers hastened south and met her. An elderly uncle gave them £200 to cover the brothers' expenses. There were two long weeks in London preparing for the transatlantic trip, but Elizabeth managed somehow to set aside her anxiety and to be notably gracious and kind to her husband's family. Then she set out for Liverpool to sail for New York, taking nine-year-old John out of school to accompany her, and leaving the other children in school or with family members.

By the time she set foot on American soil, Elizabeth Forbes had not seen her daughter for years, and she knew that Mary had already been in the USA for more than 12 months. She had no idea what the Morgans had told the girl or what they might have made her do. She must have clung to the knowledge that if the Morgans were really trying to use the girl as a way of securing money from the Forbeses, they would have to get in touch somehow.

Letters expressed Charles's worry, his kindness and his deep love and concern for his wife and children. They document the generosity of his uncle and the support of his brothers, and facts like the names of ships and the journey times. But they record nothing about what happened when Elizabeth Forbes was finally reunited with her daughter in America. Whatever occurred, Elizabeth's tenacity ensured that the teenager was returned safely to England. In May 1811, a Miss Smith wrote from London to her family in India that since their return from America, Mrs Forbes and her daughter were well.

But although there are no letters from Elizabeth, no words from Mary, not even a note from nine-year-old John, what shines through with burning clarity is a sense of family love and loyalty among the Forbeses. Charles distraught at missing his two-year-old prattling daughter, his brothers rushing around the country to help their frantic sister-in-law, the uncle doling out money as the only way he could show his support, Elizabeth not caring what risks she took or what society thought of a married woman taking a child more than half way round the globe and leaving her husband alone as she dashed to what many thought an unsafe part of the world. Charles Forbes was clear that his wife had his full support: 'I cannot of course object' to what she was doing, he said, because she was, 'determined … to rescue her daughter' who had been kidnapped in 'extraordinary circumstances'.

To underline the closeness of the family's ties, six years after the American escapade, Mary Ashburner married Michie Forbes, her step-father's younger brother. Elizabeth Cotgrave's Ashburner family and her Forbes family were united in the marriage.

On their return to England from Mumbai a few years later, Charles and Elizabeth Forbes lived in London, where his public speeches as a Member of Parliament showed to the whole world the supportive and fair man that his family knew Charles Forbes to be. It would be facile to

The formality of this engraving of Eliza Cotgrave, Lady Forbes, contrasts
with the informality of the earlier painting of her with her daughter
[© The National Portrait Gallery]

Henry Forbes Cotgrave, who did not die until 1913, was a fairly distant cousin of Eliza Cotgrave, Lady Forbes, but the family clearly remained proud of its associations with the Forbes family [Reproduced from *Somerset Leaders, social and political* by Ernest Gaskell (1907)].

pretend that he was so far ahead of his time as to think that all people really were equal, but he clearly did believe that there were no grounds for discriminating against others on the basis of their nationality or sex. He could not understand why Scottish judges should be paid a great deal less than English ones and he was such a supporter of the rights of native Indians in the British Empire that he was first person ever to have a statue honouring him paid for by popular local subscription. When it was erected in Mumbai Town Hall, he received an address signed by 1,042 of the local people. He stood up for the civic authorities in Aberdeen when they were criticised and he exposed the cant of his colleagues when they claimed to be extending the electoral franchise but were actually trying to curtail it.

Clearest of all is his empathy with women. In a Parliamentary discussion on the practice of Indian widows being burned on their husbands' funeral pyres, he dismissed the idea that the women accepted it because of their different cultural beliefs. It was, he said, 'absurd to suppose that the love of life was any less powerful in the bosom of a Hindoo woman than in other person'. When it came to Parliamentary Reform, Forbes simply did not understand how anyone could object to women being given the right to vote. He asked his fellow politicians 'on what grounds they opposed this proposition? ... if the right of voting was grounded on the possession of property, there ought to be no distinction of sex'.

In 1823, Charles was made a baronet, and Eliza became known either as Dame Elizabeth or as Lady Forbes of Newe and Edinglassie. The little girl who had been penniless, frightened and alone when her parents died in Mumbai 40 years earlier, the pregnant young widow who did not know how she would care for her infants in 1798, the unstoppable mother who had put herself at great risk to rescue her daughter, the family matriarch with a brood of nine children, had become a member of the titled classes with large and highly comfortable homes in London and Scotland.

Her children had all now grown up, the men working as merchants, doctors and military officers and all but one of the girls married to gentlemen with the same sorts of jobs. The youngest girl from Eliza's first marriage, Elizabeth Constable Ashburner, remained unmarried and lived with her mother. When Sir Charles Forbes died in 1849, Elizabeth Cotgrave, Lady Forbes as she was now known, continued to live the life appropriate to a baronet's widow, visiting friends, travelling, and attending society events. All of these things were always done with her family. When Elizabeth stayed with the Ellis family in Surrey, she was accompanied by three of her grown-up children and a daughter-in-law. When 'Milady Forbes' travelled abroad, her passport allowed for her to be accompanied by 'deux demoiselles'. At court, she was presented to the Queen by the Countess of Clarendon (a relation of Sir Charles) before going on herself to present her daughters.

Elizabeth Forbes considered that she was now a member of her husband's family, but she had not forgotten her own blood relations, and stayed in close touch with her Cotgrave family. Lieutenant Henry Cotgrave, Eliza's nephew, travelled to India on a Forbes & Company ship called the *Katherine Stewart Forbes*, named after her youngest daughter. In 1831, Henry had been formally presented to the King by Sir Charles Forbes in St James's Palace. Elizabeth's cousin Rowland Burdon Cotgrave, a former naval officer, commanded some of Forbes & Company's vessels trading between India and England. Perhaps the proudest association was in 1829, when Rowland Cotgrave captained a ship called *Lonach*, named after the traditional rallying cry of the Forbes clan. Several of the

Cotgraves took Forbes as a middle name, the last of whom, Henry Forbes Cotgrave, did not die until 1913.

In her will, written when she was about 85, Dame Elizabeth Forbes made bequests to 15 people, all close members of her family, children and grandchildren.[2] She had to write a codicil to rectify her mistake when she realised she had excluded any friends. The relationship of each family member was described in full and Elizabeth listed the qualifications and the regimental commissions of her children and grandchildren. One of her sons was 'John Ashburner Doctor of Medicine,' a grandson was 'William Ashburner Captain 3rd Bombay Cavalry' and another was 'Charles Forbes son of my daughter Mary Forbes … widow of the late Michie Forbes Esquire'.

In the original will, Lady Forbes wrote off unspecified debts due from her daughter Mary – who was now an ageing widow but who had once been the kidnapped teenager – but Mary was not given a separate bequest of her own. On reflection, however, Elizabeth changed her mind and a second codicil bequeathed Mary Forbes a legacy of £1,000.

Elizabeth Cotgrave, Lady Forbes of Newe and Edinglassie, died at her daughter's home in Wimbledon in April 1861, when she was in her late 80s. Mary, the little girl who had been kidnapped, but about whom nothing much else was recorded, lived more than 30 years as a widow; she died in her mother's old home in 1874.

Elizabeth's body was carried over 500 miles to the parish church of Strathdon in the beautiful Aberdeenshire mountains, the site of the Forbes family seat at Newe. Here, she lies among a whole clan of Forbes ancestors and descendants. The spot is within hearing distance of the field where for two centuries, the Forbes baronet has shouted the old rallying cry 'Lonach' each summer at the annual Highland games. Among the family's historic memorabilia is a beautifully simple portrait labelled 'Elizabeth Lady Forbes 1800'. It shows a young woman with her long dark hair worn loosely and informally, leaning forward to gather up into her arms a little child in a taffeta dress. The child is probably Mary Ashburner, a decade before she was kidnapped, but it does not really matter whether it is her or one of her siblings. The image says it all – the only thing that was really important to Eliza Cotgrave, Dame Elizabeth Forbes, the Lady of Newe and Edinglassie, was her family.

2   There were also charitable bequests to the parishes in London and Scotland where she had homes.

CHAPTER TWENTY EIGHT

1818

William Watson Cotgreave is sacked by the Ohio Assembly

William Watson Cotgreave was the first member of his family to be born in America. He could not have picked a more suitable time to begin a New World adventure. Born into the crucible of revolutionary fervour, he was a toddler when the Declaration of Independence was signed. His formative years were those of the War of Independence. His father lost touch with his family back home in Cheshire. His mother was closely related to the Chief Justice of New York.[1] When the Americans went to war against the former British colonists in 1812, William fought bravely for the independent country his birthplace had become and had no sympathy for the faraway land where his cousins lived. But although he was an educated, likeable, witty and able man with a distinguished military record, William Cotgreave's story shows how hard it could be for a self-made man to thrive in the uncertain early days of a new and developing nation.

William's father had come to America as a young man from Guilden Sutton, just outside Chester, but if John Cotgreave had economic ambitions for emigrating, he certainly did not fulfil them.[2] He seems to have been primarily motivated by slightly bizarre religious ideas. He wrote rambling and intransigent thoughts to the colonial authorities about the importance of arranging the seats in church and the need for cheap school uniforms as

---

1   She was described in 1780 as a daughter or niece of 'Judge Smith". The only person this could credibly have been is William Smith (1728–93), who among other roles served as the last colonial Royal Justice of New York Province and later the Chief Justice of New York.
2   See Chapter 34.

part of moral education. He concerned himself with the question of what sort of families could create perfect devoutly Protestant communities and concluded that the answer was to be found among his wife's relatives. He was also something of a conspiracy theorist, requesting that his thoughts should be kept an 'everlasting secret' and suggesting that straightforward negotiations about renting a house should remain a 'profound secret'.

Amongst all his father's delusional views, the defining feature of William Cotgreave's upbringing seems to have been constant movement. His father was in Connecticut in 1766 and New York City in 1770. In the early 1770s, he lived at Johnstown in what is now Fulton County, New York, but soon after was in Hartford County, Maryland. In 1776, he wrote his last known letter to his English family, telling his brother that he lived in Philadelphia. Soon after, John Cotgreave was back in New York State, at Dutchess County. By the time of the federal census in 1790, he and his son were living in Bennington County in Vermont but later the same year, he was again described as being of Dutchess County. In 1793, he had recently been staying in Connecticut but had left once more. Later in the 1790s, he was described as being of Albany County, New York, and by 1802, of Greene County. He then moved 450 miles to Ohio, where he died in 1814. No doubt many of his contemporaries had to move around in search of a living but even by the standards of his time, John Cotgreave was unusually nomadic. One newspaper correspondent mocked 'the peregrinations of your friend Cotgreave'. The unsettled existence and ridicule might have been worth it if the economic gains had proved commensurate, but they were not even close. John Cotgreave was declared bankrupt in New York in 1770, was bemoaning his poor quality home and his 'peculiarly' disadvantageous circumstances in the 1770s, was insolvent again in the 1780s and was classified as an 'absconding debtor' in the 1790s.

It was thus a world of religiosity, paranoia, wandering and financial failure into which William Watson Cotgreave was born in about 1773. It is hardly surprising that the earliest independent records of his life, dating from his mid to late 20s, are a notice of his own financial insolvency and a list of passengers travelling 100 miles on board a ship from New York to Philadelphia. It looked as if William Watson Cotgreave was set to imitate the pattern of his father's mistakes. That impression was reinforced in 1804, when Cotgreave appeared in court accused of attempting to 'swindle' various creditors out of $24,000.

There was, however, one big difference between the two men. While his father was a humourless bore who obviously struggled to cope with the real world, William Cotgreave was likeable and funny and understood

rejuvenate cold, wet men who needed to be fit and well for the coming season. Blisteringly harsh winter weather started as soon as the *Prince* arrived. To make things worse, the harbour was not safe from enemy attack, so as soon as the troops were disembarked, the *Prince* and her crew left the port and came to rest off the Crimean coast. Two anchors were needed to hold her steady.

Just before 9am on 14 November 1854, the wind whipped up from the southwest and the Balaklavan sea descended into tumultuous chaos. A small transport vessel smashed into the *Prince*, and the cable holding the port side anchor snapped. Being a steam-powered vessel, the captain could in theory drive the *Prince* against the wind but by now there was debris crashing about in the turbulent water and some of it became caught in the propeller. Within five minutes the starboard cable had snapped and the *Prince* began rapidly to drift towards the rocky coastline. The captain called everyone on deck and told them 'every man must try and save himself'.

The teenage Henry Cotgrave stripped off his jacket and dived into the freezing ocean. There was a hurricane, the ice cold rain turned to snow,

The Steamship *Prince* sank in the Crimea during storms in November 1854 with only seven survivors out of a crew of 150. 15-year-old Henry Cotgrave was the only surviving officer [Reproduced from the *Illustrated London News*, 16 December 1854].

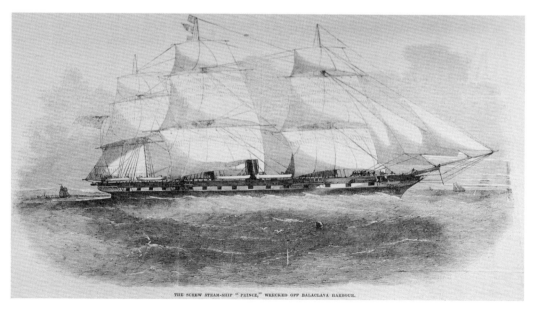

THE SCREW STEAM-SHIP "PRINCE," WRECKED OFF BALACLAVA HARBOUR.

the rocks were treacherous and the violent sea was already full of wood, bodies, cargo, netting and out-of-control boats of various sizes in various stages of disintegration. Midshipman Cotgrave became jammed between two large pieces of smashed timber and could not move. He watched helplessly as the *Prince* was dashed to pieces – 15 minutes after it first hit the rocks, there was nothing left to see. Its destruction was so comprehensive that archaeological divers did not relocate the site until 2010.

The last that anyone had seen of any of the 150 men on board the *Prince* was a melee of drowning bodies and helpless sailors clinging desperately to flotsam as they were crushed against the sharp, hard Jurassic limestone of the Crimean coastline. There was no hope.

It took a couple of weeks for news to reach home, but by 2 December, the press in London was reporting the terrible calamity. Many ships were lost in an horrific tragedy and 'foundered with their crews'. *The Times* was even more explicit about the hopelessness of the situation – the most serious loss was the *Prince,* which had sunk 'with all hands'.

That is no doubt how Henry Cotgrave's mother learned that her son was dead. Still only 37 herself, she was used to death, having been widowed twice before her thirtieth birthday. Both her sons were in high risk occupations a long way from home, with Henry's elder brother Charles serving in the Indian army.[1] But however well prepared she might have been, to lose a teenage son and learn about it from the newspapers must have been unthinkably devastating for Anna Maria Garle. Apart from anything else, she would not have the comfort of organising a funeral, or even of knowing that a burial was taking place thousands of miles away, given that most of the sailors' bodies would probably never be recovered. The young widow's desolation must have been total.

Remarkably, a day or so after the disaster, there had in fact been a search party out in a boat, trying to recover what remained of the bodies of the *Prince*'s crew. Even more remarkably, the search party included a frightened midshipman who 24 hours earlier had been battered against the rocks in the gales. When the newspapers reported there was no hope, they had been wrong. Midshipman Henry George Forbes Cotgrave had miraculously survived one of the most infamous shipwrecks in British history.

After a short while floating powerlessly in the powerful sea, Cotgrave had hit the rocks. By a fluke, the moment and place where he landed was the one point in space and time when the sea and the rocks were forgiving enough to allow the half-naked, freezing teenager to clamber on

---

1   See Chapter 30.

This painting of the port of Galle in Sri Lanka was made from the deck
of Henry Cotgrave's Steamship *Calcutta* in 1852 [© National Maritime
Museum, Greenwich, London (LOG/M/61)].

to a rocky ledge just above the violent tidal swell. Six other seamen hit the
same rocks at the same time and the seven men formed a huddle on the
freezing ledge in what was now a blizzard.

Waiting for five or six hours, they neither tried nor expected to be
rescued soon. The crews of those ships that had managed to secure
themselves safely were busy trying to rescue sailors from the sea, not just
the men of the *Prince* but those from other wrecked vessels. Eventually,
when it was clear they could do no more in the water, the rescuers turned
their attention to Henry Cotgrave and his comrades. Tied to ropes, the
seven survivors were hoisted to safety up a cliff face 200 feet high. These
seven turned out to be the only survivors from the 150 men on board the
Prince.

Almost the first thing Henry Cotgrave did once he was safe was to
write two letters. One was to his employer, the Secretary of the General
Screw Steam Shipping Company. As the only surviving officer of the
Prince, however junior, it was his duty to inform the company of what had
happened and to seek new instructions. He praised the conduct of some
of his colleagues and, recognising that without a ship he was without a
job, he signed himself 'H G F Cotgrave, late midshipman'. The other
letter began 'Dear Mama' and was signed 'your affectionate son'. The two
missives told the same story but the contrast between them is striking.
That to the company gives no indication that the sole surviving officer
was little more than a teenage trainee. That to his mother exposes Henry
as the brave but frightened child he really was. He said he expected
very soon to be taking a boat to help look for bodies, but 'please God, I

shall get home safe'. Anna Maria did not receive her son's letter until 10 December, over a week after he had been reported dead in the *Times.*

The condition of the British army in Russia following the loss of the *Prince* outraged British public opinion. The Crimean War was the first conflict that was reported in detail by the press, and the public knew as much as their political masters about what was being done in their names. When the Government came under pressure in the House of Commons on 14 December, the First Lord of the Admiralty admitted that ministers' sole source of information about what had actually happened to the *Prince* was correspondence in the *Times,* mainly Henry Cotgrave's two letters. Although the army troops on the ship had been safely landed before the disaster, the supplies had not. Tons of ammunition and tens of thousands of warm uniforms and boots were at the bottom of the Black Sea, while hordes of British soldiers froze in the biting temperatures of the eastern European winter.

So when Henry Cotgrave returned home to England at the turn of the year, Parliament was busy setting up an inquiry. On 7 February, Cotgrave, who was still only 17, attended the Palace of Westminster to appear before the Committee scrutinising 'Irregularities in Transport of Stores to the East'. Members of Parliament questioned him about why the ship had not stopped at Üsküdar (then known as Scutari). There was little point in probing Henry Cotgrave, who was too junior to have been involved in such decision making. But there was nobody else left to interrogate and he did at least know that it was Admiral Edward Boxer who had told the ship's captain not to anchor at Üsküdar, even if he could not explain why.

His brief appearance before the Select Committee was Henry Cotgrave's last involvement with the merchant navy. By the autumn, he had decided to switch to the Royal Navy in India. Between September and November 1855, he split his time between Mrs Taylor's Nautical Academy in the City of London and the Canal Iron Works in Millwall, earning certificates that he was competent as a seaman and that he understood the steam engines used in modern ships. He had a family friend, George Forbes, to recommend him to the East India Company, and signed the necessary declaration as a volunteer.[2] He sailed out of Southampton just before Christmas, and when he reached Mumbai in January 1856, he was again rated as a midshipman. It seems he could not

2   Given Henry's middle names, it seems likely that George Forbes was his godfather. The Cotgrave and Forbes families were related by marriage (See Chapter 27).

expect promotion or advancement based merely on his remarkable experiences and moment of celebrity.

For a couple of years, Henry Cotgrave lived the life of an ordinary junior officer, serving first on a ship called the *Acbar* and later the *Semiramis*. The lot of midshipmen operating out of Mumbai at the time was documented by two of his shipmates. They enjoyed using telescopes and going for trips in the captain's gig, killing a 'great cobra' and meeting the local Rajah. But largely the letters tell of how hard the life was – the heat was unbearable, the captain treated the officers 'most shamefully,' learning Hindustani was difficult, and most of all they were always broke. Their pay was gone almost as soon as they had it, falling into debt was 'very common' and the midshipmen thought it 'wonderful how quickly rupees fly out here however careful one is'.[3] Work could also be very dull – long periods on land were boring (especially the musket practice), on board ship there was a great deal of cleaning decks and inspecting holds, and there seem to have been innumerable visits from the Rev. Mr Cummings who conducted religious services on deck.

So it was no doubt with both relief and excitement that Henry Cotgrave was plucked from the deck of the *Semiramis* and sent on an expedition to the Andaman Islands, an archipelago nearer to Burma than India. His orders were to identify the best site to build a penal colony. The British had tried this before in the Andamans, but had abandoned the idea when uncontrollable tropical diseases had generated a distressingly high death rate. Moreover, the islands were inhabited by unfriendly locals who did not accept that British rule extended to their territory. Not everyone would have thought this an attractive assignment. However, Cotgrave clearly proved his worth when he was given a detachment of 20 of the best trained men and command of a cutter as part of the naval expedition to reconnoitre the islands. But the investigations of the Andamans came to an abrupt end when, on 10 May 1857, the Indian Mutiny broke out. The authorities needed more land-based troops in mainland India, so Henry Cotgrave was drafted for duty on shore at Barrackpore. He was now required to be a soldier, and he proved to be remarkably good at it. All that tedious musket drill was about to pay off.

A year later, in May 1858, Lieutenant George O'Brien Carew and his men were in deep Indian jungle when they came under fire from

3   One of the reasons was compulsory payments midshipmen made into the Indian Navy Fund, to fund their retirement pensions. In Henry's case, it turned out to be well worth it. He paid a total of 110 rupees into the fund, but his widow was still receiving £136 per year seven decades later.

the enemy. Midshipman Cotgrave and his party silenced the fire and saved their lives. Carew's despatches singled out Henry for praise. Having survived the enemy attack, the lieutenant quickly succumbed to the fetid conditions of the dirty, malarial, swampy forest and was too ill to remain in command of his troops. So Cotgrave was given a temporary promotion and it was as an acting lieutenant that he marched his men to Motihari to relieve embattled colleagues. His troops were recognised for their discipline and results, so by March 1859, Henry had come to the favourable notice of the higher command of British forces in India.

If he expected any permanent promotion, he was to be disappointed. Once the mutiny had been put down, he was back as a midshipman in the Indian Navy and it was another two years before he gained the rank of ship's mate on the *Ajdaha*. Henry Cotgrave had had enough, and he retired from active service at the age of just 24.

After the exotic excitement of a near death experience in the Black Sea, a reconnaissance mission to hostile tropical islands and a gunfight in the jungle, Henry George Forbes Cotgrave finally did something normal for a young man of his age. On 2 June 1863, he was married at Kensington in London. His bride, Ellen Caroline Morland, was also his cousin (their mothers were sisters) and came from a typical family from Cotgrave's circle. Her father was a Colonel in the Indian army. But if Ellen thought that Henry Cotgrave could settle down to boring domesticity she was mistaken. No doubt keen to impress on his new wife that he had prospects, Henry took the precaution of applying for a certificate to qualify as a ship's mate and it was issued a few weeks after the wedding. But he had no intention of returning to the tedium of language lessons, penury and a lack of respect from his superiors. Within six months of their marriage, he and Ellen were living on the other side of the world in the outback of Queensland. They had a daughter there in 1864 and a son who died when he was three weeks old.

Unlike a career in the navy, farming in the bush leaves little in the way of records and so almost nothing is known about Henry and Ellen's life together in Australia. One incident was, however, written down by the authorities, because it had fatal consequences.

On 3 March 1866, Henry George Forbes Cotgrave rode his horse out onto his land at Comet Downs in Queensland. A neighbour saw him go, but thought nothing of it – there was hardly anything remarkable about a farmer riding on his farm. When asked later, the neighbour thought that Cotgrave had been 'in good health'. When Henry failed to return home, Ellen no doubt became concerned, but it can hardly have been unusual in the nineteenth century outback for people to be delayed by all manner of situations. Early the next morning, however, a neighbour called John Brown was in the area of Race Course Creek when he found Henry Cotgrave lying lifeless on the ground. He later described how the body was face down with the head pointing towards the Creek and the left hand underneath the neck. Richard Slygh, the neighbour who had seen Henry the previous morning, then came along. The two men agreed that the only explanation for what they witnessed was that Henry had been thrown from his horse. Where the malarial swamps of India, the aggressive natives of the Andamans, the rebellious local troops of the empire, the bitter Crimean winter and the violent Black Sea had all failed, a simple accident succeeded. Henry George Forbes Cotgrave had died as soon as he hit the ground. He was just 28 years old.

The published obituary summarised Henry Cotgrave's adventures in fewer than 100 understated words. He would 'long be remembered by his friends and shipmates as a fine seaman, a man of iron nerve and great personal strength'. He had 'a handsome face and grand physique.' It was easy to see why he was 'much beloved by his brother officers'.

The shortness of Henry's life was balanced by the great length of his widow's. Ellen Caroline Cotgrave, who was 23 when her husband died, would live well into her nineties and did not die until 1936, seven decades after her husband's fatal riding accident. The ensuing years were a great deal less exciting than her time with Henry Cotgrave had been.

Within weeks of Henry's death, Ellen Cotgrave set out to return to England with their infant daughter. Somewhere between Rockhampton and Sydney, some of her precious possessions were stolen, including jewellery and miniature portraits, one of which presumably depicted the handsome face and grand physique of the dead adventurer. She remarried in 1874, to a clergyman's son who had none of Henry's fascinating stories. They emigrated back to Australia, where he worked in routine official posts as a customs collector and member of the local health board.

It was 30 years after Henry Cotgrave's death, while Ellen and her second husband were living their conventional lives, that a story came to light demonstrating that even in his final days, apparently as a steady, settled farmer, Henry had been unable to resist excitement. In 1897, the local newspaper in Brisbane was running a series of articles about the life stories of familiar characters in the area. The harbourmaster, 58-year-old John Mackay, regaled a journalist with his autobiography. In the 1860s, on his uppers, he had met a Dr Lang and Lieutenant Cotgrave

207

at Rockhampton, about 130 miles to the east of Comet Downs.[4] The two men had induced him to sign up for an expedition to explore the island of Papua. Today the island is partly a province of Indonesia and partly the independent country of Papua New Guinea. To the European population of Australia in the 1860s, it was a largely unexplored jungle.

Mackay felt bamboozled into a potentially exciting, but certainly risky, venture by Henry Cotgrave and his friend. He said he had 'fallen foul' of Dr Lang and the lieutenant. When asked why the enterprise had come to nothing, Mackay said simply 'project fell through, Cotgrave being thrown from his horse and killed'. There was no thought of carrying on without him; no alternatives were sought.

Henry George Forbes Cotgrave had become synonymous with adventure. Without him, it was impossible.

4   Henry had been promoted to the rank of lieutenant on his retirement from the navy.

CHAPTER THIRTY

1858

Mary Ann Cotgrave takes her infant daughter through the jungle

Mary Anne Cotgrave's world was dominated by men who lied to her, let her down, pretended to be something they were not and left little or no stability in her life. She eventually joined in, lying about whether or not she was married and committing bigamy, but she also showed a steely determination not to let the unreliable men around her ruin the lives of her children. She travelled half way around the world, defied the military regime and sat through the jackal-ridden darkness of the Indian jungle to force her feckless husband to care for their daughter. She risked unpopularity by pestering the London authorities, she risked humiliation by begging from her sister, and she risked complete degradation by committing a criminal act for which society would vilify her if it ever found out. All in the cause of protecting and providing for her children.

The first unstable character in Mary Anne's life was her father, William Deller, but he can hardly be blamed for his behaviour. In fact he might be praised as an honourable man doing his best for his family. His efforts, however, resulted in continual restless moving and his job was forever changing. When Mary Anne was born (in 1835), he described himself as a farmer; by the time she was six he was an innkeeper, and a year later he defined himself as a paid parish official responsible for overseeing the implementation of the Poor Law. The constant change in circumstances continued when Mary Anne was 12 because William Deller died, and she went to live with her elder brother Richard. William's attempts to keep his family reasonably well off had not been entirely deluded, and somehow or other Richard Deller had acquired sufficient investments that he could live off the income and did not need to work. Their widowed mother married a man considered a gentleman, and it seems that at this stage of her life, money was not a major problem for Mary Anne and her family.

At the age of 18, Mary Anne Deller met and married a man called Edwin Charles William Cotgrave, known as Charlie, who was about to become an officer in the British army in India. He was not rich, but once he received his commission would have some prospects, and he could expect some credit for his family's modestly distinguished record of service in India – his father had died young with an 'exemplary record' in the Indian army, his grandfather had been Chief Engineer in Chennai and his great-grandfather, who had been the first to venture outside Chester was an infantry major and had died bravely in battle.[1] It must have been obvious to everyone that this was not a carefully considered match because Mary Anne was eight months pregnant on her wedding day in August 1853, and five weeks later gave birth to a healthy baby girl called Eleanor. Soon after, Charlie caught the boat to Malta on the first leg of his journey and six months later, he was an ensign in the 3rd European Regiment at Mumbai. He went on to have what looks like a career worthy of his ancestors, being promoted to lieutenant within two years, serving at various key military moments of the coming years (with names like the capture of Rathgarh, the relief of Saugor and the battle of the Betwa), obtaining a post as a staff officer and then being posted to a different regiment over the heads of other officers, who resented him as a result.

Mary Anne Cotgrave stayed in England with the baby, and went to live with her elder sister, who had married a successful London confectioner a few weeks after Charlie had sailed. Charlie Cotgrave promised to send her £53 a year, in monthly instalments, more than enough for a woman and child to live comfortably, especially if they were staying with relations. But Charlie was a young man on the other side of the world – when he sailed to India, he was just 19. He found that out of sight, his wife was out of mind, and that his wages really were not enough for his needs and wants, let alone hers or the baby's. This was especially true because, ironically, a third of his income – 60 rupees a month – was deducted at source for the 'Military Fund,' a safety net to help out soldiers and their families in financial difficulty.

Writing to Charlie resulted in nothing except further promises that he promptly failed to keep, and at her wit's end about what to do, and perhaps frightened that her brother-in-law was tiring of paying for

1   See Chapter 27.

everything, Mary Anne Cotgrave had no option but to contact her husband's employer. She told Sir James Melville, the Chief Secretary of the East India Company, that she felt forced to 'solicit the interference of yourself on my behalf' and was careful to apologise for the trouble she was causing.

Three weeks later Melville sent the letter on to India, requesting an 'immediate' reply from Charlie Cotgrave. It took months for the demand to arrive and then weeks to be processed by the military bureaucracy. There was then a further three month delay for the reply to travel back, so that having written to complain in May, it was half way through November before Mary Anne Cotgrave received the response that her husband was sorry and would remit money home at once. Maybe he did, but he did not behave himself for long. Eight months later, Mary Anne was desperate again. She had not been able to pay her sister anything for month upon month; Cotgrave had broken his promise to pay monthly, then he had broken his promise to pay quarterly, then he broken his promise to pay every half year. He had certainly broken his promise to increase Mary Anne's allowance as little Eleanor grew up.

In a new plea to her husband's employers, Mary Anne Cotgrave made it clear that only the kindness of her friends and relatives prevented her becoming utterly destitute and walking the streets. Apologetic again, but determined to oblige Charlie to pay, she asked that the East India Company force him to accept his responsibilities. Just as before, months ensued as letters travelled from London to Mumbai and then up country to the place where Cotgrave's regiment was stationed. It was even more difficult this time against the backdrop of the Indian Mutiny. There was fighting and chaos everywhere, and Lieutenant Cotgrave had other things on his mind when he finally received a begging letter from a faraway wife he had not seen for four years and an order from his superiors to sort the problem out. This time, there was no point in pretending that he was going to mend his ways, let alone pay off the arrears. So he simply sent home a one-off payment, borrowed from the Military Fund into which he was forced to contribute, with instructions for his wife and child to join him in India.

So Mary Anne Cotgrave and her four-year-old daughter Eleanor set sail and braved the long journey to Mumbai. She had never been out of England before, and the endless peregrinations she had endured as her father kept moving the family around must suddenly have seemed trivial. Shipping technology had improved, but however someone travelled to India, it still took at least a month. When Charlie had left Hampshire on board the *Sultan* in February 1854, it had been several weeks before he arrived at Mumbai for his posting.

Once in Mumbai, Mary Anne had somehow to travel 600 miles through mutinous country to where Charlie was stationed in the outskirts of Jhansi, held by the native Indians considered by the British to be mutineers. The first step was to get to the administrative town of Mhow, 350 miles away, which she did in a cart pulled by a bullock, arriving towards the end of May 1858. Just as she arrived, the weather broke, and although the rain was 'unspeakably refreshing,' there were serious concerns that raging thunderstorms would make further travel impossible. But this turned out to be the least of Mary Anne Cotgrave's problems in Mhow.

The authorities were not happy. They could hardly allow an English woman with no experience of India and carrying a 'graceful and delicate child' to go crashing about a perilous landscape full of locals who were rebelling against their European masters. Quite reasonably, they told her straight that she could not go. But Mary Anne Cotgrave had not come all this way to fail in her bid to make Charlie Cotgrave take responsibility for his daughter, and it was at this point that she brought about the remarkable events that were later published as an example of 'woman's fortitude'.

Worried she would be detained for her own safety, she quickly hired a cart and left Mhow in the dead of night. Just four people were on the cart – Mary Anne and Eleanor Cotgrave, a native woman servant (known as an ayah) who helped looked after the child, and the driver of the cart (known as the gharry waller).

Inevitably, disaster struck.

Crashing through the thick jungle in the pitch black darkness, the cart broke down. The gharry waller tried to fix it, while the women and the child sat clinging to one another. Mary Anne Cotgrave had a particular fear of tigers and other wild animals, so she trembled in terror as the jackals around them made 'their frightful and unearthly laugh'. The women had little or nothing with them – Mary Anne had managed to send on ahead what luggage she possessed, so all they could do was sit by the side of the track listening to sounds of the wild forest, trying not to frighten the little girl too much.

In time, the gharry waller managed to complete his task and they were able slowly to move off into the night. What ensued were described as 'many delays and adventures' but sadly, nobody thought to write down the details. Somehow or other, Mary Anne reached Charlie Cotgrave at Jhansi, where he proceeded to distinguish himself at the battle that recovered the city for the British government.

MONEY, BUSINESS'S AND PROPERTY

Money and property are strong drivers of human behaviour, and many surviving records that tell us about our ancestors were originally created for financial reasons.

The life stories in this section describe how seven people have made money and how they have lost it. From a ruthlessly successful Tudor businessman to a hapless Victorian dilettante who was in constant financial difficulty, these accounts chronicle financial success and failure. One tells how an eighteenth century man's affairs were so complicated that it took decades after his death to unravel them. Two contrasting Victorian women showed both how to succeed financially in a man's world and how to waste cash on an epic scale. From the early nineteenth century, there are tales of fraud and identity theft, stories of rags to riches and of riches to rags.

CHAPTER THIRTY ONE

1570

William Cotgreve inherits a pub

Two incidents were especially remembered from William Cotgreve's term as Mayor of Chester – the hanging of a gaoler for killing a prison inmate, and the judicial burning of a woman who poisoned her husband. These anecdotes indicate something about how brutal Cotgreve's world was, but since they were considered noteworthy, they must have been exceptional even by the harsh standards of the day. William Cotgreve thrived in that tough world; he was a hard-nosed, if not a hard, man and it made him an extremely successful businessman.

The list-makers who recorded details of Chester's mayors remembered three personal facts about William Cotgreve. He had been born in the city he served, he 'kept a good house' and he 'ruled well'. He was hardly the only mayor born within the city's ancient walls, but the fact that it was recorded says something about his sense of connection with the place. It is not surprising that he entertained well, given that he owned and ran an hotel, but his constituents clearly thought it important. It reads as if he was a welcoming and accessible civic host who saw it as part of his job to retain a strong connection with his constituency. But anyone who saw William Cotgreve as a parochial, small town official would have underestimated a ruthless businessman with a wide range of heavyweight nationwide connections. And, as Chester's bakers found to their cost, he did not shy away from fights with local interests or from making himself unpopular with significant sectors of the citizenry.

When he was born in 1544, it would have been hard to predict the path of William Cotgreve's life. His brother Randle (who called himself Cotgrave) was three years older, and it was reasonable to assume that the senior of the two would inherit their father's small inn in the city centre. The most that William might have expected was a bequest of some bits

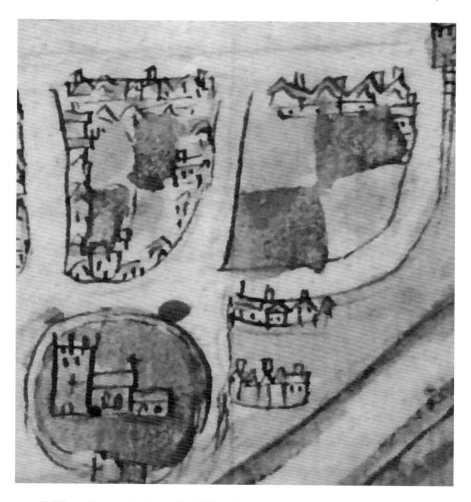

William Cotgreve's inn called The Crow occupied a number of buildings
shown on the corner at the top-right of this contemporary map of Chester,
where Foregate Street (horizontal) meets St John Street (vertical) [© The
British Library Board (Harley MS 1046 f.173)].

and pieces of real estate his father had acquired in the surrounding
villages, a few fields and the odd cottage held on longish leases.

But when their father felt his own mortality approaching in early
1570, it was to William Cotgreve that he transferred the ownership of
The Crow, a collection of adjoining houses where he ran a business
offering accommodation as well as serving food and drink. There had

219

Two painted boards in St John's Church in Chester display William Cotgreve's coat of arms as one of the parishioners who had served as the city's mayor.

been no family disagreement – the older brother Randle was not being disinherited. He demonstrated his acceptance of the deal by signing as one of the witnesses to the deed conveying the property into William's name. William's inheritance was part of a larger scheme by which his father sought to ensure all of his children has secure futures. The same deed that gave The Crow to William Cotgreve also included dowries for his sisters and made provision for their parents to retire comfortably into rooms at the inn. By this point Randle had secured the lucrative post of diocesan registrar at Chester Cathedral, a well-paid secure job for life. In fact, it was such a desirable position that the previous incumbent's son tried to argue that it was his by hereditary right. So while Randle Cotgrave settled into his life as an ecclesiastical civil servant, it was his brother William Cotgreve who took on the challenge of building the family business at The Crow into a long-term success.

Growing the company meant expanding the footprint of the hotel. In addition to the original core, William purchased the freehold or leasehold on another seven buildings, each generally described as a 'house in The Crow'. The properties were not all on the same street, and there must have been a courtyard with the sign of a crow hanging over its entrance, with the inn comprising a series of buildings along its sides, some of them opening onto perpendicular streets. Maps from the time shows buildings on at least two sides leading to gardens at the back. There were also empty plots, one of which his father had acquired, and William was responsible for constructing at least one new building in the complex.

As well as serving drinks William also provided meals for his customers. He may also have sold groceries and foodstuffs including fish (he was sometimes described as a fishmonger and he imported barrels of herrings). Like modern hotels, The Crow had rooms to let by the night and also for longer-term residents. Sir Randle Brereton, for example, had his own chamber 'wherein he is accustomed to lie'. There was secure storage space – Cotgreve was appointed by the authorities to keep an emergency supply of gunpowder and he also operated a cellarage facility for local dignitaries to keep large (and therefore valuable) quantities of their wine. Just as a modern hotel needs parking facilities, The Crow needed substantial stabling to accommodate guests' horses so the family bought a set of stables on a side street near the inn.

William Cotgreve expanded his business by ruthlessly executing a clear strategy. To guarantee success, he paid over the odds for some of the properties in The Crow. By the time he acquired the last one, a building called Twisse's House, it must have been obvious to the vendor that Cotgreve would stop at nothing to take control of the houses around the courtyard at the Sign of the Crow. In 1588, John Poole let the property to Cotgreve on a potentially long lease – a term that would last as long as any one of Cotgreve's three children was still living. This turned out to be 32 years, but given that his youngest son was just eight years old at the time, it might easily have lasted twice as long. But an uncertain lease was not enough for Cotgreve. So three years later, he bought Twisse's House outright for a sum equivalent to twenty years of the annual rent, a massive amount of money. Just five years earlier, he had acquired two houses for just over half of what he paid for this final piece of real estate to complete The Crow. The capital outlay was worth it, however, to secure William Cotgreve's place as one of the most important and powerful men in the area. In any case, he could afford it because he was rapidly becoming very wealthy. He was one of the largest contributors to a tax to alleviate poverty, assessed to pay twice as much as his older brother. He was frequently involved in the city court where people recovered debts and he clearly had good credit because he was far more often chasing debtors than being chased. His wife came from a wealthy family and she came into her inheritance in 1583. Two years later, in an ostentatious display of his wealth, William bought a 28 ounce silver gilt malmsey cup, a silver bowl weighing 15 ounces, a silver gilt ewer and an 18 ounce gilt goblet, all for £18, several years' worth of wages for an average worker.

Business acumen alone did not guarantee status. Networking and politics were important too, and William Cotgreve took these just as seriously as his financial interests. Locally, his name began to appear as a surety in the sheriff's court, the Quarter Sessions, and the assizes, supporting a range of friends and business interests. He sat on juries, testified on behalf of associates and colleagues, and served in junior official roles, such as that of leavelooker, responsible for inspecting the city's markets. He acted as a valuer of goods and property and an auditor of the local authority.

Throughout these activities, Cotgreve made sure he found ways of interacting with the great and good both within his own county and beyond. He was bequeathed a legacy from an influential alderman and was a welcome visitor at the Earl of Derby's home. When Sir Walter Leveson, a substantial landowner, magistrate and MP, needed to find a large amount of money in a hurry, he turned to Cotgreve as a source of loans. William's influence ran to the Isle of Man, where he acted as a trustee of disputed property. When he later became mayor, he was familiar and comfortable (if appropriately deferential) dealing with Lord Burghley, the queen's chief minister.

Local politics and the cultivation of interests closer to home were important too. Cotgreve had been admitted as a freeman of Chester in 1569, and elected to the Common Council ten years later when he was 34. He secured public sector contracts such as one for building a new pillory to punish wrongdoers. In the hamlet of Hargrave, a few miles outside the city walls (where he owned property) he oversaw the interests of Sir William Brereton, one of the grandest of local grandees, who would later be raised to the peerage. With all these contacts, Cotgreve was bound to be given a leg up on the greasy pole of local influence. By 1580, he was chosen as one of the city's two sheriffs, ancient and influential posts with a wide range of legal, administrative and financial functions.

Possibly the single most time-consuming job in this role was presiding over the sheriffs' court. Known as the Pentice Court, from the name of the building in which it met, it was a relatively simple system of settling mostly small-scale disputes. Perhaps because the busy sheriffs dealt speedily with the business, it was used not just by the residents of the city, but by people from the surrounding villages and countryside, and it had a huge workload. The court book for William Cotgreve's shrieval year lists over 2,500 cases, so that if the two sheriffs split the work equally, they each had to preside over 1,250 separate claims. Many (perhaps most) of the legal actions did not progress, either because the complainant did not press the matter or because the defendant conceded the debt. Even so, the court met on 69 days during Cotgreve's year in office; he must have chaired roughly 35 days of Pentice Court business.

Because the sheriffs were local appointees presiding over a court with a local jurisdiction, they inevitably found themselves deciding cases that involved their friends, neighbours and even families. During Cotgreve's year as sheriff, the Pentice Court heard cases involving his own brother, Randle, and various cousins, including Anne and John Cotgreve, who were trying to wrap up the complicated financial affairs of their late mother. In one of these cases, the Cotgreves were being sued by a man called John Banester, who was a close relative (possibly a brother) of William Cotgreve's wife. William Cotgreve was himself the plaintiff in one case, which was presumably heard by the other sheriff, Richard Bird. But in July and August 1581, there were two cases involving both Bird and Cotgreve, acting jointly as sheriffs, and it is difficult to see how the case could have received a fair hearing in their own court. Nevertheless, Thomas Whitoff thought it worth pursuing a debt of £5 from the pair, while they themselves used their own court to sue Humphrey Reynolds for £7 they believed he owed to the office of sheriff.

William Cotgreve had now acquired the qualification that was almost essential for anyone who coveted the office of mayor. The mayorality was a massively powerful post – simultaneously chief magistrate, head of the planning authority, principal coroner, leader of the local council, gatekeeper of the electoral franchise, market regulator and supreme ceremonial dignitary. Over a wide range of functions, the mayor's authority was almost absolute within the confines of the city. It was to this position that William Cotgreve aspired.

This elaborate initial from a document attested by William Cotgreve when
he was Mayor of Chester in 1589 shows a mermaid in a traditional pose
with a comb and mirror, and also a sturgeon, which may be a reference to
the fact that he traded in fish [The National Archives WALE30/41].

So in 1586, it cannot have been an easy decision for Cotgreve to face
up to an influential local interest and to risk losing popularity, in pursuit
of his private business objectives. He had already shown just how ruthless

he could be in a court battle with his cousin's widow over the ownership of a family farm,[1] but now he would take on a substantial section of the constituency that could influence his future.

William Cotgreve's problem was that the mediaeval system of guilds still controlled a good deal of trading and marketing in a range of commodities. He was himself part of the system as a member of the Innkeepers', Victuallers' and Cooks' Guild. But a large business like The Crow needed to offer a range of goods and services if it was to provide a premium product – and it was anti-competitive for any of those to be subject to restrictive practices or exclusive deals. The particular issue that vexed William Cotgreve was that making and selling bread in Chester was not permitted to anyone who was not a member of the Bakers' Guild. But how could he serve competitively-priced meals in his hotel if he had to pay premium market prices for the main staple source of starch? For the volume of business that William Cotgreve was doing by the 1580s, it made much stronger commercial sense to bake his own bread at cost price and sell it at a mark-up than it did to buy in ready-made loaves. He even had a cousin who was a miller, so perhaps he had access to cheap flour. So the proprietor of The Crow decided that the bakers' oligarchy had to be broken, and he made sure that anyone who ate at his hotel had the benefit of fresh bread, homemade on the premises. There were no doubt up-front investment costs setting up a bread kiln and buying equipment, and it was risky to pay them when his right to serve his own bread might be challenged and he might lose.

With their ancient privilege under threat, the officials of the Bakers' Guild sprang into action. Their problem was not so much that one hotel, however large, was making its own bread, but the idea that others would follow suit. Maybe butchers, cheesemakers and fishmongers would start making bread to sell with their products. The bottom would fall out of the lucrative market in overpriced loaves. When the bakers' reaction to William Cotgreve's effrontery came, it was a legal and political attack on several fronts simultaneously.

The case formally began in January 1586 in the Exchequer of Chester, which was mainly a court of equity – a forum in which a complainant set out in plain English why they felt that simple fairness and justice were not being observed. The leading lights of the Bakers' Guild wrote down how Cotgreve was failing to honour their traditional and previously-undisputed rights, as established by centuries of custom and practice. The Exchequer could only proceed to judgment if the facts were plain.

1   See Chapter 15.

Doubts would need to be decided in a common law court, where a panel of jurors could determine the disputed facts. The Exchequer delayed for a month (which was not at all unusual; cases could drag on for years) before deciding that the Court of Great Session would need to get involved by empanelling a jury who would hear what the two sides had to say. This suited William Cotgreve because it bought him time. He was not going to waste the opportunity sitting around passively, but submitted a strong new argument to the Exchequer that the matter was not one for either equity or common law. It was, he pointed out, essentially a private matter concerning the privileges of the city and could only be dealt with by the authority of the mayor. So before the assize court had even had chance to list the case, the issue had become more of a political decision than a legal technicality. The mayor, Edmund Gamull, was much more susceptible to influence than any judge or unpredictable jury would have been. The Innkeepers' Guild could now helpfully lubricate the process by paying for wine when 'Mr Cotgreave and others' went to see Gamull. They were friends and a few years later Cotgreve's daughter would marry Gamull's son.

Despite the fact that the case was now running very much in Cotgreve's favour, he took no chances. He also put in a visit to the Earl of Derby, one of the most powerful men in the north west of England and someone you wanted on your side in any local dispute. The political effort paid off and three months after the Bakers' Guild had started its case, the Assembly of the Corporation of Chester recorded that 'the controversy between the Bakers and William Cotgreve, innholder, concerning the baking of bread is decided in favour of the latter'. The lawyers who had been filing papers in the Exchequer and looking forward to racking up fat fees for lengthy arguments at the assizes were dismayed. They were not going to be put off by a nepotistic stitch-up and as late as September 1587, the Court of Great Session was still concerning itself with a lawyer's 'brief of the matter in question' while the aldermen of the Guild of Bakers continued to sue Cotgreve for a 'breech of liberties of their corporation'. But in the end this amounted to nothing more than a job creation scheme for the legal profession. The determined hotelier had outsmarted the baking fraternity, and he could afford to continue outspending them to the bitter end; the Innholders' Guild recorded more expenditure by 'Mr Cottgreve and our bretherin,' in 1587, presumably in legal fees or bribes. It was a comprehensive victory for a canny and effective businessman, who had now established the permanent right to sell a high volume product at a significant mark-up.

As the 1580s drew to a close, William Cotgreve had achieved a great deal both commercially and politically. The mayorality of the city was perhaps finally in sight. But when the councillors and aldermen met to elect their new mayor each year, there were no doubt many political aspects to their decision. It was by no means guaranteed that a man like William Cotgreve would secure election.[2]

In the autumn of 1589, Cotgreve was 45 and it was almost 20 years since he had taken over The Crow from his father. He had spent two decades securing his position as a leading businessman and cultivating influential local and national contacts. Moreover, he had used his business to good effect, offering lavish hospitality to his constituency – or keeping 'a good house' as it would be remembered. It was true that none of the city's bakers was going to vote for him, but he had spent decades canvassing enough support elsewhere. All that effort paid off, and on 10 October, William Cotgreve was installed as the Mayor of Chester, the post he had clearly coveted for decades.

William was now the supreme civic dignitary in Chester, the largest city in the northwest of England, and one of great historical and economic significance. He governed around 10,000 people, and presided over a whole range of areas of their lives – trade, local democracy, aspects of the criminal law, planning and development, ceremonial celebrations and politics.

Perhaps naively, one of Cotgreve's first decisions was to curtail his own power. One of the last acts of his predecessor had been to order two freemen to be imprisoned for something they had allegedly said during a meeting of the city's assembly. A week later, Cotgreve agreed that in future the mayor should not be able to incarcerate men in that way. As head of the assembly, the mayor had the exclusive duty to admit new free citizens. Cotgreve admitted 27 freemen during his year in a variety of trades including three shoemakers, a hatter, two butchers and a plasterer. Two were bakers who had served seven year apprenticeships, and whose masters had therefore been part of the losing side of the trade's dispute with Cotgreve three years earlier.

It is difficult to avoid the impression that many of the functions of the mayor were actually rather dull. One for example, was witnessing a kind of bond called a Statute Merchant. These were simply ways of

---

2   Of the 10 men who served as mayor during the 1580s, eight had previously been sheriff, but of the 21 men who served as sheriff only five would go on to become mayor (there were 21 because one died in office and was replaced part way through the year). So while those with mayoral ambitions generally needed to secure a term as sheriff to qualify, it was not a guarantee.

tradesmen securing repayment of their debts and William Cotgreve had no particular interest in the outcome. But 300-year-old legislation dictated that in provincial towns the documents were only valid if they were sealed in the presence of the mayor, so he had no choice but to turn up and witness them. Nor can it have been enjoyable receiving a string of petitions requesting that court cases be removed from the sheriffs' court to be dealt with by the mayor, and then finding that having agreed, he had to sit and listen to evidence about two cows and a heifer.

Despite his great local power over the citizenry, Cotgreve also found that many people on a national scale had even more over him. Chester may be 180 miles from London, but communication was remarkably good, and the local mayor was expected to enact central government policy. A letter with instructions from the authorities in Westminster took less than a week to reach William Cotgreve from the Secretary of State's desk, and he acted on it and replied the same day it arrived. He also had to respond to the instructions of the Lord Lieutenant on military matters such as keeping defensive arms and ammunition and supplying conscripts for the army – the city was required to provide 100 soldiers, who were trained by a local tanner.

But despite the rather tedious duties, there is no doubt that being mayor was a matter of great prestige. Something of the pomp associated with the job is obvious from the fact that when Cotgreve sacked one of his serjeants-at-mace, who walked in front of him carrying his symbol of office, there were three others in post to fulfil the duties, not counting a separate swordbearer and a serjeant of the peace. William Cotgreve's will lists various cloaks and gowns, at least one of which was a ceremonial outfit designed to make an impression – a scarlet gown with a tippet (a sort of scarf that serves no purpose other than to make a garment look fancier). Scarlet livery gowns are known to have been worn by successive mayors, and were treated with special pride. Their use was regulated. Ceremonial processions with the mayor in his scarlet, wearing a gold chain, carrying a staff of office and preceded by his serjeants and sword-bearers, formed a long-established element of Chester's identity as an independent regional centre. Given that Cotgreve's gown was subsequently valued at £5, it must have been a genuinely luxurious item.

As he handed over the symbols of office to William Massey, his successor as mayor, the 46-year-old William Cotgreve probably wondered what would come next. He had achieved his ambition to hold the highest local office, he was popular, he was rich, and he had a successful business. His wife had died in 1583 and his unmarried sister looked after the family. Their elderly mother was still alive, and William had two surviving sons and a daughter. No doubt in the fullness of time, he would be able to leave his hard-won business, lands and money to them to secure a leading role for the Cotgreve family in the running of local affairs. But there was plenty of time for that.

Given his track record, it seems extremely likely that William Cotgreve had a plan for the coming years – to expand the business at The Crow, to set up his children with advantageous marriages and their own businesses, to buy more land or seek even more influential posts. He certainly had expansion plans for the property portfolio; the house he was living in when he died was 'yet not finished'. With such a long career potentially ahead of him, it was not beyond the realms of possibility that he might even aspire to sit as the one of the city's two members of Parliament.[3]

Whatever he had in mind, it was not to be. Within 18 months of standing down from the mayorality, William Cotgreve was dead. His plans would come to nothing. His children were too young to inherit immediately. His eldest son died soon afterwards, and it would be 12 years before the younger, also called William (but who spelled his surname Cotgrave), would successfully get the courts to liberate his inheritance. In the interim, those appointed as guardians and executors would take advantage of the situation, creating endless, expensive legal disputes and financial problems. When William Cotgrave died in 1620, he was still rich, but the momentum had gone out of his father's schemes. The Crow was not the business it had once been, William Cotgrave himself never served in any municipal office, and there is no evidence that he was on personal terms with the nobility or the more important local dignitaries. His father would not have considered him a worthy successor.

In the end, for all his ambitions, his drive, his ruthlessness, his charm and his ability, what people remembered about the late William Cotgreve was that he was 'born in the city' and 'kept a good house'.

3   One of Chester's MPs was Richard Birkenhead, a friend and colleague of Cotgreve, and few years later, the city elected William Brock, whose mother was a Cotgreve and who was a friend of William Cotgreve's son.

CHAPTER THIRTY TWO

1776

Thomas Cotgreave becomes a mortgage trustee

Thomas Cotgreave's study at his home in St John's Lane in Chester must have been well organised. The volume of paperwork needed for his public duties, business and property dealings would have been vast. He was on charity committees and local authority bodies, he owned an array of houses and lands and he lent all sorts of people money as mortgages. He was a powerful man – for 40 years a senior member of the city's governing Corporation and a Justice of the Peace – and he was seen as a trustworthy holder of that power. The colonial administrator Henry Hulton, who had 'a very large acquaintance with persons of different countries, professions and characters' rated Cotgreave as one of his most valuable friends because their connection was 'founded in truth and sincerity'.

Because of this, throughout his life Thomas Cotgreave was chosen as a trustee and executor, administering money and property for other people. He was elected as a Governor of the Foundling Hospital, he was a trustee of Chester's almshouses, one of the most active members of the Board of Chester Infirmary, a director of turnpike trusts, and he was treasurer of the charitable Bluecoat School.

These were high profile roles, where any maladministration might be easily exposed. The true measure of Cotgreave's trustworthiness was the number of times others chose him to deal with private matters. As a young man, he was appointed by a local bricklayer as trustee of his estate, and this was the first of many occasions when the local population considered him the best person to take care of their affairs.

Thomas Cotgreave trained as a linendraper, but he must always have suspected that he would not need to work for a living. His father was a landowner who had been Mayor of Chester and, when Thomas was a teenager, he bought the manor of Netherlegh on the outskirts of the city. While his younger brother John moved to Manchester and made his living as a trader, Thomas remained at home and became a local dignitary. He was granted the freedom of the city in his early twenties, served as sheriff before his thirtieth birthday and was elected as an alderman at the age of 36. He sat on a committee to review the state of local hospital, was one of seven leading citizens who signed a report on the corporation's finances, and was appointed as a commissioner for implementing Parliamentary legislation. As murenger – the officer responsible for the city walls – he completed repairs to the ancient bridges, two of which still bear inscriptions commemorating his role. Outside of official business, he owned some fine horses and was President of the Farndon Hunt.

Although he never married, he clearly had a wide circle of friends, and he was deeply affected by the death of his sister in 1780, when a friend sent condolences on the 'severity of your distress to be separated from one whom you had been united by the tenderest affection from infant years'.

By the time he (inevitably) served as mayor – in 1758 – and became a magistrate, Thomas Cotgreave was rich, and his name appears on title deeds and mortgages as the owner of various properties in Cheshire and the neighbouring counties in North Wales, where he owned a farm and seems to have been known as an approachable source of both capital and advice. He administered the estate of a colleague in the drapery trade, although he was not in fact the nominated executor, and did the same for a shopkeeper from Pwllheli in Caernarfonshire. He was trustee of a complicated deed for partitioning an estate among a group of sisters, involving lands in Cheshire, Shropshire and Denbighshire. He lent money against property in St Asaph, and was the trustee of a mortgage on other property nearby. The record-keeping for these activities was extensive. As a single example, his involvement as a mortgagor of a few houses and pieces of land at Ysceifiog in Flintshire produced at least 26 surviving title deeds, bonds, assignments, receipts and memoranda.

By Cotgreave's time, the concept of a mortgage – borrowing money against the value of real estate – had become routine. But lenders wanted to make sure that if a borrower defaulted, they could actually take possession of the property that had been offered as security. The standard solution was for the borrower to give a long lease – 500 or even 1,000 years – to the lender. If anything went wrong, the lender enforced the lease. Thomas Cotgreave regularly used funds in this way, helping out friends by lending them money or investing capital in building projects,

This plaque records that Thomas Cotgreave was Chester's murenger, responsible for upkeep of the gates and walls, when the Bridgegate was restored in 1782.

including an impressive town house that was bought by a cousin who spelled his name Thomas Cotgrave.

However, this method of lending money had a problem. If the borrower paid off the mortgage, it was theoretically possible that for hundreds of years to come, the lender's heirs could produce the lease, point out that it had never been cancelled (there was no legally robust mechanism for doing so) and claim that it gave them the right to occupy the property. It was astonishingly unlikely, but it was legally untidy. The normal solution was for the lender to assign however many years remained on the long lease to a friend, relative, or lawyer of the owner. This meant that for the foreseeable future, the only person who could even try to pretend they had some right to the lease was someone whom the owner trusted. Moreover, there was a firm legal basis demonstrating that the trustee's only rights were – in the legal jargon – 'to attend the inheritance'. It worked, but it was messy and for property that had been mortgaged more than once, it could be difficult to follow in the large parchment deeds exactly who owned what.

When Thomas Cotgreave became a trustee for a property deal in North Wales in 1776, even he could not have predicted the absurdity of what would happen in the coming years. The byzantine nature of the arrangements became clear only when they risked unravelling more than half a century later.

The Myddelton family of Chirk Castle had known Thomas for years, possibly all his life and Cotgreave had acted as a trustee for their lands near Wrexham in 1764. At some point later, John Myddelton had borrowed money against the value of property in Flintshire and Denbighshire, and the lender had been granted the standard 500-year lease as security. When the debt was cleared, the remainder of the lease was assigned to Thomas Cotgreave 'to attend the inheritance,' meaning that he had a nominal vested interest in the property, even though nobody believed he had any real rights. Then in 1784, John Myddelton again borrowed money, this time from a man named John Hignett, who happened to be Cotgreave's brother-in-law. The residue of the old 500-year lease remained with Cotgreave.

Thomas Cotgreave died a few years later, leaving two executors in his will, John Hignett and a local dignitary called Sir Foster Cunliffe. But with Hignett doing all the work, Cunliffe decided there was no need for his involvement in Thomas Cotgreave's estate and he formally withdrew. So Hignett was granted the sole right to handle Cotgreave's estate by the probate court in Chester on 29 April 1791 and had that reaffirmed by the Prerogative Court of Canterbury two weeks later. As the sole representative of Cotgreave's estate, Hignett now became the formal owner of the nominal rights to the remaining years of the lease. Hignett then died himself, leaving his sister, a widow called Sarah Litherland, as his heir, and a cousin who was also called John Hignett as his executor. These two people had now acquired the utterly valueless, nominal right to the 500-year lease, which only existed because there was no legal way of cancelling it. Since the second mortgage on the property was not yet paid off, the Myddeltons were still making regular interest payments to the current mortgagee (who was now Sarah Litherland because she had inherited it from her brother, the original John Hignett).

The Myddelton family then decided to sell some – but not all – of the lands, which involved paying off the mortgage and conveying all the rights to the new purchaser. Sarah Litherland (the ultimate owner of the mortgage) and the younger John Hignett willingly agreed, and in January 1806, a complicated deed was signed by which they recouped all the money that the original John Hignett had loaned to the Myddeltons 30 years earlier, in return for which they gave up any interest in the property. The nominal rights to the 500-year lease were assigned to a new trustee (a man called Thomas Lloyd, presumably a friend of the new owner), everyone was happy and the legal difficulty about the dangling lease was apparently no longer anything to do with the Cotgreave family, the Hignetts or Mrs Litherland. But the Myddeltons had only sold some of the lands, so it was possible to argue that the nominal 500-year rights had in effect now been split into two.

Decades passed and nobody worried about the arrangements, however unnecessarily complex they seemed. But then in 1845, 69 years after Thomas Cotgreave has first been assigned the lease, the Myddelton family wanted to prove they owned the remaining lands, so they could sell them. A clergyman called Robert Myddelton and his son found that they were 'unable to make a good Title' to the property. Some eagle-eyed lawyer had spotted that a 500-year mortgage lease had been granted on the property, it could not be extinguished, it may have been split in two, or perhaps not, and its ownership was complicated and unclear.

It now came to light that when Sir Foster Cunliffe had declined to act as one of Thomas Cotgreave's executors, even though he had signed a formal renunciation, he had not, in a technical sense, cancelled Cotgreave's wishes. So in the tortuous labyrinth of deeds, mortgages and inheritances, it was at least arguable that when the older John Hignett had died, Cunliffe had become the rightful owner of the nominal right to the residue of the original 500-year lease. Cunliffe himself was dead by now, and since he had declined to be involved in Cotgreave's estate, he had never tried to make any provisions about the dangling lease.

All sorts of people could, on one legal argument or another, be thought to have a vested interest in the pointless lease. The Hignetts and Sarah Litherland's heirs were all contenders, as were Cunliffe's family, Thomas Lloyd, and the people who had inherited the meaningful parts of Thomas Cotgreave's large estate, represented in 1845 by a young cousin who was also called Thomas Cotgreave. But the Cotgreave estates had been put into a trust and the situation was further complicated because the current Thomas Cotgreave was legally a minor, so his affairs were in the hands of his guardians. The whole thing was further complicated because the Bank of England had refused to allow some of Thomas Cotgreave's stocks to be sold after Hignett died, and a relative called Elizabeth Johnson had taken out a second authority from the probate court, but by 1845 she and her husband were both dead, and her inheritance was split between three of her children. None of these people wanted anything to do with the Welsh lease, everyone acknowledged that it was a meaningless construct of no value, and nobody had the slightest interest in preventing the Myddeltons from doing whatever they wanted with the land that nobody disputed was theirs. But the lawyers had spotted the legal difficulty, and the buyer would not proceed until the uncertainty was resolved.

To the nineteenth century legal establishment, there was only one solution – to create a new and complicated document of more than 2,500 words. Its effect was simple – admitting the confusion, it conveyed whatever rights remained in the original 500-year lease to yet another trustee, someone called Thomas Hastings, acknowledged as nothing more than 'a person for that purpose named'. There could be no further arguments because the document did not try to define what the rights in question actually were, or ascertain who actually owned them, it merely said that whatever form they took, Hastings could have them for the purpose of allowing the Myddeltons to sell. And so it was not until January 1845, more than 50 years since Thomas Cotgreave's death, that the Proctor of the Diocese of St Asaph finally wound up the last of his trusts.

Half a century before, as the 1790s had begun, when Thomas Cotgreave was in his seventies, he had been one of the most esteemed characters in Cheshire. He was accounted the 'senior alderman' of the city Corporation. When George III recovered from his first bout of madness, it was Cotgreave who signed Cheshire's congratulatory address. When the courts were looking for a particularly fair and experienced justice to bail some defendants, it was ordered that they appear before 'Mr Cotgreave (if here)' and only if he could not be found would one of the other magistrates be allowed to do it. But he was not a soft touch, and had no hesitation in punishing criminals – fining fraudsters or arranging the transportation of more hardened convicts.

Alderman Thomas Cotgreave's will is a microcosm of his life, for two reasons. It is a large and wordy document of the kind that came to typify his everyday existence, and it is scrupulously fair almost to the point of absurdity. His brother John was seventy and had never married, but to make sure that nobody was left out of their inheritance, Thomas made provision for up to seven legitimate sons that John Cotgreave might yet father. Knowing that this was an unlikely scenario, Thomas Cotgreave provided for his estate to pass to his cousins, a family called Johnson.[1] But even though Charles Johnson had not been heard of for many years and everyone thought he was dead, Cotgreave also made sure that up to seven of Charles's potential sons could inherit if they were ever proved to exist.

As his fortune passed to others, with a bequest to fund a perpetual charity for Chester's four oldest inhabitants, and as his fine horses were auctioned off, Thomas Cotgreave's fairness and trustworthiness shone through. His obituary said simply that 'as a magistrate he was active and impartial; as a man, friendly and sincere'.

1   See Chapter 17.

CHAPTER THIRTY THREE

1811

Sidney Cotgreave thinks she has married well

Nineteenth century literature is full of plots that rely on the reader believing in smooth and rapid social mobility. Oliver Twist goes from street urchin to wealthy gentleman, Pip Pirrip cashes in his 'great expectations' and the Mayor of Casterbridge plummets in the opposite direction from wealth to beggary. Readers suspended their disbelief because these sorts of things really could occur. The Georgians and Victorians knew that their social positions could be precarious. What they also knew was that appearances mattered. If you looked and acted like someone who belonged to the more genteel levels of society, then posh people would probably reciprocate.

Sydney Cotgreave and her husband worked hard to convince their peers that they had a status above the ordinary middle class. But fine words could not hold back the tide of poverty, and her death came as a miserable end to a lengthy incarceration in a depressing workhouse.

She was born Sydney Parry in 1776, the daughter of a blacksmith. It now seems unusual that a girl might be called Sydney, but at the time it was not uncommon.[1] Not much is known about her early life, but in 1810, she certainly came to the attention of her neighbours. Sydney was one of three young women living together who were accused of breaching the peace and 'living in a disorderly house,' a euphemism for prostitution.

---

1   It may have been common in the Chester area; towards the end of Sydney Cotgreave's life, at the time of the 1841 census, 555 women in England and Wales were called Sidney or Sydney, compared with 2,723 men; 58 percent of the women were recorded in Cheshire, Lancashire, or North Wales although these counties were home to just 15 percent of the total population of England and Wales.

There is no report of any further action being taken, so presumably Sydney and her friends thought better of their lifestyle choices.

The following year she married an ambitious shoemaker called John Cotgreave. His family was highly respectable, but its members were not wealthy, held no special offices, did not live anywhere out of the ordinary and had no claim to be any better than the families of other tradesmen who held the hereditary office of city freemen. John himself was admitted as a freeman in 1812. In 1797, he had married a young woman called Mary Edwards and conducted his trade, apparently successfully, from premises that must have looked just like those of his brother, his father, his uncle and cousins, all of whom made a living by making and mending footwear for the people of Chester.[2]

The couple had no children, in part because Mary was sickly. Within a few years, she died and John Cotgreave was on the lookout for a new partner in life. But in an early sign of John's attempts at public relations, his first wife was portrayed as a very hard act to follow. Mary Cotgreave was said to have been 'a woman of pious character' and John very publicly announced that 'her loss will be deeply regretted by a large circle of acquaintance'; moreover, she was presented as a sort of saint whose death came as the stoical fulfilment of a long and painful illness. Sydney Parry, the flighty blacksmith's daughter with a disreputable past, hardly seemed like a suitable replacement. In one regard, however, Sydney was superior to her predecessor. She could sign the marriage register with clear, confident handwriting whereas Mary Edwards had been illiterate, unable to do more than scribble a shaky 'X' in the space left for the bride's signature.

In a sign of his attempts to appear important, John Cotgreave used the kind of published family announcements that were normally reserved for the better classes. Not only was his first wife's death lamented in the local press, it was announced in the *Monthly Magazine*. She was described as the wife of 'Mr J Cotgreave of Martin's Ash' as if John were the owner of a property; Martin's Ash was actually the name of a road, and in reality the couple lived on one of the less impressive side lanes that branched off it. When he married Sydney, the *Chester Courant* reported somewhat officially that Mr J. Cotgreave had married Miss S. Parry. None of his brothers or cousins ever published details of their weddings and the other Cotgreaves to appear in posh magazines were a lawyer, an alderman, and a Lord of the Manor.

Like her predecessor as John's wife, Sydney Cotgreave had no

2   See Chapter 25.

children. The couple continued to be ambitious for worldly property. In 1821, John managed to buy a house worth nearly £200; he needed the help of a building society (a relatively new phenomenon) and he had to find a 50 percent deposit, some of which he may have inherited from his father who died in the same year. Some combination of business success, careful stewardship of resources, a lack of expenditure on children and an overweening desire to better themselves meant that deeds were drawn up transferring a newly built house in Cuppin's Lane in Chester into the ownership of a shoemaker called John Cotgreave. From his proud base in the centre of the city, John Cotgreave was presenting an image not of an ordinary tradesman but of an entre-preneur, building a business and a life that put him above the ranks of his neighbours, brothers and cousins.

In truth, with the exception of owning his house, he was no more successful than any of the others. Unlike several of his relatives, he was not even chosen as the Steward of the Cordwainers' Company, the ancient guild that protected the rights of shoemakers trading in the city.

In 1829, at the age of 58, John Cotgreave died, and despite his lifetime's efforts, was promptly forgotten. The record of his burial accords him a modicum of status by calling him 'John Cotgreave Shoemaker' with the occupation underlined, implying perhaps that he was perceived as one of the leading men of his profession. Everyone else on the page is simply given a name. But that was the end of Cotgreave's claim to any social advancement. There was no newspaper announcement, although in a painful twist, his brother Ralph, also a shoemaker, was briefly commemorated in the *Chester Chronicle* when he died the following year. Nobody thought John's possessions of sufficient value to justify bothering the probate court about who should inherit them. John Cotgreave was gone, and with him his parvenu pretensions; Sydney Cotgreave was on her own.

In a male-dominated society in which families were important, a childless widow in her 40s was hard to categorise. Unless they were financially secure, most middle-aged women would probably expect to remarry. At her age, and having failed to produce offspring during 18 years of marriage, no man who wanted children was going to take the risk of marrying Sydney Cotgreave. Without any genetic connection through children, she could not expect her late husband's family to have much direct interest in her future. Similarly, with no experience of childrearing, she was hardly desirable to any widowed man who needed someone to bring up his children while he was out working. If she still owned the house in Cuppin's Lane and if the cobbler's business was successful, it would perhaps have made her an attractive prospect but if she still had any real estate, she did not retain it for long.

Perhaps Sydney Cotgreave could not keep up the payments to the building society, perhaps she had to sell the property to convert her equity into ready cash. Whatever happened, within a few years, she had left Chester and was living in central London where she worked as a seamstress. The house where she stayed appears to have doubled as a dressmaking business and a boarding house for respectable men and women.[3]

No longer a member of the propertied class and unable to rely on a husband's business, Sydney Cotgreave had to work for a living. But her trade needed two characteristics that old age could not guarantee, good eyesight and nimble fingers. The first evidence that she could not make ends meet came in 1837, when she was 60. She broke her arm and, unable to work or afford a doctor, she was forced to receive the basic free care available at the infirmary on Castle Street in Westminster, classified as a pauper.

As she aged, it is perhaps not surprising that eventually the old widow could not even earn enough to pay her rent and basic living costs. So Sydney Cotgreave ended up not in the Poor Law infirmary but in the main workhouse. This was not an emergency admission of a patient to the only local institution that could provide any kind of medical care. It was a hideous reality of Victorian Poor Law, designed to ensure that nobody should die from absolute want, while strongly discouraging anyone from voluntarily claiming publicly-funded benefits. Desperate people might stave off death by entering the institution, but nobody would choose it unless they had no alternative. Sydney languished in the workhouse for at least 18 months.[4] In some ways, the Marylebone institution was not the worst of its kind – the inmates were not forced to do hard manual labour as they were elsewhere. But having nothing at all to do may have added to the boredom, and allowed the paupers more time to notice that their conditions were miserable. There were two meals a day, each consisting of eight ounces of bread and half a pint of gruel or soup. Forty women slept in a room 36 feet by 16 feet; the beds must have been packed in

---

3   A few years later, when the same landlady still owned the house on Villiers Street, there were six other women occupied as dressmakers and seamstresses, a clerk and two gentlemen.

4   There is no surviving admission register to record when she first went into the workhouse, but she was there in the census in June 1841 and died there in early 1843.

with just a few inches between them on each side. Not long after Sydney Cotgreave died, overcrowding became so serious that 'adequate standards of management were impossible'. It was a far cry from owning her own home in Chester.

When she died, nobody placed an announcement about Sydney Cotgreave's death in any newspaper or middle-class journal, and they could not mark her grave because she shared a pit with the other poor souls who died in the workhouse. Unlike her husband and his first wife, there could be no attempt to position her as someone who had benefitted from social mobility. Mobility works both ways, and Sydney had fallen so low that she died at the abject bottom of Victorian society.

Sydney Cotgreave was one of seven workhouse inmates buried in St Marylebone Church's graveyard on 25 February 1843, no doubt put collectively and without any great ceremony into the communal grave. Despite the great fall in her living standards, she was luckier than the others; perhaps those earlier years of upward mobility had given her a persistent strength or built a resilient constitution. Sydney had survived longer than the four month old boy, the girls of five and two, or the other adults in their forties and fifties with whom she now lies. The authorities recorded that she was 63, not an unreasonable lifespan for the period. In fact, she was nearly 67 – the destitution of her final years had not ravaged her appearance as much as it might have done. That was no doubt because she had enjoyed better times in a youth spent in Chester, dreaming of climbing the social ladder that she eventually fell off.

CHAPTER THIRTY FOUR

1815

William Cotgreave absconds under a false identity

When Thomas Cotgreave set out from Chester for London, he was presumably confident that there were great opportunities in the capital. He hoped to thrive economically, and an elaborate mausoleum in Tarvin graveyard proves that he achieved this wish. What the grave does not record is that after his death, his sons would overreach themselves and get into debts that would plunge them into bankruptcy, lies, subterfuge and shame.

Thomas and his brother John Cotgreave evidently decided their greatest chance of success was to get away from the tiny village of Guilden Sutton where they were born in the 1730s. John ended up in the USA and never really achieved his ambitions,[1] while Thomas was either luckier or shrewder in moving to London. He set up a cheese factory in Southwark, which was rapidly successful. The business grew and acquired new premises, which together with the stock and equipment were insured for a huge sum.

Thomas and his wife had several children, not all of whom survived infancy, and in 1779 they moved house, having previously lived at the same address as the business he ran with a man named John Roden. Cotgreave became active in politics, as part of a committee to support the re-election of local Members of Parliament.

At some point in the second half of the 1770s, Thomas changed the

---

1   See Chapter 28.

An elaborate tomb immediately outside the door of Tarvin church gives
William Cotgreave and his family a place of great distinction, but it hides
the fact that for much of his life, he avoided prison by operating under a
false name and living hundreds of miles away.

spelling of his surname from Cottgrave to Cotgreave.[2] The reason for the
change is not obvious, although his brother John, thousands of miles away
in America, did the same thing. The most likely possibility is that they
wanted to be more closely associated with another branch of the family
which had become wealthy, and which happened to use the spelling
'Cotgreave'. Status mattered.

Soon after his wife died in 1780, Thomas Cotgreave moved back
to Cheshire and used his now considerable wealth to buy property in
the towns and villages around Chester. A farm in Burwardsley, two
in Tattenhall, property in Newton. Most significant was his home in

2   In 1768, he had signed the church register Thomas Cottgrave. His company
was listed in trade directories as Cottgrave and Roden, and in 1775, he had used
the name Cottgrave on a mortgage deed; from the late 1770s, the directory listings
were entered as Cotgreave or occasionally Cotgrave. His name and signature on
subsequent documents, including property deeds from 1778 and 1795 and his will,
dated 1803, is always spelled 'Cotgreave'.

Tarvin, just a couple of miles from where he had been born. He acquired Tarvin Hall along with 137 acres of farmland and became Lord of the Manor. He was rich – the contents of his home were insured for £470, at a time when £50 was a perfectly comfortable annual income. Cotgreave remarried, had more children, and retired from active involvement in the firm, which in consequence changed the order of the proprietors' names, becoming 'Roden and Cotgreave'. He was now generally called a merchant, although the company partnership, still based in Southwark, always went by the description of 'cheesefactor'.

In semi-retirement, Thomas Cotgreave appears in surviving records as an ordinary member of the gentry. He occupied his own pew in Tarvin church, subscribed to a book of poetry, purchased a game licence so that he could shoot partridges and other birds on his land, and made a massive donation when citizens were asked to contribute to the war effort against France. His interest in politics was still active; he attended a meeting at Chester Castle to discuss new tax legislation and he was the first to sign a parish resolution about securing affordable corn for the poor.

In his 60s, Thomas Cotgreave's heath deteriorated and he died in January 1803 while seeking treatment at the hot wells in Bristol. The *Chester Courant* observed that he was 'most deservedly respected and sincerely lamented by all who knew him'. His will shows just how wealthy he had become, with generous annuities for his widow, sister and second son, and very large settlements for his daughter and his eldest and youngest sons, Thomas and William. William appears to have been responsible for carrying on the Southwark business, while Thomas operated either a separate company or an additional factory at Faringdon in Berkshire. Both were routinely referred to as 'cheesefactors,' although William Cotgreave also ran his own farm in Cheshire and operated for a while as gamekeeper on his elder brother's estate at Tarvin. Both men married well – Thomas to the daughter of a distinguished surgeon in Faringdon and William into a well-to-do family of landowners and lawyers who lived just over the Shropshire border from the family's Cheshire lands.

William Cotgreave was now living the life of a country gentleman. He served on local juries and was sufficiently important to sit on 'special' juries, chosen from an elite. As well as his Cheshire estates, Thomas had a house in Faringdon with land attached, became a churchwarden – one of the bells in the parish church there still bears his name – and acquired a game licence so he could shoot with a shotgun made by the prestigious firm of Bond. He read Hulme's *History of England* and had a copy of Shakespeare's works, played cards and the board game bagatelle, and kept a well-stocked cellar with 240 bottles of port and 70 gallons of beer. He also began to take business risks, branching out into financial services.[3] He and some friends started a private bank called Ward, Cotgreave & Company. They issued their own bank notes and lent one customer £400 as a mortgage in 1808. It seems that William Ward was the main instigator of the scheme and in 1814, he personally lent £1,000 jointly to Thomas and William Cotgreave. Perhaps they wanted capital to expand the cheese-making firm. Whatever was behind the loan, it was at this point that their financial affairs began to unravel, and the whole relationship with Ward started to seem unwise.

The banking company collapsed and the partnership was dissolved. Rumours spread about Thomas Cotgreave's finances and most of his creditors were pressing him for immediate payment. Like most owners of a small business, he simply could not pay all his debts at once. In an attempt to avoid ruin, Cotgreave appointed two respectable friends (including his wife's brother) to handle his affairs and in October 1814, they called a meeting with the creditors at a local inn to discuss how to satisfy their demands. The plan failed and before the end of the year, Thomas Cotgreave was declared bankrupt.

There were now rapid moves to liquidate all of Thomas Cotgreave's assets to meet his debts. An auction sold off the furniture, silverware, crockery, and household goods. Cotgreave's superfine Brussels and Kidderminster carpets, feather beds, mahogany clock, tea service and kitchen utensils were all sold to the highest bidder. Shakespeare's works, the *History of England*, the gun, the port and the beer all went under the hammer. Back in Cheshire, the farmhouse in Burwardsley was sold with 117 acres. Thomas even had to sell his notional future rights to half of his late father's property in Tattenhall (two farms, a garden, an orchard and just over 100 acres), which depended on his sister dying without children or if she had any, on her genealogical line dying out at some undefined point in the future. In the sale notice, she was described as 'a single lady aged 29 years,' presumably to indicate that it was a good bet that she might never marry.

But Thomas was not the only one in financial difficulties. His brother William Cotgreave had also been party to the loan from William Ward, who was himself now in trouble that was causing

---

3   The family had already experienced some success offering financial services. In 1775, Thomas Cotgreave senior and John Roden had lent £113 to a Surrey homeowner, secured against the value of the property, and three years later when the borrower could not repay, they took possession of the house.

knock-on effects. Ward was a stamp distributor – he sold the stamps that people had to stick onto some legal documents to make them valid (the origin of the phrase 'stamp duty'). But he was short of cash and could not reimburse the Treasury for the stock of stamps he had been allocated. Rather than punish him directly, the government was more interested in getting its money back. With Thomas Cotgreave officially bankrupt, it was hopeless even to try and get extra funds from him, but there was still the theoretical possibility of squeezing money out of William. William Cotgreave, however, was ahead of the game. He had conveyed much of his property into the names of other family members, and had hurriedly exited the farming business in Cheshire. He sold his livestock, farming equipment and cheesemaking machinery a few weeks after the auction that had sold off his brother's effects. The suddenness of the decision is clear from the fact that many of the sale lots had only recently been bought. His horse's harness, the cheese presses and milk coolers were all 'nearly new'. Household effects were also included and some of them look suspiciously as if they may have been spirited away from the Faringdon house to avoid being lost in the earlier sale. The 'handsome eight-day clock in a mahogany case' that was sold in Tarvin in March could have been the item of an identical description that was supposed to have been auctioned in Berkshire in January. William let out Tarvin Hall and sold his own farm at Wheetwood, throwing in the 'considerable' standing crop of wheat for a quick sale.

Then he ran away and changed his name.

When the government came around to considering William Cotgreave as a source of cash to pay off William Ward's debts, it concluded that Cotgreave was 'greatly decayed in credit and must go to gaol,' the idea being that his accomplices would then pay up to clear the debts and free him. But he could not be sent to prison because he had absconded and nobody knew where he was, at least nobody official.

He was in fact in Cumbria, 150 miles away from Tarvin and over 300 from the London authorities who were busy fulminating about imprisoning him. At first, Cotgreave seems not to have taken too much trouble to hide his identity and remarkably, one of the first things he did was to get remarried under his real name (his first wife had died in 1814 just as all the trouble had been starting).

By this time, William's brother was dead, perhaps broken by the shameful and stressful experience of falling from wealth to bankruptcy within a matter of a few weeks. Thomas Cotgreave was buried in what became Southwark Cathedral, a sign of his former status, leaving several children and a widow who had been pregnant during the bankruptcy crisis and had given birth to another baby girl in 1815.

William Cotgreave had left his daughter from his first marriage safely with her mother's family[4] and with Thomas dead, there seemed little point in attempting to go back into his former life. He adopted a false name – William Chatterton. This was hardly an original choice – it had been his gamekeeper's name in Tarvin. William and his new wife settled into life in Cumbria, registering at the census as William and Sarah Chatterton, but taking their children 30 miles into Carlisle to have them baptised with their real name of Cotgreave.

Twelve years elapsed before William Cotgreave returned home, but he possibly sneaked into Chester briefly when his other brother James died in 1827 because his signature appears on the documents arranging probate of the estate. It was not until May 1831 that he finally had the cash to clear his problems, more than 16 years since he had fled. It was then that his stepmother died, and left him the money that would allow him to liberate himself from debt and persecution, if not from the shame of his former problems. Perhaps she realised that her well-to-do lifestyle was based on money that William's father had made before she had married him. She arranged to pay off 'such debts of my … stepson … as were contracted by him prior to his leaving Cheshire in or about the month of March 1815 and which remain … due and unsatisfied'.

By now settled at Bridekirk in Cumbria, William Cotgreave did not move back to Tarvin on a permanent basis, but he was able to operate freely again and visit Cheshire. Soon afterwards, in 1832, he was in Chester finally to arrange the estate of his sister, who had been dead for 12 years. He voted in the General Election in Cheshire in 1837; his right to do so was based on his ownership of property in Tarvin which he had somehow managed to retain. He was now considered a gentleman, and owned at least one boat that operated from the harbour of Maryport.[5] In 1833, he was elected, as William Chatterton, to the Board of Trustees for implementing an Act of Parliament for improving Maryport and its Harbour, he acquired a licence to shoot game and he was on the Maryport committee for building a local railway. In short, he was once again a man of standing in his local community. As a former fugitive, it was perhaps cheeky of him to host meetings of the local Association for the Prosecution of Felons, but by now, he seemed to be firmly back on his feet with his financial difficulties behind him.

---

4   See Chapter 36.
5   Sadly it sank in 1832 and three of the four crew died.

Then he over-reached himself again.

In 1838, William Chatterton, as he persisted in calling himself, took over an inn, the Senhouse Arms Hotel, and tried to develop it by introducing gigs and chaises for people to hire, offering 'sumptuous' celebratory meals to local groups and opening a bowling green. It was an establishment 'of the best quality,' but the investment needed to set up such a venue was not justified by the level of business. He tried to supplement his income by farming a small quantity of land leased from the owner of the local estate, but it was doomed to fail. Moreover, once again William was involved in opaque legal cases, on one occasion withdrawing an action from the assizes at the last minute. At the beginning of 1841, less than three years after he had bought the pub, the *Carlisle Journal* announced that Chatterton had taken steps to avoid bankruptcy. He conveyed all his property and personal belongings to a local lawyer, who gave Chatterton's creditors three months to come forward and accept whatever proportion of their money could be recovered. If they refused, they would get nothing, even if they subsequently forced William into bankruptcy. The creditors duly sent in their accounts and the Senhouse Arms was sold. Complete ruin was avoided by the narrowest of margins, but having learned his lesson William Cotgreave, alias Chatterton, never tried his hand at commerce or serious financial dealings ever again.

By the mid 1840s, in his sixties, William Cotgreave had developed cardiac problems, hardly surprising in someone who must have suffered great stress in his life. Soon after Christmas 1846, his flesh started to swell and become puffy, possibly caused by his heart condition. Six weeks later, he died at home on the windswept Cumbrian coast, at the age of 68. In his will he described himself as 'William Cotgreave formerly of Tarvin in the County of Chester but now of Tallentire in the Parish of Bridekirk in the County of Cumberland (where I have assumed the name of Chatterton)'. With his stepmother's help he had preserved his Cheshire interests, and was able to make provision for the daughters of his second marriage. All of his sons were dead, and the daughter of his first marriage was already rich through her late mother's family.

Freed from the shameful association with her husband's financial irregularities, William's wife, now calling herself Sarah Cotgreave, moved to Tarvin. She could not say she was going home, because she had been born in Cumbria and had not met William until after he had run there. She died at Tarvin in 1862 and was buried there, where an impressive mausoleum stands to commemorate the family, immediately outside the main door of the parish church.[6] It recasts history, claiming that William's son 'Thomas Sinclair Cotgreave' had died in 1840 when the name on the death certificate and the Maryport burial register is Thomas Sinclair Chatterton.

William Cotgreave was not born in Cheshire, he did not spend his childhood there, he lived in the county for just one fifth of his life, and in his prime had been forced to sell up, run away and pretend that he was nothing to do with the place. For decades, he could not openly appear in the locality. Yet his monument, larger and more imposing than the others in the pretty rural churchyard, stands as a deliberately misleading symbol of the permanence of William Cotgreave's presence in Tarvin. This enduring artefact was possible only because Cotgreave had managed to avoid incarceration by hiding far away on the Cumbrian coast for more than 30 years. Something of how he felt while he lived there is surely evident in the name he gave to the boat he owned. It was called *Freedom*.

6   It commemorates William Cotgreave himself, both of his wives, four of his children, one of his brothers and someone from his adopted home in Cumbria whom it is impossible to identify because the passage of time has eroded the inscription (Anne Marian [illegible surname, presumably daughter of] John and Isabella [illegible surname] of Maryport [illegible dates]).

denied his own identity. The investigator happened to speak Welsh and fell into easy conversation with the old woman in her native tongue and she confirmed that the man in her home really was the one who had written to 'noblemen and gentlemen of ancient pedigree' with offers to make those pedigrees even more ancient and noble. Although Spence was shabbily dressed and manifestly not wealthy, he must have been making reasonable sums from his scheme. The old woman confirmed his level of industry – he was 'in the habit of sending a great number of letters' – and this is patently verifiable. At least 45 examples are still known over 150 years later, some published and others in the victims' family papers. William Spence tried to charge each family £5 for proof of their glorious ancestry and although some men negotiated, he usually received at least £3. Even if he was only writing two letters a week and having a 25 per cent success rate, Spence's little business was turning over around £80 a year, with minimal expenses, comparable to the £100 that had been considered an appropriate annual allowance for his sister in her status as a knight's widow.

So when Harriet Cotgreave died in 1848, Spence had no intention of giving up the enterprise. Without his sister's help, he needed the connivance of one of her children. Whether Thomas Cotgreave refused or whether it was thought more convincing to use a woman, it was Thomas's sister Eleanor Gamull Cotgreave who began to attest to the truth of the nonsense that her uncle was peddling. The scam did not survive for long, however, because William Spence died a few months after Lady Cotgreave. Without his ludicrous enthusiasm for the fraudulent scheme, there was little point in continuing. Eleanor Cotgreave soon admitted that the whole thing had been a fraud and the shameful tale began to be exposed in the pages of respectable journals, especially *Notes & Queries*, which carried a series of articles under the heading *The Cotgreave Forgeries*. It was the Spence siblings who had perpetrated the scam, but the name of Cotgreave that was publicly and shamefully associated with it.

With Lady Cotgreave dead, the massive extent of her foolish financial entanglements was exposed. Not only had Matthew Harrison profited by purchasing her annuity for a knock down price, he had acquired a life insurance policy in her name and another on Thomas Cotgreave's life. He had supplied all sorts of clothes and shoes on credit and then convinced Thomas to sign blank bills accepting the debt. Year after year before her bankruptcy, Harriet had been buying fancy goods more or less oblivious of how they were to be paid for, and expecting her teenage son to take responsibility. Harrison had been egging her on and taking advantage, forcing the family further and further into his debt. He knew the estate could eventually bear the cost.

Soon after Harriet's death, Harrison tried to collect his money, almost £1,000, but Thomas Cotgreave and his court-appointed trustee fought back. Although he was an adult by the time the matter came to court, Thomas Cotgreave had been legally an infant when most of the papers had been signed. The courts held that children could not be held liable for debts.

In the assize court in 1848, where there was no doubt about Cotgreave's date of birth, the judge accepted the argument but ruled that Cotgreave must pay for any 'necessary' items that Harrison had supplied. Moreover, given Thomas's status as a landowning son of a knight, the definition of necessary would be liberal. But Cotgreave's lawyer had further arguments up his sleeve. First, many of the payments Harrison was claiming were for women's clothes supplied to Lady Cotgreave, not the young Thomas. Since she had been declared bankrupt and taken advantage of the Insolvency Act, it was legally impossible now to recover the money. The lawyer also alleged that at least some of the items on the list had never been supplied at all, and were fraudulent entries by Harrison trying to bump up the amount he could claim.

Matthew Harrison himself was portrayed in court as a dishonest trickster who preyed on silly women and children. What was left of Harriet Cotgreave's reputation was shredded. She had been a vain, foolish, inadequate manager of her children's future prospects, more interested in finery and frippery than income and expenditure. The official trustee was humiliated, ridiculed by one of the barristers for taking exception to the suggestion that he drank beer rather than wine and exposed for taking backhanders from tradesmen wanting to secure Cotgreave family business.

On paper, the winner was undoubtedly Thomas Cotgreave. Although he had to pay Matthew Harrison for the most essential of his supplies, he ended up with hundreds of pounds worth of goods for which he never paid. The financial stupidity he had displayed was put down to the 'imprudence and profligacy of youth'. The judge pointed out that many people had shown similar juvenile folly but then become 'most profitable members of society'. Thomas's status as a 'gentleman of fortune' was enhanced and he had established that he was the boss of his own affairs even if the official trustee was nominally in control of the money.

In theory, the young Thomas Cotgreave was now set for the enjoyable life of a man with a large income, freed by the courts from the depredations of Matthew Harrison and by death from the folly of his mother and the embarrassment of his uncle. In practice, he never really recovered from the trauma of the whole affair.

Cotgreave continued to live in Chester but he sold Netherlegh House, the beautiful villa his father had built in the nearby countryside, choosing instead to live in a much less impressive townhouse. He married but had no children and in the 20 years that he survived, he failed to shrug off the shameful association of fraud, financial stupidity and vanity that had attended his earlier years. Although it was completely untrue, a myth grew up that the Cotgreaves had lost their property by gambling it away in a card game with the Duke of Westminster, a rumour the Duke's family was still denying over a century later.

When the railways came, Thomas Cotgreave fought a reactionary and futile battle against the Shrewsbury and Chester Company for their line at Saltney, where he owned land. In 1859, Thomas Cotgreave's agents threatened to remove the rails, to go to court, and to 'offer any opposition to the line' over what he believed was 'wanton' invasion of his private rights as a landowner. Lawyers even had apologise for the 'warm zeal' of Mr Hope, the trustee who had been so heavily involved in the earlier court case, because he felt that the company had stolen what he held in trust. The correspondence went on for years, long after the trains had started running. But the company's policy was not to risk litigation over 'so small a matter.' So in the end, it settled the issue by paying the Cotgreave estate £1 a year to compensate it for its loss of vegetation, which would otherwise have been used as fodder for cattle.

Thomas Cotgreave and his wife Eliza drank heavily and it affected both his health and his reputation. When a working class drunk said in court that he had enjoyed a glass of ale with Thomas Cotgreave, the public erupted in knowing laughter. The extent of Cotgreave's drinking problems was revealed when he was caught hammering on the door of a pub on a Sunday morning, demanding that it open up and serve him. He racially abused the arresting officer as an 'Irish bastard,' and was convicted and fined. Eventually, alcohol would kill both Thomas and his wife. The cause of Eliza Cotgreave's death in October 1876 was medically certified as cirrhosis of the liver. Thomas Cotgreave passed away of the same disease, just three weeks later. Perhaps he had found in her someone he could trust and respect after the dishonesty and stupidity that had characterised the role models that surrounded him in youth. Perhaps they spent their time drinking together so they could forget the public ridicule.

It does not seem very fortunate for 'a gentleman of fortune'.

CHAPTER THIRTY SIX

1848

Jane Cotgreave goes to court on her neighbours' behalf

Jane Nickson Cotgreave saw almost the entire nineteenth century. She was a baby when Nelson died; a child when Jane Austen was publishing; a young woman when Robert Peel invented the modern police force; middle-aged when Florence Nightingale sent back reports from the Crimean war; elderly when Gladstone became Prime Minister; and decidedly old when Queen Victoria celebrated her Diamond Jubilee.

Jane Cotgreave witnessed more change than anyone could have dreamt about when she was born. Nobody had even begun to imagine the steam railway at the time of her birth but by the time she died, Britain had tens of thousands of miles of railway track and she presumably took the train when she went on seaside holidays. Almost none of the people she knew as a child had the right to vote in elections, but many more of those she knew in old age did so – at least among the men. For all the progress she experienced, Jane Nickson Cotgreave lived and died in a world where women remained second class citizens.

Even at the end of her long life, Jane Cotgreave could not vote or hold any kind of office, even though she was a substantial landowner. Had she been a man, she would certainly have been a magistrate, a sheriff, an alderman, or a guardian of the poor. Because Jane never married, her identity could not be subsumed into a husband's, and she was lucky enough that some of her male relatives recognised in her the positive qualities and capacities that many men, including her own father, lacked. This gave her the financial and social status to be a successful woman in a man's world.

Jane Cotgreave's father was a moderately well off gentleman, who was born in London, but had moved back to his family's home area.[1] He set himself up as a landowner in various towns and villages outside Chester, living at Tarvin. Jane's mother, Elizabeth Nickson, was also from a well-off family that owned property in the neighbouring parishes and over the Shropshire border in the market town of Wem. When her younger brother died as a toddler, Jane was left as the couple's only surviving offspring. Elizabeth Cotgreave died a few years later, when Jane was nine, and from then on, the girl's life centred on her late mother's family. She adopted Nickson as a middle name, and seems to have had nothing much to do with her father or the half brothers and sister she acquired when William Cotgreave married again. She was eventually buried in what was called her 'family vault' but was in fact the last resting place of the Nicksons, not the Cotgreaves.[2]

When Jane was still young, her father moved 150 miles away to Cumbria and changed his name, because he was threatened with gaol over financial irregularities. Jane stayed behind with her mother's relatives, and they seem not only to have cared for her but also genuinely cared about her. They went out of their way to keep her separated from her wayward father; when her grandfather Nickson left her a large amount of money, he put it in trust and instructed the trustees to suspend payment if they ever suspected that any money was reaching William Cotgreave. The Nickson family produced few sons that lived to inherit the family wealth, so Jane started to become the beneficiary of her mother's relatives. In 1817, when she was 12, her grandfather left money to pay for her education and maintenance until she was 24, then her grandmother left her another £200 (£50 a year would have been plenty to live on comfortably) and her cousin left her a half share of an investment portfolio. She must have been a likeable young woman; although her grandfather Cotgreave's second wife had blood relatives of her own, she nevertheless chose to leave Jane an assortment of luxury items including a silver tea canister, a lacquered chest, sugar basket, cream jug and silver candlestick.

As a young woman, Jane lived with her aunt, Mary Nickson, spending at least some of the time in Worcestershire, where Mary had been born. Then in the mid 1840s, when Jane was still only in her thirties, she and Mary jointly inherited houses and land in Wem. Mary transferred her

---

1   See Chapter 34.
2   The other people commemorated on the sepulchre outside the door of Wem parish church include two different Jonathan Nicksons, Sarah Jane Nickson, Mary Nickson, and the aunt with whom Jane lived throughout her adult life, Mary Brown Nickson.

share of the property into Jane's name as a trustee and they set up home at a newly built house in Chapel Street, employing three servants. Jane Cotgreave's new home was not far from her Cheshire roots and she clearly stayed in touch with old friends throughout her life; in her eighties, she gave two glass baskets as a wedding present to a young couple getting married in the parish of Tarvin where she had been born.

From these early days, Jane clearly had a religious zeal, and throughout her adult life she made donations to the Church of England Bishopric in Jerusalem and the Irish Church Missions. When she died, she left £500 each to the Church Missionary Society and the Society for Promoting Christianity amongst the Jews. But her charity was not constrained to the strictly religious. For 30 years, she regularly gave financial support to the Ragged School Union, which provided education for destitute children, and she was a financial a supporter of a charity for homeless boys.

It was in 1848, when she was in her mid forties, that Jane Nickson Cotgreave proved that she could hold her own as a woman in a man's world. One of the ways in which she deployed her finances was to lend money on commercial terms to the local farmers. For example, William Teese of Alderton Farm about five miles from her home took out a mortgage, borrowing £3,400 from her at an interest rate of four and half percent, and secured against land and cottages that he owned. Teese obviously paid the interest regularly because when he was short of money again two years later, he borrowed another £200 from Miss Cotgreave, using the same property as security.

But when another local landowner, Thomas Ireland, died without paying back his debts, Jane Cotgreave was angry not only on her own behalf but for 'all other unsatisfied' creditors. Ireland was a neighbour who had borrowed £300 from Cotgreave in March 1846 and handed over title deeds as security. Despite this, he did not even service the interest on the loan, let alone pay back the capital, and when he died the following year, he owed both the original debt and the accumulated interest. However, his executor, John Walmsley, refused to pay, claiming that there was simply not enough money in the estate to meet the claims. Jane was having none of it, not merely because she was considerably out of pocket herself but because other, less well-off neighbours had lost smaller amounts.[3] She took Walmsley to the Court of Chancery on behalf of all her friends and neighbours. The essential feature of

3   For example, the transactions recorded in the case include a debt of £6/10/9, not a trivial sum but possibly not on its own worth the expense and effort that Jane Cotgreave went to in pursuing her Chancery suit.

Chancery cases, made famous by Dickens in *Bleak House*, was that their workings were excruciatingly slow. Jane Cotgreave's attempt to recover debts from Ireland's estate demonstrated this very clearly, with the case scheduled to be heard again and again and again, year after year, without reaching a conclusion. Between March 1853 and November 1857, the case of Cotgreave versus Walmsley was listed on at least 23 separate occasions. Some of the delays were relatively minor but other interruptions lasted for months. Having already been postponed for years, the case was due to come before Sir Richard Kindersley, one of the Lord Chancellor's deputies, on Monday 30 June 1857, but he did not get around to it, so it was scheduled again for the Tuesday. Then it was supposed to be dealt with on the Wednesday, then the Thursday, and then the weekend intervened, so it was rescheduled for Monday of the following week. But Sir Richard still had too many suits to hear, so the case was pushed back to the Tuesday, and when that still proved to be overoptimistic, it was abandoned for a further four months.

In the end, after years of inactivity punctuated by bursts of legal wrangling, Jane Nickson Cotgreave triumphed and the court found that Thomas Ireland's property was sufficient to cover his debts. Apart from anything else, sensible creditors like Cotgreave had ensured they had proper security – she could wave title deeds in Walmsley's face, or at least her male lawyer could. The simple solution, ordered by the court on 19 November 1857 – a full decade after Ireland had died – was to sell his property and use the money to reimburse his creditors. Jane got her money back, and more importantly, so did her neighbours.

Not much of note happened during the rest of Jane Cotgreave's life as it is recorded in surviving records. She had always remained highly active, travelling back to Worcestershire, where she had lived as a young woman, for social occasions and even in her 80s, she was returning to her home village at Tarvin for Conservative Party events. She, her aunt and cousins took fairly regular holidays on the North and mid-Wales coast at Llandudno, Aberystwyth, Barmouth and Rhyl and occasionally much further away on the Isle of Wight. Otherwise, Jane Cotgreave continued to live at the house in Chapel Street until Mary Nickson died in 1872, when she moved to another of her houses just outside the town. Her tenants farmed her land, she continued giving money to charity and her importance in the local community was never in doubt. In 1877, she signed a document promising to produce the title deeds to the entire Manor of Wem, once owned by the Nickson family, if they were ever needed to prove ownership by the people who had subsequently acquired some of the individual plots, fields and houses in the parish. She was not exactly mistress of all she surveyed, but if anyone wanted to sell land and property anywhere in the local area, they needed the Nickson archives, and so they needed Jane Nickson Cotgreave.

The extent to which society assumed the supremacy of men had been clear when the Chancery Clerk who recorded the process of Cotgreave versus Walmsley in a massive ledger had assumed that the plaintiff must be a man and recorded Jane's name as 'John' Nickson Cotgreave. It was even more blatant when the census taker came to Northwood Villa in Wem on the evening of 5 April 1891. He reported that an 85-year-old spinster called 'Jane Nixon Cotgreave' (the age was wrong by one year and the middle name was misspelt) was a boarder in the home of a man called Robert Williams, who was recorded as the head of the household. But Williams was actually Jane's 'faithful servant'. Robert Williams and his wife looked after Jane Cotgreave in her last years, living in her large house on the outskirts of Wem. Well into her 80s, she was sending donations to charity and presents to local weddings.

Jane Nickson Cotgreave died at home in March 1898, at 'the ripe age of 93'. Sometimes doctors used fancy, medical-sounding names like 'senectus' when old people died, but the one who certified Jane Cotgreave's death did not bother – the cause was straightforwardly 'old age'. She would, according to the local newspaper, be greatly missed because she was 'a helper to many'. The funeral must have been an impressive affair. She was buried on a Friday afternoon in the presence of a large crowd of her tenants, friends and family.

After her death, Jane's name lived on. The sale of Thomas Ireland's assets had generated more than enough funds to reimburse those creditors who came forward, so a substantial amount of cash remained with the Court of Chancery waiting to be distributed either to others who had not been identified or to someone else who could be recognised as the proper heir. The money remained unclaimed 'in Chancery,' and it appeared on the official lists published periodically to remind creditors and heirs that they might try their luck at releasing the funds. The unclaimed proceeds of Cotgreave versus Walmsley continued to appear in the list until 1914; and they only disappeared then because someone decided there was little point in wasting time, effort and paper printing names year after year when it was clear that nobody was coming to claim the money. When the next list appeared in 1917, it omitted hundreds of old cases, including Jane Cotgreave's, and merely suggested that earlier lists could be consulted for information about long-dormant funds. It was nearly 60 years since the last transaction had occurred on the account in Cotgreave versus Walmsley. Ironically, Jane's name disappeared just on the cusp of the first real step in women's enfranchisement. The following year, in 1918, women obtained the vote, not on the same terms as men, but the franchise would certainly have encompassed Jane Cotgreave if she had still been alive.

Jane Nickson Cotgreave's legacy may yet live on. If anyone ever manages to claim the money in Chancery, they should remember that it is only there because in a world absolutely and utterly dominated by men, a society that assumed Jane Cotgreave's manservant was head of the household or that she was a man called John, a system in which Jane had financial freedom only because her male relatives trusted her, that it was Jane Nickson Cotgreave who employed a male lawyer to take on the male executor of a male debtor in a court presided over by a male judge and staffed by male clerks, and recovered the money owed not just to her but also to her male neighbours.

CHAPTER THIRTY SEVEN

1903

Richard Cotgrave unlocks his inheritance

Richard de Malpas Farmar Cotgrave was 'the invisible man'. It says so in a tiny footnote in the biography of the author Mary Wesley, famous for writing *The Chamomile Lawn*. Cotgrave was Wesley's uncle but there is no evidence that they ever met. Indeed, her immediate family shunned him, probably because financial embarrassment followed him around. When recording the family history, Mary Wesley's father simply ignored Cotgrave as if he had two brothers instead of three. But Wesley's biographer cannot bring himself to leave Cotgrave alone, and he is given his own footnote (not an endnote at the back, which some readers might well ignore). Decades after his death, there is something about Richard de Malpas Farmar Cotgrave that draws people to him.

Cotgrave was born in December 1853, the son of a valiant army officer and his well-to-do wife, herself the only child of a naval commander of some distinction. It was Richard's mother who was a Cotgrave, and his original name was Richard de Malpas Farmar. The name 'de Malpas' was an attempt to advertise his mother's mediaeval family in Cheshire. Ancestry clearly mattered and Richard's own children would be given an assortment of names that reflected centuries of distinguished antecedents.[1]

When his mother Alicia died at the age of 36, Richard Farmar (as he was then known) was just seven years old, and he was already at boarding school, so it is hard to know how well he knew her, let alone what kind of relationship they had. Alicia's demise appeared to give Richard great

---

1   Christopher Russell Farmar Cotgrave (born in 1891) was named after Colonel The Honourable Christopher Russell, an eighteenth century Governor of Minorca who was a direct ancestor of the Farmars, and Hugh Hovell Farmar Cotgrave (born in 1882) was named after Hugh Hovell Farmar (died 1812), a friend of the Prince Regent.

financial security, however. His one-eyed naval grandfather, who lived in retirement with little to do but attend garden parties and balls, now had nowhere else to leave his considerable wealth but directly to Richard Farmar and his two younger sisters. So Captain Edward Stone Cotgrave left the bulk of his £25,000 fortune in trust for his grandson, with a handful of provisos, including that before 1 July 1882, he changed his

Richard de Malpas Farmar Cotgrave with his wife Amelia [Reproduced by kind permission of Linda de Malpas-Finlay].

Thomas Manson Cotgrave became inadvertently embroiled in his cousin Richard's dodgy financial dealings [Photograph from Phyllis Scott Morgan reproduced by kind permission of Joy Davidson].

name to 'Richard de Malpas Cotgrave only and none other'. It was not simply a matter of wanting his grandson to perpetuate the surname Cotgrave, he wanted the name Farmar obliterated. Richard and his sisters would even lose everything if they married 'any person connected either by blood or marriage with their father Major William Roberts Farmar,' except a handful of specific exceptions who had given 'unbounded kindness' to Alicia before her untimely death. The family had to wait for the money until the children came of age; in the meantime, Captain Cotgrave's will allowed £150 a year to be drawn to pay for Richard's upbringing, and £100 for each of his sisters.

Major Farmar remarried in 1863 to a woman with money of her own, so to any objective observer, it seemed obvious that whatever life unfolded for Richard, he would not have to worry about money. He was the only son of his father's first marriage, with a guaranteed annual allowance equivalent to a professional salary and the prospect of inheriting a fortune when he came of age, his father had a successful military career and his stepmother was independently financially secure. Even when the family solicitor absconded with the bulk of the Farmar family fortune, Cotgrave's half-brother had a concept of poverty that extended to nothing worse than 'bad cooks and poor quality nurses'. In any case, by then Richard Cotgrave had married Amelia Morison at Kensington Register Office and his father had signed over to him all rights to his mother's fortune. Richard de Malpas was independent of the rest of the Farmars and their cheap, lousy servants.

It was in 1881, when he was in his late twenties, that Cotgrave's spectacular talent for financial mismanagement began to manifest itself. He was by now running a brewery in the Cotswolds and his affairs had to be 'liquidated by arrangement'. Quite how he came to be in such a dire financial position when he had inherited a fortune just a year earlier is baffling. It was presumably a short-term cash flow issue because his status was soon described as a 'gentleman' and he moved into a large manor house. Fourteen years after his grandfather died, he finally made the formal, legal change to his name that had been demanded by his inheritance. He did so by signing a deed poll on 13 June 1882, just a fortnight before the deadline that had been set in Edward Stone Cotgrave's will.

It is from this time that the first evidence emerges of just why Richard de Malpas Cotgrave (as he now was) was so popular. He threw himself into the social life of his community, a leading member of both the local hunt and the cricket team. He and Amelia were involved in ensuring that the inmates of the workhouse were treated well, helping to serve the New Year's meal in 1883 and again showing his warm and outgoing personality by contributing to the entertainment. But it is also from this period that the first signs emerge that someone of such a strong personality could rub people up the wrong way. A local alderman refused him permission to hunt hares on his land, but Richard Cotgrave blithely took three greyhounds and a terrier onto the fields anyway. Convicted of trespass, he was admonished by the mayor, who thought that 'considering Mr Cotgrave's position, he ought to have known better'.

Later in 1883, Richard Cotgrave moved to Guernsey, to make a fresh start. He ran a social club, and was yet again a leading light of the sports world. His interest in hunting continued, and he kept his own foxhounds. On one occasion, when he took six wickets for just 11 runs in a cricket match against the soldiers of the Middlesex Regiment, the local newspaper reported that 'the bowling of Mr Cotgrave was very remarkable'. Richard Cotgrave seems to have enjoyed any sporting activity with a social element, and was a keen supporter of the Guernsey

Bicycle and Tricycle Club. A good public speaker, he made a 'humorous speech' at the club's annual dinner. He clearly liked a party, attending the annual Governor's Fancy Dress Ball, but where others went as an Easter Daisy, a Neapolitan fisherman, a domino and (rather specifically) 'the Countess von Neipberg in 1485', Cotgrave chose to dress up in his regular recreational outfit and go simply as a 'huntsman'. It is easy to believe that Richard de Malpas Cotgrave, despite his grand sounding name, was an affable and generous soul who was good at team sports, and had a natural facility with all kinds of people, so that many were drawn to his gregarious nature.

Eventually, this way of life also failed. Presumably the sports club was not successful and the hounds too expensive. So the Cotgrave family moved yet again for another new beginning, this time much further away, to Cyprus. Richard and Amelia now had two infant sons and over the next few years in the Mediterranean, three daughters would be born. There is little evidence for how the family made a living and perhaps they simply lived prudently on the income from the Cotgrave family inheritance. But in 1886, Richard wrote to the Secretary of State for the Colonies to apply for the post of Local Commandant of Police. Perhaps he was advised by his cousins Henry and George Cotgrave, who were Police Superintendents in India, that the colonial police service was a good career.[2] The incident turned out to be embarrassing for all concerned, however, not just because other candidates were 'better qualified' but more seriously because the job was not actually vacant. The Cypriot authorities politely blamed the mistake on a 'misapprehension' but the Governor's staff were clearly riled that they had been embarrassed in front of the Secretary of State.

So somewhat predictably, Richard Cotgrave moved again and was living back in England later the same year, although his family must have stayed on in Cyprus because another daughter was later born there. They all soon returned, however, and eventually settled together in Bedford. As usual, it is not entirely clear how Richard was making a living, although when he joined the town's Freemasons in September 1892, his occupation was listed as 'none'. The family increased, with two more boys born in the early 1890s.

During the 1890s, Richard de Malpas Cotgrave continued to demonstrate the sporting and social personality that made him popular. He helped to organise and officiate at gala sports events arranged for fun, played cricket for a variety of amateur teams almost every week, kept and

2   See photograph, p. 190, for a portrait of Henry Cotgrave.

showed fancy pigeons and indulged his interest in cycling – he was even prosecuted for riding on the pavement. He was a committee member of the cricket club, a member of the local rugby association and one of the organisers of the steeplechase races, where he insisted there should be a competition for novice farmers as well as the well-practised idle rich. His personality shone through when he sang a solo at a dinner to honour one of a handful of survivors of a shipping disaster.

The good times could not last and it was in 1898 that Cotgrave's financial ineptitude became obvious once more. A local loan company pressed for Richard to be declared bankrupt, presumably as a way of recovering a substantial sum of money. But Richard saw a way to avoid having to pay up, while simultaneously throwing off the monetary shackles with which his grandfather had encumbered him.

Although his grandfather had left him a lot of money, it was tied up so that he could only spend the interest, not the £15,000 lump sum of capital. Clearly, Captain Cotgrave had known that his grandson could not be trusted with money, and he had gone even further than simply putting the capital in trust. If Richard ever tried to give the money to someone else, or in any way pass it out of the trust– in legal parlance if it were ever 'alienated' or even if Richard 'agreed' to alienate it – then the legacy would be void. If this happened, the money would go to Richard's cousin Thomas Manson Cotgrave, who spent his career in the Indian civil service before retiring to rural Devon. But when it came to financial jiggery-pokery, Richard de Malpas Cotgrave was not going to be beaten by his grandfather's clever lawyers.

Richard evidently told Thomas Manson Cotgrave that his wife Amelia was suffering financially because of their inability to access the massive tranche of capital. Thomas Cotgrave fell for the old charm, and went along with his cousin's scheme because of 'pity for the family'. The first step was for Thomas Manson Cotgrave to sell to Amelia (for £500) his theoretical future interest in the money. In the immediate term, this had no effect other than to make Thomas a bit richer and Richard and Amelia a bit poorer, but it was a legally binding contract. If the relevant clause of the original will were ever triggered, Thomas had given up all rights to the capital in favour of Amelia. All Richard had to do now was to set in motion an attempt to 'alienate' the fund, but he had to do it in a risk-free way; he could not risk actually giving the £15,000 over to someone whom he did not trust completely. Cleverly, he declared himself bankrupt. The bankruptcy process involved temporarily putting a person's assets into the hands of a court-appointed receiver. Until the bankruptcy was discharged, the capital was no longer technically Richard's – it was in the possession of the receiver. Legally, it had been alienated. The rest was simple. There were manifestly enough assets to cover Richard's liabilities, so the bankruptcy could be discharged straight away, but the brief period that those assets had been out of his control constituted a legal 'alienation' and were enough to trigger the clause in his grandfather's will. Amelia Cotgrave was now the rightful owner of the capital. No doubt because his lawyers had thought the language foolproof, Captain Cotgrave had not made any stipulations tying up the capital in these circumstances. At least theoretically, the money was no longer in trust, it was Amelia's outright to spend, give away, burn, waste or invest as she pleased.

The sheer beauty of the plot was that as soon as the bankruptcy order was issued, Richard was almost literally penniless – the money was his wife's – and however hard the loan company pursued him, they would struggle ever to recover their money. Legal uproar broke out; the judge admitted he would have blocked the bankruptcy if he had known what was planned, and lawyers for the loan company accused all of the Cotgraves of fraud. Thomas Manson Cotgrave was gravely upset at the slur on his reputation after half a century in the service of the Crown, in which he had repeatedly been praised for his diligence, innovation, zeal, judgment and loyalty.

The trustees of the original settlement had no idea what to do. Should they surrender the money and if so to whom – the receiver appointed by the court, Thomas Cotgrave as the will stipulated, or Amelia Cotgrave as the deal seemed to suggest? Or did the evidently-contrived nature of the bankruptcy and the judge's reversal of opinion render it meaningless? The issue could only be settled by a higher authority. On 5 August 1903, the matter came for judgment in the High Court and Mr Justice Kekewich had no doubts. The bankruptcy petition had – rightly or wrongly – been allowed, it had had the legal effect of alienating Richard de Malpas Cotgrave's property, and the clause in Captain Cotgrave's will was triggered.

The outcome was that Thomas Manson Cotgrave had £500 but felt his reputation had been assailed, Richard and Amelia had their money but were very publicly embarrassed, and the proprietors of the loan company were substantially out of pocket and risked being sued for libel after injudicious talk about fraud. The official receiver was concerned that costs might be attributed to him when all he had tried to do was his job. A private discussion in judge's chambers six months later sought to settle everyone's difficulties. The loan company withdrew the accusation of fraud and the judge made it clear that nobody thought Thomas Cotgrave had acted improperly. £1,000 was paid to the loan company to cover the substantial losses it had suffered from the legal proceedings; for the benefit of the receiver, it was made clear that he was not expected to fund any of this payment – it had to come out of the estate. Amelia and Richard Cotgrave got the bulk of the money and experienced a valuable lesson that they seem finally to have learned. At any rate, they never ran into financial difficulty again.

Throughout the period, Cotgrave had kept up appearances. His cricketing career continued and he joined the local football club. He even sat on the Grand Jury for the Quarter Sessions. A few years later, it must all have seemed like a pointless dream.

Richard de Malpas Farmar Cotgrave (as he was now calling himself, subtly reinserting the name Farmar) was 60 when the First World War broke out, too old to fight. But he had four sons, ranging in age from 22 to 32. With their family backgrounds stuffed full of majors and colonels, commanders and captains, it was obvious they would join the military services, and there was a high chance that some or all of them would receive officers' commissions. In short, there was a very strong probability they would die young. By the time of the armistice in 1918, two of the four were dead, and so was their sister's husband.

Captain Montague Lewis Farmar Cotgrave was severely wounded and gassed in France in 1915. Back in action after recovering, he was killed at Passchendaele in 1917. 'His gallantry and utter disregard for his own life were in very large measure the factors which made for the greatest success of the engagement ... [he] fought bravely and ... fell like a gentleman and a brave soldier that he was.' His body was never recovered and he is commemorated on the Menin Gate Memorial in Belgium.

Captain Christopher Russell Farmar Cotgrave was attached to the 100th Trench Mortar Battery. Once he reached France in 1916, he served continuously without leave, and was at almost all the engagements on the Somme. He was killed in 1918 when a prematurely exploding mortar accidentally shot from a howitzer and smashed into his abdomen and buttocks. Described as 'an extremely good officer and a fine soldier,' he was buried with full military honours.

The young men's former headmaster wrote to their father, 'Two more blameless, splendid boys never fell in the service of humanity and England than yours'.

But despite the accolades awarded to his sons' memories, Richard Cotgrave struggled to cope. Because Christopher's death was an accident, there was a military Court of Inquiry and it turned out that it was 'contrary to published instructions' to use the particular kind of bomb that had killed him. Christopher had been in personal charge, so 'the

Three of Richard Cotgrave's sons died violent early deaths. Christopher
Cotgrave was accidentally killed by a mortar on the Somme [Reproduced
from *The Sphere*, 9 March 1918]. Montague Cotgrave died at
Passchendaele [Reproduced from *The Sphere*, 12 January 1918]. Reginald
Cotgrave was shot in the back by a Nigerian policeman while working as a
colonial administrator [Reproduced from the *Illustrated London News*,
25 March 1922].

responsibility for the sad occurrence' appeared to lie with Captain Cotgrave himself. Desperate to exonerate his son, Richard de Malpas Cotgrave wrote repeatedly to the War Office demanding to see the official papers. 'I consider … there is a stigma resting upon his name,' he wrote, 'I am entitled to see the details of the Court of Enquiry'. Officials tried to make him understand that whatever had happened, Christopher's memory was unsullied. 'It cannot for a moment be supposed that the sad occurrence can be in any way a stigma on his memory'. The Commanding Officer's official opinion as to 'whether the man was to blame' was an unequivocal 'no'.

Richard Cotgrave, however, was hardly thinking and behaving rationally. He railed against the ministry for misspelling his name, and said he would 'take advice in the matter,' presumably a threat to involve a lawyer. He took offence when officials wrote to his other son when the letter should have been addressed to him as head of the family and he threatened to involve his local MP. Eventually, when he wrote 'I do not accept the conclusions arrived at,' ministers and officials realised there was nothing they could ever say or do to ease the crushing pain of losing his children. As he had pointed out, 'I have lost two sons and a son-in-law in less than two months killed in France'. So 'after much thought,' the War Office decided not to reply to Cotgrave's latest letter.

It is impossible to imagine how Richard de Malpas Farmar Cotgrave felt as he waited hopelessly for the War Office to send him a report that could not bring back either of his sons. Five years later, he was still railing against the authorities who were 'a perpetual disgrace' because of their inadequate plans for a war memorial to the local men who had given their lives.

The legal games over his inheritance, the failed attempt to become a colonial police chief, the foxhunting and hilarity of the bicycle club party must have seemed pointless and empty. Even worse was to come. Just a few years later, one of his two remaining sons, Reginald Walsingham Farmar Cotgrave, who had fought in the Boer War and the First World War before joining the colonial service, was shot dead in the back by a Nigerian policeman whom he had reprimanded. What had been the point in unlocking his grandfather's inheritance when Richard de Malpas Cotgrave was rapidly running out of offspring to leave it to? Of his five sons, one had died in infancy and three as young adults. Only Hugh Hovell Farmar Cotgrave outlived his father; he had been invalided out of the army in 1917, deprived of his commission because of a scar on his eye that meant he could not see properly. But he had fought as an officer in the Royal Engineers at Gallipoli and in France so no doubt Captain

Edward Stone Cotgrave would have considered Hugh a worthy inheritor of the Cotgrave name and fortune. But it was not to be.

Although the terms of the inheritance had been unequivocal on the issue of his name, Richard had never really given up the name Farmar. He died quite suddenly in 1926, after an illness that lasted just two days, and his death certificate recorded that his name was Richard de Malpas Farmar-Cotgrave. That is how he had been recorded in the 1901 and 1911 censuses. Each of his children was given Farmar as a middle name and Hugh used it as the first half of a double-barrelled surname, calling himself Hugh Hovell Farmar-Cotgrave. As if that was not insulting enough to Captain Cotgrave's wishes, when Hugh died (as late as 1971), the registrar wrote the name in slightly scruffy handwriting, and anyone trying to find the official record of his death must look under Farmar-Colgrave. Hugh and his wife never had children, so the next generation of Richard's descendants contained his daughters' offspring, known by the surnames of those daughters' husbands – none of Richard's grandchildren was called Cotgrave, Farmar-Cotgrave, Farmar or any of the names that had so obviously mattered to Richard and to his grandfather.

The names had disappeared, what money was left had passed to in-laws, many of the surviving records told stories of bankruptcy, embarrassment, grief and disappointment. His own half-brother had tried to erase him from the family's story and in an age still dominated by men, he had suffered the indignity of being dependent on his wife for his income. He might have slipped quietly into the past and allowed his distinguished father and grandfather, his brave and sacrificed sons, or even his loyal, kindly, hard-working cousin to occupy the pages of the family history. But this was a man who could bowl out an entire cricket team, make the ladies laugh at the bicycle club ball, look dashing in his hunting pinks and repeatedly charm his way out of financial oblivion. And as well as advertising his distinguished Cheshire roots by calling himself 'de Malpas,' he could blatantly use a surname that was expressly forbidden.

No wonder that his niece's biographer could not resist allowing his readers a tiny glimpse of 'the invisible man'.

Acknowledgements

You cannot write a book about your relations without some help from your family. I would never have been able to start my research if I had not been encouraged as a teenager by my parents Roger and Val Cotgreave. A large number of older family members, most now sadly dead, helped and provided information, including Sheila Hughes, Marjorie Stockbridge, Ellen Thornton and others. It has been a great pleasure to make new friends, distantly related genetically but close in interests, and in particular I am lucky that my hobby introduced me to Tony and Leah Cotgreave and to Bill and Chris Cotgreave and their families. Bill has tirelessly tracked down all of our living relatives, uncovering wonderful stories, photographs and friends, while Tony has painstakingly gone through thousands of pages of records to learn new things about our common ancestors.

It has also been a great pleasure to correspond with and meet many people with whom I have some distant relationship or common interest, and in many cases to have been invited into their homes to share their memorabilia and photographs. They are far too numerous to thank everyone individually, but among others Gillie Turner, Elspeth and George Hardie, Keith Dodds, Linda de Malpas-Finlay, Joy and Angus Davidson, Sir Hamish and Lady Forbes, and Hilarie and Colin McNae have been particularly generous.

You also can't write a history book without a lot of assistance from librarians, archivists and curators. There are far too many institutions to list here, let alone each of the helpful and friendly individuals who work in them; the references section gives the details of dozens of different places where I have been able to consult unique old documents and books.

I am very grateful to everyone who has given permission to reproduce pictures and I would especially like to thank Gillie Turner, Rosemary Walker and Jonny Hardie, Linda de Malpas-Finlay and Joy Davidson. The Louisiana State University Museum of Art has been especially generous in waiving its normal fees.

I gave up history at school when I was 13, and if you had suggested that one day I would have the privilege of being on the council of a history charity, I would have laughed. But being a trustee of the Record Society of Lancashire and Cheshire has brought me into contact with proper historians, and they have been enormously encouraging. Through it, I met the two experts who have been so generous with their time as to read and comment on the whole book. If it has any credibility as a piece of historical research, it is no small part because Alan Crosby and Colin Phillips helped. Alan is the editor of *The Local Historian* and writes a regular column for *Who Do You Think You Are?* magazine, so it would be hard to find someone better placed to comment on a book about local and family history. When it comes to the history of the north west of England, Colin literally wrote the book – his *Lancashire and Cheshire from AD 1540* remains invaluable more than two decades after it first appeared; his detailed criticisms of individual Chapters were invaluable in helping me avoid mistakes.

Fulsome thanks must go to Anna Goddard at Carnegie Publishing for taking on the project. As soon as you say your book is based on research about your family, most people involved in publishing switch off; they think that because your grandmother's date of birth is a boring detail, it must be the case that none of your ancestors ever did or said a single interesting thing. They either rudely ignore you or send you a patronising rejection. Anna's very first reaction was completely different. She kindly wrote that the book 'deserves to see the light of day' and offered a route to making that happen. I hope she was right and I thank her and the team for their confidence.

Lastly of course, I must give posthumous thanks to the people whose stories I try to tell in the book. As it happens, they did and said a great many interesting things, and I hope I have done them justice.

References

Abbreviations

BL	British Library
CALS	Cheshire Archives and Local Studies
CGPA	Calendar of Grants of Probate and Administration in England and Wales
HC	History Centre
LMA	London Metropolitan Archives
NLW	National Library of Wales
ODNB	Oxford Dictionary of National Biography
Ormerod	Ormerod, G. (1882) *The History of the County Palatine and City of Chester*, 2nd Edition, Revised and Enlarged by Thomas Helsby, 3 Volumes, George Routledge and Sons, London.
RBEW	General Register Office Register of Births in England and Wales
RDEW	General Register Office Register of Deaths in England and Wales
RMEW	General Register Office Register of Marriages in England and Wales
RO	Record Office
TNA	The National Archives, UK

Chapter 1: Thomas de Cotegrave

Charters and deeds that mention him are in BL: Harley MSS 2022, ff. 33v. 34r, 35r, 55r, 55v, 56r; CALS: D/BW/A/A/A/1; Reference to his family's salt works in is Landsdowne MS 644, ff. 9–11; His ancestry and family are described in Cotgreave, P. (2008) The Barony of Malpas in the Twelfth Century, *Transactions of the Lancashire and Cheshire Historic Society*, Vol. 157, pp. 1–32; The political situation in December 1259 is described in Jones, D. (2012) *The Plantagenets*, Harper Press, London, p. 264; References to his colleagues on the jury are in Manchester University Library: RYCH/1375, 1386, 1400, 1475, 1573; CALS: DDX553/3; DLT/A/8/5; DLT/A/8/60; Lancashire RO: DDSC37/2; The suggestion that his family were foresters is in *The Cheshire Sheaf*, Series 3, Vol. 4 (1902), p. 40; The roll with the earliest mention of his name is in TNA: CHES29/1; Near and Far Cotgreaves are listed in TNA: IR29/5/86.

Chapter 2: Eleanor Cotgrave

Her portrait is Louisiana State University Art Museum: 59.9.2 and is described in Walker, H. (2010) Madame Savage: Recovering Lady Eleanor Savage, Hans Eworth The Complete Catalogue Raisoné; available at www.hanseworth.com and *The Connoiseur*, Vol. 26 (Jan 1910), p. 12; Family relationships are in BL: Harley MSS 380, f. 161; 1535, f. 92; 2153, f. 258v; Queen's College Oxford, MS 80, f. 105; TNA: C1/1295; C24/50; C54/533; CALS: ZSBC10, f. 94r; Disputes with the Pexall family is described in Burrows, M. (1886) *The Family of Brocas of Beaurepaire and Roche Court, London*, and Squibb, G. D. (1991) *The Visitation of Hampshire and the Isle of Wight*, London, p. 197; The surviving deeds which she was alleged to have destroyed are at Bodleian Library, Oxford: Dep.Deeds. Brocas; Information about her marriages and husbands is in Williams, S. (1861) *Letters written by John Chamberlain*, London, p. 53; Laing, D. (1875) *Correspondence of Sir Robert Kerr First Earl of Ancram and his son William Third Earl of Lothian*, Edinburgh, Vol. 1, p. xxviii; LMA: P69/AND2/A/002; Metcalfe, W. C. (1885) *A book of Knights*, p. 158; Ormerod, Vol. 3, p. 716; Shaw, W. A. (1906) *The Knights of England*, Vol. 2, pp. 93, 143; CALS: DCH/F/817; DLT/B4, p. 174; TNA: C3/349/43; MS Eng.hist/c.479, ff. 227–8; PROB11/17, ff. 141–2; PROB11/53, ff. 337–8; PROB11/99, f. 321; Relationship with the Brocks is in CALS: WS Robert Brock 1588; C2/JASi/R12/38; Legal disputes among the various families she married into are at TNA: C2/ELIZ/C16/27; C2/ELIZ/S3/19; C2/ELIZ/S15/55; C2/JASi/M6/24; C2/JASi/M8/15; C2/JASi/S18/10; C2/JASi/S20/44; C2/JASi/S23/59; C2/CHASi/S57/52; C3/261/77; C7/49/79; C21/S43/11; E134/42Eliz/East9; E134/42Eliz/East12; E134/42Eliz/Hill0; E134/JASi/East22 REQ2/93/29; STAC5/B17/19; STAC8/21/7; STAC8/60/3; STAC8/260/11; Her burial is in Millard, J. E. (1882) *The Book of Accounts of the Wardens of the Fraternity of the Holy Ghost in Basingstoke AD 1557–AD 1654*, London, p. 94.

Chapter 3: Randle Cotgrave

His book is Cotgrave, R. (1611) *A Dictionarie of the French and English Tongues,* London and subsequent editions; Its evolution, production and reception can be traced in Arber, E. (1876) *A Transcript of the Registers of the Company of Stationers of London 1554–1640 AD,* London, Vol. 3, pp. 381, 432; Smalley, V. E. (1948) *The Sources of A Dictionarie of the French and English Tongues,* Baltimore; Cunningham, P. (1842) *Extracts from the accounts of the revels at court,* London, p. 31; Miege, G. (1677) *A new Dictionary, French and English,* London; Rickard, P. [transl. J. Considine] (2012) The French-English Dictionarie of Cotgrave (1611), *Ashgate Critical Essays on Early English Lexicographers: Volume 4 The Seventeenth Century,* Ashgate, Farnham, pp. 377–85; Royal Commission on Historical Manuscripts: Manuscripts of the Duke of Rutland, Vol. 2 (1889), p. 353; His biography can be traced through Cooke, W. H. (1868) *Students Admitted to the Inner Temple 1571–1625,* London, p. 66; Private communication, A St G Walsh, King's School, Chester, Aug 1988; Eccles, M. (1982) Randle Cotgrave, *Studies in Philology,* Vol. 74, Part 4, p. 26; John Leigh, 'Cotgrave, Randle (fl. 1587–1630?)', *ODNB,* 2004; Cotgreave, P. (1995) A Note on Randle Cotgrave, *Notes & Queries* New Series, Vol. 42, pp. 346–7; Venn, J. and Venn, J. A. (1922) *Alumni Cantabridgiensis,* CUP, Part 1, Vol. 1, pp. 313, 401; Liverpool RO: 920 CHES/2/82; BL: Harley MSS 2099, f. 115v, 166v; The Cheshire Sheaf, 3rd Series, Vol. 4 (1902), p. 89; His employment with the Cecils is in Burghley House: Accounts 10/3; TNA: C2/CHASi/E5/31; C3/35/63; C24/460, 518, 537, 593, 622; E215/466; The surviving letter to him is at Wiltshire RO: 9/1/426; Letters he wrote are at BL: Harley MS 7002, fol. 126; *Notes and Queries,* 3rd Series, Vol. 8, pp. 84–5; For Sir Robert Heath, see Kopperman, P. E. (1989) *Sir Robert Heath: Window on an age,* London; Information about words he first recorded is from Oxford English Dictionary online www.oed.com, accessed November 2011.

Chapter 4: Ellen Cotgreave

Family information is in CALS: P121/2; RDEW: Jan Q 1915, King's Norton, Vol. 6d, p. 86; TNA: HO107/97/1, f. 3; HO107/2171, f. 386; RG11/2980, f. 28; RG14/17888; The formal record of the Coroner's inquest is filed at TNA: ASSI66/12 and there are fuller details in *Chester Chronicle* 15 May 1838 and Return of Coroners of England and Wales of Inquisitions where death was caused by poisoning, *House of Commons Accounts and Papers,* Session 1839; The doctor's career can be traced in CALS: WS Robert Bostock 1835; TNA: HO107/98/10, f. 6; HO107/2171, f. 346; RG9/2624, f. 152; RG10/3719, f. 24; *Kelly's Directory of Cheshire* 1865, p. 298.

Chapter 5: Sibella Cotgrave

Family information is in Cornwall RO: P119/1/8; P251/1/1; Curgenven, J. B. (2006) *The Family of Brendon and their descendants, additional material by Anthony D Bell*; RDEW: Jun Q 1849, Plympton St Mary, Vol. 9, p. 278; Somerset RO: D/P/ba.ab 2/1/13; Her husband's career can be traced in TNA: ADM9/26, #830; ADM51/3508; ADM175/78, p. 139; ADM196/2, f. 255; HO107/1113/13; HO 107/1880, f. 96v; PROB10/7442; Taylor, M. (1882) The Story of My Life, Edinburgh & London, p. 274; Her son's career can be traced in BL: IOR/L/AG/34/27/404, f. 59; IOR/L/MIL/9/216, f. 72; *London Gazette* 14 Mar 1871; *Morning Post* 9 Jun 1849, 4 Jul 1850, 15 Mar 1871; *The Times* 9 Jun 1849, p. 8; Details of the state of Plympton asylum is from Commissioners in Lunacy: Report to the Lord Chancellor, *House of Lords Papers* (1844), pp. 60–3, 260–1; Life in Fairford Asylum is described in Gloucestershire RO: D1070/VII/78; Trusham Church and its circumstances are described in *Transactions of the Devonshire Association*, Vol. 53 (1921), Twelfth Report of the Committee on Church Plate, p. 123; *Weekly Express* 16 Nov 1865; *Western Morning News* 21 Mar 1873.

Chapter 6: Robert Cotgreave

Biographical and family details are from CALS: DTD/67/5; 68/5; P87/1/2; P87/4; P91/3/2; CGPA: Robert Cotgreave 6 Jun 1866, Robert Cotgreave 15 Jan 1874; *Chester Chronicle* 3 Jul 1840, 31 Aug 1849; Grosvenor Archives: Letter to S Cotgreave dated July 1989; RDEW: Dec Q 1861, Lambeth, Vol. 1d, p. 259; Jun Q 1868, Great Boughton, Vol. 8a, p. 254; Dec Q 1874, Great Boughton, Vol. 8a, p. 273; RMEW: Dec Q 1869, Holborn, Vol. 1b, p. 723; History, Gazeteer & Directory of Suffolk (1855), p. 141; *Post Office Sussex Directory* (1859), p. 1429; TNA: ASSI66/5-6, 17; HO107/2172/609, p. 12; HO107/90/12; RG9/362, f. 138; Flintshire RO: BP9310; His early cartographic work is at Suffolk RO: E18/700/2/2/4; His patent on the plough is GB Patent (1850) 13,076; Details of its use and success are in *Chester Chronicle* 16 Nov 1850, 15 Feb 1851, 15 Nov 1851, 26 Mar 1853; *Illustrated London News*, Vol. 31, p. 166; *Leeds Times* 4 Aug 1855; Munn, B. (1856) *The Practical Land Drainer*, Saxton & Co, New York, p. 173ff; Museum of Rural Life: TR/RAN/MP3/17, p. 197; TR RAN/P1/A105; Phillips, A.D.M. (1989) *The Underdraining of farmland in England during the nineteenth century*, London; Royal Agricultural Society, *A catalogue of the various agricultural implements … exhibited at the Society's Show* (1854, 1855, 1856, 1857, 1858); *Scientific American* 11 Aug 1855, p. 383; *The Times* 7 Aug 1856.

Chapter 7: Charles Cotgreave

Family and biographical information is in CALS: MFR/13; WS Jane Latchford 1851; Z/CR22/19; Z/D/T/1/1850; RDEW: Jun Q 1872, Vol. 8a, p. 253; *Satirist*

27 Jan 1849, 24 Nov 1849; The Poll Book for the General Election: List of Voters who polled at the election for representatives of the City of Chester, Fletcher, Chester (1820); A Narrative of the Proceedings at the memorable contest for the representations of Chester in 1826, Chester (1826); TNA: HO107/129/6, f. 18; HO107/2172/ f. 317; RG9/2955, f. 11; RG10/3731, f. 59. Hughes, T. (1856) *Stranger's Handbook to Chester*, Chester, p. 38; *Cheshire Observer* 6 Feb 1858, 10 Apr 1858, 12 Feb 1859, 10 Oct 1863; *Chester Chronicle* 29 Dec 1837, 20 Jul 1838, 31 Jul 1840, 7 May 1841, 7 Dec 1841, 20 Apr 1842, 16 Jun 1848, 21 Dec 1849, 25 Aug 1850, 21 Jan 1856, 26 Nov 1859; *London Gazette* 8 Feb 1842, 12 Mar 1844, 15 Mar 1844, 19 Apr 1844, 30 Apr 1844; *Wrexham Advertiser* 8 Jun 1867; Horseraces and related information is in *Bell's Life in London and Sporting Chronicle* 26 Nov 1848, 31 Dec 1848, 24 Jul 1850, 28 Jul 1850, 4 Aug 1850, 15 Sep 1850, 29 Sep 1850, 17 Nov 1850, 12 Jan 1851, 21 Sep 1851, 19 Oct 1851, 16 May 1852, 27 Jun 1852, 17 Oct 1852, 6 Mar 1853, 13 Nov 1853, 5 Mar 1854, 17 Jun 1855; *Berrow's Worcester Journal* 10 Jun 1854; *Carnarvon & Denbigh Herald* 25 Oct 1851; *Freeman's Journal* 23 Jun 1851; *The Era* 19 Oct 1851, 16 Nov 1851, 5 Mar 1852, 20 Jun 1852, 18 Jul 1852, 13 Nov 1853, 14 May 1854, 16 Jul 1854, 12 Nov 1854; Green, R. (2000) *The Grand National: Aintree's official illustrated history*, London, p. 18; *Hampshire Advertiser* 21 Jun 1851; *Hull Packet* 2 Feb 1849, 4 Oct 1850; *Lancaster Gazette* 6 Mar 1852, 5 Mar 1853; *Liverpool Mercury* 5 Mar 1852; *Lloyd's Weekly Newspaper* 29 Sep 1850, 7 Mar 1852; *Manchester Times* 24 Nov 1849, 4 Mar 1854; *Morning Chronicle* 28 Feb 1854; *Morning Post* 26 Jan 1849, 23 Nov 1849, 9 Oct 1850, 17 Nov 1851, 4 Mar 1852, 9 Jan 1854, 28 Feb 1853, 2 Mar 1854, 9 Mar 1854, 15 Apr 1854, 8 Nov 1854, 15 Jun 1855; Munroe, D. H. (1931) *The Grand National 1839–1931*, London, p. 23; *North Wales Chronicle* 19 Jan 1847, 7 Mar 1848, 23 Oct 1858; *Nottinghamshire Guardian* 1 Aug 1850, 12 Sep 1850, 19 Sep 1850, 9 Oct 1851; *Preston Guardian* 24 Nov 1849, 6 Mar 1852, 11 Mar 1854, 15 Apr 1854; *Racing Calendar* 1848–58 editions; *Racing Times* 16 Apr 1851, 17 Feb 1852, 24 Feb 1852, 29 Jun 1852, 8 Mar 1853, 12 Jul 1853, 11 Oct 1853, 1 Nov 1853, 22 Nov 1853, 7 Mar 1854, 14 Mar 1854, 18 Apr 1854, 18 Jul 1854, 14 Nov 1854, 30 Jan 1854, 19 Jun 1855, 25 Feb 1856, 4 May 1857, 20 Jul 1857; www.allbreedpedigree.com; *York Herald* 25 Nov 1848, 13 Jul 1850, 17 Aug 1850, 12 Oct 1850, 6 Mar 1852, 12 Jun 1852, 26 Jun 1852, 15 Jul 1854, 8 Aug 1857; Greyhound coursing information is in *Coursing Calendar for the Spring Season 1867*, p. 25; *Coursing Calendar for the Spring Season 1870*, p. 9; *Bell's Life in London and Sporting Chronicle* 4 May 1862.

Chapter 8: Alfred Cotgreave

His publications include Cotgreave, A. (1891) *Guile-Alles Library and Museum: Encyclopaedic Catalogue*, Guernsey; Cotgreave, A. (1896) *Borough of West Ham Public Libraries, Catalogue of the Books in the Central Lending Library, London*; Cotgreave, A. (1901) *Views and Memoranda of Public Libraries*, Library Aids Company, London; GB Patent applications 188409171, 188710706, 188716444,

189110375, 189117947, 189306228, 189319827, 189319986, 189424659, 189506274, 189520268, 189600896, 189609883, 189715191, 189722160, 189815449, 189816346, 189816678, 190006503, 190120212, 190108123, 190124648, 190209913, 190427963, 190517120, 190626102, 190818543, 190817121, 190801732; His early life and naval career is documented in *Cheshire Observer* 3 Sep 1870, 14 Oct 1876; Maritime History Archive, Canada: Crew list: Athene 18686, 1864, 1865, 1869; National Maritime Museum: C/L 25330 (1862) Edmund Graham; Masters Certificates number 82.838; RMEW: Dec Q 1870, Liverpool, Vol. 8b, p. 97; RG9/362, f. 138; HO107/2172, f. 609; The important legislation is *Public Libraries Act 1850*; His professional career as a Librarian can be followed in detail from *Academy*, Vol. 59 (1900), p. 521; *Birmingham Daily Post* 25 Sep 1879; Bishopsgate Institute Library: SPL/1-2; BL: Mic.B.53/34-58; CALS: MF240/26; *Chelmsford Chronicle* 3 Feb 1896, 12 Jun 1896, 3 Feb 1905; *Country Life Illustrated* 8 Apr 1899, p. 424; *Freeman's Journal* 2 Oct 1884; *Glasgow Herald* 6 Oct 1880, 12 Sep 1883; Guille-Allès Library Archives: Address from the staff to Alfred Cotgreave, September 1890; Letter from Cotgreave to Mr Pitt, 20 August 1905; Letter from Cotgreave to Mr Roswell, 16 July 1906; *Invention* 2 Sep 1893; *Leisure Hour: A monthly magazine for home reading* 1901, p. 962; *The Library Assistant* Vol. 1, pp. 129–37; Vol. 2, p. 261; *Library Association Record*, Vol. 8, p. 115; *The Library*, Vol. 6, pp. 324, 417; Vol. 7, p. 200; Vol. 8, p. 583; Vol. 10, pp. 240, 284; *Library World*, Vol. 1 (1898), pp. 32, 87–8; Vol. 5, p. 190; Vol. 6, p. 172; Vol. 7, p. 270; *Manchester Courier* 1 May 1874; Manchester Metropolitan University Special Collections: F027.441/PUB; *Mona's Herald* 17 Jul 1878; *Municipal Journal* 12 Dec 1902, pp. 190, 1017; *National Review*, No. 40 (1886), p. 571; Newham Archives and Local Studies: Public Libraries and Technical Institution Minutes, Vol. 1898–99, 11 September 1899; Vol. 1900–01, 16 September 1900; Vol. 1903–06, 6 March 1905; Richmond Local Studies Library: R/L/1-3; Sandwell Community History & Archives Service: B/W/1/9, 027.44246 (*First Printed Report of the Free Library Committee 1878*); *Royal Cornwall Gazette* 13 Sep 1900; Royal Historical Society: Roll of Fellows; Council Minute Book 1886–1894, p. 193; *Souvenir Presented by the Public Libraries Committee to Andrew Carnegie Esq in Commemoration of his Opening the Passmore Edwards Public Library, Plaistow on May 9th 1903*, West Ham; *Star* (Guernsey) 29 Jan 1895; UCL Special Collections: Library Association Archives, Series D, Box 11; United Grand Lodge of England, Membership Registers, Mariners Lodge, Guernsey; Woodgrange Lodge, London; *West Ham Library Notes* Vols 1–9; *Whitstable Times and Herne Bay Herald* 5 Nov 1898; Records of Cotgreave's Indicators Ltd are in TNA: BT34/2975/69144; Reference to his personality is in Munford, W.A. (1968) *James Duff Brown 1862–1914*, London, p. 30; Library of Birmingham: BCC1/AT/1/1/3; Information about the modern Library of Birmingham is from www.libraryofbirmingham.com; His will is at CGPA: Alfred Cotgreave 20 Oct 1911; His death is registered at RDEW: Sept Q 1911, Yarmouth, Vol. 4b, p. 9.

Chapter 9: Robert de Cotegreve

The list of soldiers with his name on is in E/47/1, m.1; Other references to his name are in TNA: CHES3/30; CHES24/26, 40; CHES26/12; Details of the campaign, his likely compliment of horses etc is in Barker, J. (2005) *Agincourt*, Abacus, London; Cheshire soldiers more generally are described in Morgan, P. (1987) *War and Society in Medieval Cheshire 1277–1403*, Manchester; The career of his commander is described in G.L. Harriss, 'Fitzalan, Thomas, fifth earl of Arundel and tenth earl of Surrey (1381–1415)', *ODNB*, 2004; His father's purchase of a property for him is in CALS: DVE/1/SI/18; The coat of arms is at BL: ADD MS 62,541, f. 78r; Information about relationships with the other Cheshire men in the list and his relationships with them is at Harley MS 2075, f. 28r; Ormerod: Vol. 3, p. 51.

Chapter 10: Richard Cotgreve

The Cotgreves' case is analysed by Clayton, D. J. (1990) *The administration of the County Palatine of Chester 1442–85*, Manchester, pp. 25, 100, 176, 243; The relevant ballads are in Hales, J. W. and Furnivall, F. J. (1868) *Bishop Percy's Folio Manuscript: Ballads and Romances*, Vol. III, London, pp. 205–14; and the significance of key characters described in Weir, A. (2013) *Elizabeth of York*, London, pp. 144–52; William Cotgreve's training in London is in Boyd, P. (1934) *Roll of the Draper's Company of London*, p. 46; Personal communication from the Archivist of the Draper's Company, November 2001; Biographies of Calveley and Stanley are in Kenneth Fowler, 'Calveley, Sir Hugh (d. 1394)', *ODNB*, 2004; Michael J. Bennett, 'Stanley, Sir William (*c.* 1435–1495)', *ODNB*, 2004; Family relationships are in Queen's College Oxford: MS 80, f. 105r; BL: Harley MSS 360, f. 161, 1925, f. 148v, 2011, f. 4r; 2059, f. 139; Cheshire men at Bosworth are described in Skidmore, C. (2013) *Bosworth: The Birth of the Tudors*, London, pp. 265–6; The recognizances to keep the peace are all in TNA: CHES2/132-178; The brothers' other dealings in the Cheshire courts are in TNA: CHES3/52; CHES19/6; CHES20/3; CHES24/44; CHES25/15-6; CHES26/19; CHES29/166.

Chapter 11: Robert Cotgrave

The detailed depositions are in E178/3636; The cursory trial is described in CHES29/360; Details of careers and deaths of the various protagonists are from Armytage, G. J. and Rylands, J. P. (1909) *Pedigrees made at the Visitation of Cheshire 1613*, Record Society of Lancashire and Cheshire, p. 253; Rylands, J. P. (ed.) (1882) *The Visitation of Cheshire in the Year 1580*, London; CALS: WS Edward Dutton 1617; WS George Cotgrave 1612; WS Hugh Bromley 1628; WS Hugh Davenport 1622; WS Thomas Booth 1624; WS William Cotgrave 1620;

P21/3607/1/2; BL: Harley MS 2041, f. 69; LMA MS 9050/5, f. 192r; Sefton's will and burial are at CALS: P29/1/1; WS Thomas Sefton 1605; Previous conflict between the Cotgreaves and Seftons is described in BL: Harley MS 2063, f. 27v; TNA: CHES14/5, p. 740; The sale of property during his lifetime is at BL: Harley MS 2131, f. 146v; for the Cotgraves in Staffordshire see Staffordshire RO: Q/SR/291/28; Parish Registers of Burslem and Stoke-on-Trent, 1649–1660s.

Chapter 12: Ralph Cotgreave

Court cases and appearances involving him and his son are at CALS: QJB1/3; QJF28/2, ff. 35, 45, 49; 30/3, ff. 32, 37, 38, 54; 34/3, ff. 33, 100; 43/2, f. 60; 50/2, f. 89; 52/3, f. 1; 62/4, f. 15; 71/4, ff. 5, 6, 7, 21; Z/M/B28b; Z/SBC50, ff. 94r–v; 51; 52, ff. 297v, 311v; 53, ff. 342r, 435v; 54, ff. 31r, 389r; 56, ff. 355r, 605r; 57, ff. 181v, 499v; Le Hardy, W. (1936) *County of Middlesex Calendar to the Sessions Records*, New Series, Vol. 2., Radcliffe, London, p. 131; TNA: C93/12/5; CHES5/11; CHES6/1, ff. 155v, 170r, 225r, 280r; 6/2, ff. 64v, 98r, 184r, 226r, 251r; 6/3, ff. 78r, 85r, 96v, 101r, 108v, 122v, 161–2; 6/4, ff. 47r, 130v, 210r, 314r, 324r, 358r, 370r, 373r; 6/5, ff. 10v, 83v; CHES13/5, 7, 20–2; CHES14/7, f. 144v; 14/9; 14/9; 14/12; 14/13; 14/36, ff. 160r, 166r, 188v, 245r, 274v, 277r, 285r; 14/37; 14/38, ff. 94v, 151r, 190v, 212v, 215r, 236r; 14/39, ff. 6v, 7r, 10r–v, 17r, 34r, 45r, 55v, 155r, 157r, 163v; 14/40, ff. 16r, 26r; 14/41, f. 90v; 14/42, f. 169v; 14/43, ff. 18r, 134r; 14/51; 14/60; 14/61, f. 65v; 14/62, f. 168; 14/63; 14/64; 14/65, ff. 84v, 88v, 121v, 123v, 90v, 112r, 133r, 170v, 196v, 200v, 204v, 216v, 222r, 227r, 253r; CHES15/32, 50, 52; CHES16/10-12, 15-17, 20-1, 23-4, 28, 32-4, 36, 30-41, 44, 46; CHES21/2, ff. 46r, 60v, 90; 21/3, f. 75r; CHES24/110/2; CHES29/370, 376; CHES35/4, ff. 46r, 68r, 71v, 69r, 73v, 103r, 122v; 35/5, ff. 32v, 105r; CHES38/5-6; 38/28/9; Other references to property are at: BL: Harley MS 2020, f. 107r; CALS: DVE/1/SI/18-21, 29-30; EDD10/1/5; His son's career as a juror in the context of others is described in Morrill, J. S. (1976) *The Cheshire Grand Jury 1625–1658: A Social and administrative study*, Leicester; His relations are described in CHES31/56; Thrush, A. and Ferris, J. P. (2010) *The History of Parliament: the House of Commons 1604–1629*, London/William Brocke; Widden's marriage is in CALS: P65/1/1.

Chapter 13: Isaac Cotgrave

Family information is from TNA: PROB10/4151; Walford, E. (1865) *The County families of the UK*, Robert Hardwicke, London, p. 240; *York Herald* 22 Aug 1801; O'Callaghan, E. B. (1860) *Names of persons for whom marriage licences were issues by the Secretary of the Province of New York previous to 1784*, Albany, NY, p. 31; *Gentleman's Magazine*, Vol. 84, part ii (1814), p. 87; *Miscellanea Genealogica et Heraldica*, 5th Series, Vol. 4, p. 122; LMA: CLC/B/192/F/001/MS11,936/357, p. 191; His career can be traced via *An address to the people of the United Kingdom of Great Britain and Ireland containing an account of the sufferings of Thomas O'Neill, A British Officer*, London, 1806, pp. 26–8; BL: IOR/B/85, p. 143; IOR/L/MIL/12/1, f. 17v; *Bury and Norwich Post* 26 Aug 1801; *Carlisle Journal* 22 Aug 1801; *Chester Chronicle* 21 Aug 1801; *Gloucester Journal* 24 Aug 1801; *Hereford Journal* 26 Aug 1801; *Hull Packet* 15 Apr 1806, 25 Aug 1801; *Ipswich Journal* 22 Aug 1801; *Lloyds Evening Post* 30 Jun 1794; Long, W. H. (1899) *Naval Yarns*, London, p. 177; *Morning Chronicle* 8 Sep 1808, 9 Mar 1811, 3 May 1813; *Morning Post* 19 Aug 1801; National Army Museum 1968-07-183-5; National Maritime Museum: CRK3/97; *Northampton Mercury* 8 May 1813; *Oxford Journal* 22 Aug 1801; Plymouth and West Devon RO: 1/674/1/36, 1/702/56, 413/133-6; *Reading Mercury* 24 Aug 1801; Ronald, D. A. B. (2009) *Young Nelsons: Boy Sailors during the Napoleonic Wars*, Osprey Publishing, p. 96; *Staffordshire Advertiser* 22 Aug 1801; *Stamford Mercury* 21 Aug 1801; Sugden, J. (2012) *Nelson: Sword of Albion*, London; TNA: ADM1/1653#233; ADM1/3755, 3757, 3764, 5333; ADM6/88; ADM36/5671, 7287–9; 7307–8, 7467, 7539, 7577, 7688, 7903, 9127, 9944, 9946, 10898, 12694, 13968; ADM 48/97/26, 48/98/211; ADM106/1178, no. 348; ADM107/6, p. 78; *Trewman's Exeter Flying Post* 17 Apr 1806, 20 Sep 1810, 30 Aug 1810, 25 Jul 1811, 12 Sep 1811, 24 Oct 1811, 30 Sep 1813; Information about Dartmoor is from Stanbrook, E. (2002) *Dartmoor's War Prison and Church*, Tavistock, pp. 77–84; *The Collected poems of the late N. T. Carrington*, Vol. 1 (1834), London, p. 162; *The Prisoners' Memoirs, or Dartmoor Prison* (1815), New York; Thomson, B. (1907) *The Story of Dartmoor Prison*, London, p. 35; Rhodes, A. J. (1933) *Dartmoor Prison*, London; ADM99/213.

Chapter 14: Hugh Cotgrave

The engraving of him is British Museum: 1892,0628.194.6 and is described in Hind, A. M. (1952) Engraving in the Sixteenth and Seventeenth Centuries, London, Part 1, p. 107; Cotgrave's Ordinary is at the College of Arms and is described in Wagner, A. (1950) *A Catalogue of English Mediaeval Rolls of Arms*, London, p. 60; Nicolas, N.H. (1829) *Rolls of Arms of the Reigns of Henry III and Edward III*, London; His career including taxation and property ownership is tracked in Noble, M. (1804) *A History of the College of Arms*, London, pp. 154, 182; Nichols, J. G. (1848) *The Diary of Henry Machyn from AD 1550 to AD 1563*, London, pp. 88, 101, 174, 176, 193, 210, 243, 256, 264, 293, 294, 306; BL: ADD MSS 6113, f. 147r; 10,110 ff. 148r, 278r; *Collectanea Topographica and Genealogica*, Vol. 3 (1836) p. 195; Bodleian Library, Oxford: Ashmole MS 840, ff. 453, 457; TNA: C2/Eliz/P11/59; E179/251/16; E179/145/252; LC2/4/2-3; SP12/46, f. 53; Essex RO: D/AER/12; The visitation record he owned and wrote is Queen's College Oxford, MS 80; Pedigrees that omit him include: College of Arms MS H14, f. 14; BL: Harley MS: Harley MSS 380, ff. 160–1; 1070; 1424; 1505; 2187; 5182; Other documents he wrote include BL: Harley MSS 890, 3967, and can be traced through Wright, C. E. (1972) *Fontes Harleiani*, London,

p. 112; Records of his attendance at funerals are in Barrett-Lennard, T. (1908) *An Account of the Families of Lennard and Barrett*, London, p. 358: Bartlett, A. D. (1850) *An historical and descriptive account of Cumnor Place, Berkshire*, J. H. Parker, Oxford, pp. 65, 67; Gibbs, R. (1888) Worthies of Buckinghamshire and Men of Note of that County, London, p. 310; Godfrey, W. H., Wagner, A. and London, H. S. (1963) *The College of Arms*, London, p. 145; Gower, G. L. (1883) Genealogy of the Family of Gresham, London, p. 10; Bradney, J. A. (1993) *A History of Monmouthshire*, Vol. 3, Part 1, p. 83; College of Arms: I10, ff. 2, 4, 6, 74, 110, 142; I12, ff. 7r, 18v, 19v, 23r, 27v, 28v, 31r, 33r, 42r, 55r; I13, ff. 13–16, 32r, 53v; L16, ff. 15–28, 132v, 142v; Muller, J. A. (1933) The Letters of Stephen Gardiner, Cambridge, pp. 504–17; King, T. W. and Raines, F. R. (1869) *Lancashire Funeral Certificates*, Record Society of Lancashire and Cheshire, p. 3–4; His burial is recorded at Littledale, W.A. (1903) *The Registers of St Vedast Foster Lane and of St Michael le Quern*, London, p. 134; For Antonio Toto see Surrey HC: LM/1892; LM 1893; z/407/MS L.b. 17, 19, 21, 261.

Chapter 15: Eleanor Cotgreve

For family relationships and references to women as men's wives and daughters, see Queen's College Oxford: MS 80, f. 105; TNA: CHES15/8; For other people called Welshman, see WS Richard Barker 1586; CHES21/1, f. 43v; CHES24/97/1; Details of the dispute with William Cotgreve are in BL: Harley MS 2063, f. 23–4; CALS: QJB2/3; QJF 28/4, f. 49; TNA: CHES13/3; CHES14/5, 51, 58–60; CHES14/3, p. 263; For taxation see Gonville and Caius College Cambridge: MS197/103, p. 33; TNA: E179/85/60, 70, 78, 82, 85; E179/369/3; For dispute with a neighbour see TNA: CHES38/2, 24; For William Cotgrave in Ireland see BL: ADD MS 5754, f. 93; Morrin, J. (1862) *Calendar of the Patent and Close Rolls of the Chancery of Ireland*, Dublin, Vol. 2, pp. 337, 338; For the Owens see CALS: EDC7/1; P40/1/1; Peter's status is described in QJB1/3; QJF25/1, ff. 17, 60–1; His children are in CALS: P8/1; P9/1/1; P282/4554/1; For Godfrey Wynne see CALS: WS Godfrey Wynne 1629; Ormerod Vol. 1., p. 214; TNA: CHES16/8; For financial success, see TNA: CHES14/51; CHES14/60; CHES15/20; CHES16/12-13; The sale before her death is in TNA: CHES31/116; For the Cotgreaves still at the farm in the twentieth century see CGPA: Hannah Cotgreave 18 Jun 1937.

Chapter 16: Margaret Cotgreave

The case and most of the details are described in CALS: WC Charles Aldcroft 1749; Family wills are in CALS: WS Elizabeth Cotgreave 1737; WS John Cotgreave 1725; WS John Cotgreave 1768; Reference to her grandson owning the building by the bridge is in BL: Additional MS 9415, no. 1311; Her ownership of land in Whitby is in CALS: DPB/1186/11; Backford parish register recording the marriage is CALS: P32/1/3; The bishop's copy of the parish register is CALS: EDC7/12; EDB/Backford/1734; The right to the bridge tolls is in CALS: Z/A/B/3, f. 234v; Z/A/B/4, ff. 50v, 65v; Z/TCD/28; Her burial is at CALS: P20/1/3.

Chapter 17: Sir John Cotgreave

Family information is from CALS: DPB/1021/15, p. 164; DWS/MTD/24/8; P20/14/2; WS Sir John Cotgreave 1836; WS Thomas Cotgreave 1815; Z/ CR38/2–3; Z/QCI/28/9-15; Z/QRJ/1, ff. 175v, 182v, 198v; *Bath Chronicle* 2 Jul 1829; Lancashire RO: WCW 1773 Johnson, John of Scowcroft, chapman; WCW 1773 Johnson, John of Scowcroft, minor; Biographical information is in Anon (1818) *The Last Elections*, Bensley & Sons, London, p. 66; Armstrong, J. (1901) *Freemasonry in Cheshire*, London; Bennett, J. H. E. (1908) *The rolls of the freemen of City of Chester, Part 2, 1701–1800*, Record Society of Lancashire and Cheshire, p. 411; BL: Additional MS 9415, no. 1311; Burke, J. (1834) *A Genealogical and heraldic history of the commoners of Great Britain and Ireland*, London, Vol. 1, pp. 531–2; *Cheshire Observer* 23 Jan 1869; *Chester Chronicle* 12 Feb 1813, 3 Sep 1813, 11 Feb 1814, 15 Apr 1814, 19 Aug 1814, 30 Aug 1814, 21 Oct 1814, 23 Dec 1814, 15 Jul 1815, 3 Nov 1815, 10 Nov 1815, 1 Mar 1816, 7 Jun 1816, 12 July 1816, 2 Aug 1816, 16 Aug 1816, 20 Dec 1816, 13 Jun 1817, 20 Jun 1817, 17 Aug 1817, 24 Oct 1817, 26 Dec 1817, 2 Jan 1818, 15 May 1818, 11 Sep 1818, 9 Oct 1818, 23 Apr 1819, 11 Feb 1820, 10 Mar 1820, 15 Sep 1820, 16 Sep 1820, 16 Oct 1821, 30 Oct 1821, 22 Apr 1825, 20 Jun 1826, 6 Oct 1826, 17 Nov 1826, 5 Oct 1827, 3 Jul 1829, 25 Aug 1848; *Chester Courant* 14 Jul 1795, 19 Nov 1805, 3 Jan 1809, 25 Oct 1814, 3 Jan 1815, 28 Nov 1815, 23 Jul 1816, 10 Sep 1816, 8 Oct 1816, 15 Oct 1816, 21 Jan 1817, 21 Jan 1823, 29 Jul 1823, 8 Jun 1824, 1 Nov 1825, 8 Nov 1831; Flintshire RO: DC/319; *Gentleman's Magazine* Vol. 99 (1829), Part 1, p. 640; Hanshall, J. H. (1823) *The History of the County Palatine of Chester*, p. 292; Hemingway, J. (1831) *History of the City of Chester from its foundation to the present day*, Chester, Vol. 2, pp. 230–1, 352; John Cotgreave's original commission in the militia in private hands; Lack, W., Stuchfield, H. M. and Whittemore, P. (1996) *Monumental brasses of Cheshire*, London, p. 72; *Leeds Intelligencer* 18 Aug 1826; Library of the United Grand Lodge of Masons: AR/217, SN/217/11; *London Gazette* 16 Jun 1795, 29 Sep 1798, 6 Jul 1816; *Morning Chronicle* 8 Oct 1816; *National Advocate* 23 Nov 1816; *Newcastle Journal* 26 Aug 1837; *Observer* 3 Nov 1799; Ormerod Vol. 1, p. 180; *Schedule of Deeds and Monuments in the Muniment Room at Eaton and elsewhere*, privately printed (copy available at CALS), pp. 53, 145, 154; Shaw, W. A. (1906) *The Knights of England*, London, Vol. 2, p. 317; *The Times* 19 Oct 1821, 27 Sep 1824; TNA: CHES38/30/8; IR23/6; References to the erroneous use Johnson as a first name are in *Chester Courant* 27 Feb 1796, 9 Nov 1813; *Chester Chronicle* 14 Oct 1814; CALS: P20/14/2; TNA: C13/638, no. 24; Books he patronised include Roberts, R. (1816) *Daearyddiaeth, yn Rhoddi hanes am yr*

Amrywiol Wleddydd, Teyrnasoedd ac Ardaloedd y sydd yn Ewrop, Asia, Affrica, ac America, Chester; Anon (1822) *A memoir of Hawarden parish, Flintshire, by a parishioner*, Chester; His gardening is recorded in *Bell's Life in London and Sporting Chronicle* 1 Aug 1830; *Catalogue of Fruits cultivated in the Garden of the Horticultural Society of London at Chiswick* (1826), p. 191; *Chester Chronicle* 3 Sep 1813, 23 Dec 1814; *Newcastle Journal* 26 August 1837; The pedigree and arms he registered when he changed his name is at College of Arms: MS 7D14, pp. 260–1.

Chapter 18: Mary Cotgreave

Family information is available in *Birmingham Gazette* 8 Nov 1858; Burke, J. (1833–8) *A Genealogical and Heraldic History of the Commoners of Great Britain and Ireland*, London, Vol. 1, pp. 530–2; CALS: DPB1021/30, pp. 432–3; DWS/MTD/12/32; DWS/MTD/24/8; P51/1/4; WS Sir John Cotgreave 1836; WS Thomas Cotgreave 1815; WS William Cross 1808; Z/TRT/7/7k; *Cheshire Courant* 6 Aug 1811; *Cheshire Observer* 6 Nov 1858, 12 Dec 1874, 9 Apr 1887; College of Arms: Burke's Collections for Commoners; MS 7D14, pp. 260–1; *Coventry Herald* 11 Dec 1874; *Crockford's Clerical Directory for 1868*, London, p. 157; Deed of Sir John Cotgreave dated 10 July 1824 in private hands; *English Reports* Vol. 63, pp. 961–2; *Gentleman's Magazine*, Vol. 99 (1829), part 1, p. 640; Dec 1858, p. 659; *Leamington Spa Courier* 6 Nov 1858; Leicester, Leicestershire and Rutland RO: DE1110/640; *London Gazette* 6 Jul 1816; Somerset RO: D/P/WAL.SW2/1/26; *The Times* 5 Dec 1846; TNA: C14/497/C65; C33/958, f. 256r; HO107/1198/10, f. 44; HO107/2067, f. 634; The poem is in *The Old Cross: A Warwickshire Quarterly Magazine*, Vol. 1 (1879), p. 260; Her will is at CGPA: Mary Cotgreave 18 Jan 1859 and a draft at Coventry Archives; PA/101/4/94; Her death and Catherine's are at RDEW: Dec Q 1858, Coventry, Vol. 6d, p. 269; Dec Q 1874, Coventry, Vol. 6d, p. 351; Both burials can be found at Coventry Archives: London Road Burial database.

Chapter 19: Matilda Cotgreave

Family information is in RBEW Jun Q 1877, Chester, Vol. 8a, p. 435; Mar Q 1874, Chester, Vol. 8a, p. 408; Mar Q 1909, Chester, Vol. 8a, p. 377; Sep Q 1889, Chester, Vol. 8a, p. 411; RDEW: Mar Q 1910, Chester, Vol. 8a. pp. 253, 254; Sep Q 1895, Chester, Vol. 8a, p. 280; Sep Q 1895, Liverpool, Vol. 8b, p. 189; RMEW, Sep Q 1895, Liverpool, Vol. 8b, p. 189; Her life can be tracked through CALS: P29/2/5; TNA: HO107/129/10, f. 7; 130/14, f. 9; HO107/2172, f. 322; RG9/2629, f. 77; RG10/3730, f. 24; RG10/3731, f. 21; RG11/3558, f. 72; RG12/2878, f. 124; RG13/3368, f. 106, p. 27; RG14/477/33/25435; *Notes and Queries*, 9th Series, Vol. 6 (1900), p. 275; RBEW: Dec Q 1869, Great Boughton, Vol. 8a, p. 373; *Cheshire Observer* 10 Oct 1863, 22 May 1869, 5 Oct 1889.

Chapter 20: Thomas Richardson Cotgreave

Family information including his marriage and death is at RDEW: Dec Q 1895, Vol. 8a, p. 292; RMEW: Mar Q 1838, Shrewsbury, Vol. 18, p. 181; CALS: P1/6; P29/3/4; TNA: HO107/2172, f. 121, p. 47; RG9/265, f. 93, p. 8; RG10/3722, f. 7, p. 8; RG11/3554, f. 104, p. 8; RG12/2862, f. 75; Electoral Register for Cheshire Mid 1874; Information about his employment is at CALS: Z/C2C/54; CGPA: 1885 under Wood, John Brock; *Cheshire Observer* 17 Oct 1863, 3 Sep 1870, 12 Nov 1870, 21 Nov 1874, 13 Nov 1875, 20 Nov 1875, 13 Oct 1877, 8 Dec 1877, 15 Dec 1877, 29 Dec 1877, 6 Jul 1878, 29 Mar 1879, 4 Oct 1879, 8 Sep 1883, 31 Mar 1888, 17 Nov 1888, 23 Nov 1889, 4 Jan 1890, 17 Jan 1891, 11 Jul 1891, 1 Dec 1894, 26 Jun 1897; *Chester Chronicle* 23 Apr 1859, 22 Sep 1860; *Liverpool Mercury* 11 Nov 1853, 21 Dec 1878; *Manchester Courier* 22 Dec 1877; NLW: Hawarden MS 1886; *The Times* 7 Jan 1852; *Wrexham Guardian* 23 Oct 1875; *White's History, Gazetteer and Directory of Cheshire* 1860, Sheffield, p. 134; References to Gladstone are from Gladstone, W. E. (1986) *The Gladstone Diaries*, Clarendon, Oxford, Vol. 9, p. 171; Matthew, H. C. G. (1994) *The Gladstone Diaries*, Vol. XIII 1894–1986, Clarendon Press, Oxford, pp. 419, 421; *Nottingham Evening Post* 3 January 1931.

Chapter 21: Ranulph de Cotegreve

The sale of land in his father's lifetime is at TNA: OBS1/819, pp. 31, 32, 36; Charters and deeds naming him are found in BL: Add Charter 72,442, Harley MS 2007, ff. 127–9, 139v; 2065, ff. 73v, 77r, 124r; *The Ancestor*, Vol. 6, (July 1903), p. 34; *The Cheshire Sheaf*, 3rd Series, Vol. 4, p. 47, Vol. 54, p. 17; CALS: DVE1/S1/1; Accounts relating to his wardship are in BL: Landsdowne MS 644, ff. 9–11; Inferences about the importance of the Cheshire Grand Jury are in Skoda, H. et al. (2012) *Contact and Exchange in Later Medieval Europe*, Boydell, Woodbridge, pp. 221–46; His career in the Cheshire courts is tracked through TNA: CHES2/44, 57; CHES3/12, 14, 18, 19, 21–6, 29–31; CHES19/2-4; CHES23/5; CHES24/13-16, 20, 24, 26, 28; CHES25/4, 8, 10; CHES26/4-12; CHES29/89; CHES38/15/4, 22/3-4; Near and Far Cotgreaves are listed in IR29/5/86; His family connections and wife's identity is given in Queen's College Oxford: MS 80, ff. 105–6; BL: Harley MS 139, ff. 134, 150.

Chapter 22: John Cotgreve

His freedom of Chester and that of his brother are in Bennett, J. H. E. (1906) *The Rolls of the Freemen of the City of Chester*, Part I, pp. 15, 17; William Cotgreve's training in is Boyd, P. (1934) *Roll of the Draper's Company of London*, p. 46; Personal communication from the Archivist of the Draper's Company, November 2001; Robert Cotgrave's career with Plantagenet is in

Byrne, M. St. C. (1981) *The Lisle Letters*, University of Chicago Press, Vol. 3, p. 384, Vol. 4, p. 45, Vol. 5, p. 493, Vol. 6, p. 152; Plantagenet's career is in David Grummitt, 'Plantagenet, Arthur, Viscount Lisle', *ODNB*, 2004; Family relationships are in Queen's College Oxford: MS 80, f. 105; Brereton's career is described in E. W. Ives, 'Brereton, William (*c.* 1487×90–1536)', *ODNB*, 2004; Information about his wife is in TNA: C1/1295, ff. 51–4; 2153, f. 258v; 2177, f. 83v; Information about his brother's treason and Dutton's case against him is in TNA: SP1/94, ff. 3,5,7; Dutton, E. (2015) *The Ruler of Cheshire*, Leonie Press, Northwich, pp. 82–3; *Memorials of the Duttons of Dutton in Cheshire*, London, 1902, p. 127; His will is at CALS: DEO192/12; His career in the Cheshire courts is at CALS: EDC2/2, f. 69; Z/QSF2, f. 8; Z/SB5i; Z/SB7a, e; Z/SB7e; Z/SB9b; Z/SBC/1-5; Z/SR531-534; BL: 2057, f. 121; Other landholdings are in BL: Harley MS 1994, f. 94; 2063, f. 63v.

Chapter 23: Randle Cotgreyve and John Cotgreve

Randle's career as a monk and his family's benefit of the abbey's lands is touched on in *Transactions of the Lancashire and Cheshire Antiquarian Society*, Vol. 13 (1895), p. 16; BL: Harley MS 2063, f. 25r; 2071, ff. 20v, 48r; TNA: C1/1295, ff. 51–4; 1994, f. 315r; As a clergyman after dissolution, his career can be tracked in Borthwick Institute: V1578-9 Chester; Queen's College Oxford: MS 80, f. 105; *The Cheshire Sheaf*, 3rd Series, Vol. 1, p. 34; CALS: EDV2/4, f. 23r; EDC2/4, ff. 168–70; EDD3913/1/1-2; EDV1/1, ff. 16v, 76v; Lichfield RO: B/A/1/14iii, f. 38v; His more secular career in Cheshire is in CALS: DEO192/12; TNA: CHES5/4-5; CHES15/8-9; E179/85/28; Z/SBC10, f. 72v; Wills that left him property are at CALS: WS John Massie 1564, Richard Done 1579; BL: Harley MS 2067, ff. 75v, 78r; Piccope, G. J. (1860) *Lancashire and Cheshire wills and inventories*, Vol. II, Chetham Society, p. 152; John's career can be tracked in Furnivall, F. J. (1897) *Child Marriages*, Early English Text Society; *Miscellanies Relating to Lancashire and Cheshire*, Vol. 4, Part 2 (1903) Record Society of Lancashire and Cheshire; John's burial is in BL: Harley MS 2177, f. 9r; Randle's is in CALS: P51/1/1.

Chapter 24: Elizabeth Cotgrave

Prosecutions are detailed in BL: Harley MS 1994, f. 121r; Borthwick Institute for Archives: V1578-9, Chester Papers, Call Rolls; V1590-1, Court Book 2, ff. 87r, 94r; V1595-6, Court Book 2, ff. 370r, Court Book 3, f. 3r; CALS: EDB64 (June 1608); EDV1/10, f. 19v; EDV1/12a, f. 16r, 20v; EDV1/12b, f. 40r; EDV 1/14, f. 18v; QJB 2/2-3; QJF35/3, f. 36; WS Ralph Cotgrave 1588; Z/QSE 4/3; Catholic Record Society (1916) *Recusant Roll Number 1 1592-3*, London, p. 13, 23; Catholic Record Society (1961) *Recusant Records*, London, p. 67; TNA: CHES16/23; CHES 21/1, f. 164v; CHES 21/2, ff. 18v, 23r, 28r, 64r, 76r, 125r;

CHES 21/3, ff. 15r, 33r, 34r, 103v, 113v, 153v, 183r; CHES 24/109/1; CHES 24/113/3, part 1; CHES 24/115/1; E377/8; Her cousin's prosecution in Sussex is in Cockburn, J. S. (1975) *Calendar of Assize Records, Sussex Indictments, James I*, London, p. 79; Examples of women recusants and their activities are described in Childs, J. (2014) *God's Traitors: Terror and faith in Elizabethan England*, London; The burial is in Surrey HC: P5/1/1.

Chapter 25: John Cotgreave

Records relating to freedom of Chester, the franchise and the city's Cordwainers' Company are in Bennett, J. H. E. (1908) *The Rolls of the Freemen of the City of Chester, Part II, 1701–1805*, Record Society of Lancashire and Cheshire, p. 228; CALS: MFR/13; Chester Company of Cordwainers, private records; *Chester Chronicle* 23 Apr 1859; *Chester Election, List of The Freemen and Householders who polled at the last General Election*, 1859, p. 2; Journal of the House of Commons, Vol. 25, 21 Geo II, 9 February 1747/8, p. 505; Other family information is in WC Charles Aldcroft 1748; RDEW: Jun Q 1867, Great Boughton, Vol. 88, p. 229; Information related to the trial is in J. M. Beattie, 'Garrow, Sir William (1760–1840)', *ODNB*, 2004; *Chester Courant* 4 Sep 1821, 27 Nov 1821, 4 Dec 1821; *Westmorland Gazette* 22 Sep 1821; Travel between Chester and Shrewsbury is from www.carlscam.com/coach.htm; Reports of the inquiry into election corruption are from *Hansard*, House of Commons, 30 Mar 1881; House of Commons (1880) *Shorthand writer's notes of evidence and judgment on trial of the Chester election petition*, p. 13; House of Commons Command Papers (1881) *Royal Commission to inquire into Existence of Corrupt Practices in City of Chester, Report and Minutes of Evidence*, pp. xix, xx, 134, 137, 195, 331, 340–1, 623.

Chapter 26: Jonathan Cotgrave

His family and early life in Chester is documented in College of Arms; Howard MS, pp. 188–9; CALS: WS Thomas Cotgrave 1800; CALS: DPB/1021/19, p. 163; HI/51; P1/9; P63/1/2-3; *Chester Chronicle* 15 Jan 1790, 22 Jan 1790, 5 Feb 1790; *Manks Advertiser* 15 Sep 1840; His subsequent medical career is in Personal communication from the Library at Royal College of Surgeons of England, Jan 2007; Peterkin, A. and Johnston, W. (1968) *Commissioned Officers in the Medical Services of the British Army 1660–1960*, London, p. 88; Anderson, P. J. (1889) *Fasti Academiae Mariscallanae Aberdonensis*, Aberdeen, Vol. 2, p. 152; Letters from President of the College of Surgeons on Charter, *House of Commons Accounts and Papers*, 1844 Session, p. 2; Westminster Abbey Archives: CWIC652310652, available on www.londonlives.org; TNA: ADM103/494; WO4/405; WO12/4955-8, 7695; WO25/3910, no. 39; Personal communication from Dr Tim Smith, Chair, Berkshire Medical Heritage Centre, Sep 2014; Military matters are described in Anon (1861) *The Campaign in Holland 1799*, *by a Subaltern*, 1861, London, p. 81; Army List 1798, p. 315; Bonnici, W. (1997) The 'Very Long Hiccup' and the emergence of the Army Medical Services in Malta. *Journal of the Royal Army Medical Corps*, Vol. 143, pp. 124–8; Sugden, J. (2012) *Nelson: The Sword of Albion*, London, Chapter XI; War Office Intelligence Division (1884) *British minor expeditions* 1746–1814, London, pp. 31–45; *London Gazette* 5 May 1795, 18 Jul 1797; Monument in St Peter's Church, Chester; Information on his time and contacts in Rotherfield Greys can be constructed from TNA: HO107/874/6/38; PROB11/1471/158; PROB 11/2075/160; PROB 11/2221/269; Bangor University: Catalogue of the Dinam Hall Manuscripts (GB 0222 DIN); His death is at RDEW: Dec Q 1844, Henley, Vol. 16, p. 53, and his will at TNA: PROB10/6285. His funeral is described in *North Wales Chronicle* 14 Jan 1845; *Liverpool Mercury* 10 Jan 1845.

Chapter 27: Elizabeth Cotgrave

Family information is in BL: IOR/L/AG/23/2/4, p. 109; Z/N/3; Her journey is in part documented in BL: IOR/L/MAR/B/38A; Her later life can be traced in TNA: HO107/686/9, f. 24; HO107/1605, f. 5; RG9/454, f. 43; Information about the Forbes family and Charles Forbes's career is in Tayler, A. and Tayler, H. (1937) *The House of Forbes*, Aberdeen; *Elgin Courant* 30 Nov 1849; *Hansard* 20 Feb 1822, 16 May 1825, 16 Jun 1825, 7 Mar 1831, 8 Jul 1831; *The Times* 28 Apr 1831; *Morning Chronicle* 28 Apr 1831, 25 Jun 1831; *Royal Ladies Magazine*, Vol. 1 (1831), p. 431; Copies of family letters are available at Cambridge University Centre for Asian Studies: Forbes Collection; Information about the current status of Charles's company is available at www.forbes.co.in; Family members working for and associated with the company are mentioned in TNA: ADM9/26, #829; *The Morning Chronicle* 2 Dec 1829; Horsburgh, J. (1841) *India Directory, or Directions for sailing to and from the East Indies, China Australia*, Vol. 1, p. 15; *Hampshire Telegraph and Sussex Chronicle* 13 Dec 1830; *Morning Post* 13 Dec 1830; *Asiatic Journal* 28 Mar 1830, p. 138; *Bombay Calendar* 1828, p. 145; Wills are at CGPA: Dame Elizabeth Forbes 23 Jul 1861; Henry Forbes Cotgrave 7 Nov 1913; Mary Forbes 13 Jun 1874.

Chapter 28: William Watson Cotgreave

Family information is in College of Arms: Bigland Pedigrees Vol. III, p. 170; His earlier life is recorded in *Albany Sentinel* 15 May 1798; *Calendar of NY Colonial Manuscripts Indorsed Land Papers 1643–1803*, Albany (1864) p. 816; *Litchfield Monitor* 7 Feb 1786, p. 4; Palmer, T. H. (1816) *The Historical Register of the United States*, Vol. 4, Philadelphia, pp. 248–9; Passenger Arrivals at the Port of Philadelphia 1800–1814, Genealogical Publishing (1986), p. 141; US National Archives: M33 92, p203; RG94, entry 12; Yeates, J. (1819) *Reports of Cases Adjudged in the Supreme Court of Pennsylvania, Philadelphia*, Vol. 4, pp. 230–4; Information relating to his time in Ohio is in *A compilation of the laws, treaties, resolutions and ordinances of the General and State Governments which relate to lands in the State of Ohio*, G. Nashe, Columbus (1825), p. 250; *Acts of a General Nature passed at the First Session of the 24th General Assembly of the State of Ohio*, Columbus (1826), pp. 122–3; *American Watchman* 24 Feb 1813, p. 2; Brinkerhoff, R. (1993) *A Pioneer history of Richland County, Ohio*, Ohio Genealogical Society, pp. 59, 65; *Cleveland Herald* 29 Nov 1881; *Daily National Intelligencer* 30 Jun 1814; Dawson, H. B. (1858) *Battles of the United States*, New York; Gilpin, A. R. (1958) *The War of 1812 in the Old Northwest*, East Lansing, pp. 168–9, 243; Green, K. M. (1988) *Pioneer Ohio Newspapers 1802–1818*, Galveston, pp. 50, 117, 119, 156, 218, 220; *History of Trumbull and Mahoning Counties*, Cleveland (1882), Vol. 1, pp. 68, 248, 294, 297, 317, 336; *Journal of the House of Representatives of the State of Ohio*, 1815–16, pp. 4, 22, 34, 43, 176, 321, 326, 330, 338, 347, 351, 355; *Journal of the Senate of the State of Ohio*, 1815–16, pp. 33, 48, 314, 317, 325, 327, 332, 335; Knopf, R. (1962) *Document Transcriptions of the War of 1812 in the Northwest*, Columbus, Vol. 10, Part I, pp. 85, 106, 119, 133, 145; Part II, p. 178; Mansfield Courthouse, OH: Richland County, Commons Pleas Book 1822–33, pp. 6–8, Court of Commons Pleas Journal 1822–35, pp. 11, 24, 54, 77, 83, 95, 101, 120; Richland County, Deed Book 1, pp. 230, 232, 358, 415, 417; Book 3, p. 441; Book 5, p. 203; New York State Library: SC7005; *Niles' Weekly Register* 9 Jul 1814; Ohio Genealogical Society Library: Common Pleas Packets 1816-4-5a, 1818-10-36c, 1819-11-50; 1819-2-3; 1820-9-50; 1831-6-11; 1831-10-32: Ohio Historical Library: R977, 1280OH-3: *Ohio History*, Vol. 28, p. 318: Ohio Laws: 16th Ohio Legislature, Chapter MMCCXX; 17th Ohio Legislature, Chapter MMCCXXIV, 23rd Ohio Legislature, Chapter MMCCCXXXV; *Ohio Register* 9 Oct 1816, 17 Jul 1818, 23 Sep 1818, 30 Sep 1818, 7 Oct 1818; Richland County, Ohio: *Original Land Purchases, Richland County*, Genealogical Society (1999), pp. 80, 153, 173: *Roster of Ohio Soldiers in the War of 1812*, Vol. 1, p. 208; Vol. 2, p. 239; *The American Whig Review*, New Series, Vol. IX–XV (1852) pp. 60ff; *The Life of Major-General William Henry Harrison*, Philadelphia (1840), pp. 48–9: *The Pastfinder* Vol. 27 (2007), pp. 28–9, 32–3; *The Supporter* 12 Dec 1815, 2 Jan 1816, 9 Jan 1816; *True American* 13 Jul 1814; US Bureau of Land Management Acc CV Vol. 40, p. 332; US Congressional Serial Set, Vol. 56, Session Vol. 9, 16th Congress, 2nd Session, Letter from the Postmaster, p. 206; Warren Courthouse, OH: Trumbull County Probate Records 1813–1819, p. 219, 1819–1825, p. 287; *Western America* 20 Jan 1816; Western Reserve and Northern Ohio Historical Society Historical and Archaeological Tracts, No. 12 1872, Selection 3 of War of 1812, p. 1, No. 92 1913, Northern Ohio During the War of 1812, pp. 75–7, 99–101; *Western Reserve Chronicle* 29 Jun 1823; Western Reserve Historical Society: MS 2729, Container 1, folder 3, MS 3122, Container 39a, MS 3133, Container 1, folders 2, 4; Western Reserve Historical Society: MS 3133: Container 1, folders 3, 4.

Chapter 29: Henry George Forbes Cotgrave

Family details can be found in *Cheltenham Looker-On* 2 Dec 1854; *The Courier* 28 Nov 1863, 9 Dec 1863; *Hampshire Chronicle* 21 May 1853; RMEW: Jun Q 1863, Kensington, Vol. 1a, p. 91; Mar Q 1874, Bedford, Vol. 3b, p. 421; *The Times* 12 Dec 1854, 3 Jan 1855; HO/107/1529 f. 127v; *Worcester Journal* 2 Dec 1854; His naval career is in TNA: BT98/3442; BT98/3879; Low, C. R. (1877) *History of the Indian Navy 1613–1863*, London, Vol. 2, pp. 456, 459, 461, 469, 488; National Maritime Museum: Master's Certificate No. 74,628; LOG/M/61; RUSI/NM/143/3,4,5; *Papers relating to Committee to inquire into Irregularities in Transport of Stores to the East*, House of Commons, Session 1854–1855, Minutes of Evidence, pp. 601–2; *Public Ledger and Advertiser* 17 Nov 1853; *Hansard* 14 Dec 1854; *Liverpool Mail* 2 Dec 1854; LMA: Ms 12818/16, p. 84; *London Evening Standard* 16 Nov 1854; *Morning Advertiser* 29 Apr 1853; *Morning Chronicle* 10 May 1853, 2 Dec 1854; *The Advertiser* (Adelaide) 9 Jun 1936; *A history of our relations with the Andamanese*, Calcutta, Office of the Superintendent of Government Printing (1899), Vol. 1, p. 232; *Banner of Ulster* 19 Jul 1853; BL: IOR/L/MAR/C/708; IOR/L/MAR/C/713, pp. 800–24; IOR/L/AG/23/18/3, p. 107; IOR/L/AG/23/18/6, p. 295; IOR/L/MIL/12/77, no. 262; IOR/MSS EUR C345; *East India Register for 1838* (ii), 1857–1864; Information relating to his time and death in Australia, and his widow's return is in Queensland Archives, Australia: ID348611 No. 51 H G F Cotgrove [sic]; Queensland Government Registry of Births, Deaths and Marriages: Births 1864/C1430, 1866/C2103; Deaths 1866/C1185; *Queensland Police Gazette* 1 Aug 1866; *The Queenslander* 4 Aug 1866, 16 Oct 1897; *The South Australian Advertiser* 15 Jul 1881, 17 Mar 1882; *South Australian Weekly Chronicle* 27 Jan 1883, 18 Mar 1882; *The Standard* 3 Jan 1855; *Sydney Morning Herald* 25 Nov 1863; *The Brisbane Courier* 4 Aug 1866, 14 Aug 1866.

Chapter 30: Mary Anne Cotgrave

Family information about the Dellers is available at www.dellerfamily.com, and other family information is from Ford, John, 'Ackermann, Rudolph (1764–1834)' and 'Ackermann, George (1803–1891), *ODNB*, 2004; *Daily News* 10 Mar 1863; East India Register for 1858 (ii), p. 43, 1860 (i), pp. 18, 43; *Hampshire Advertiser* 25 Feb 1854; LMA: ACC/1785/024; P76/PET1/008; Monument in St James's Church, Mumbai; RDEW Dec Q 1874, Marylebone, Vol. 1a, p. 378, Mar Q 1915, Fulham, Vol. 1a, p. 371, Jan Q 1953, Bideford, Vol. 71, p. 372; RMEW: Sep Q 1853 Lambeth, Vol. 1d, p. 510, Jun Q 1854, Pancras, Vol. 1b, p. 19, Dec Q 1854, Winchester, Vol. 2c, p. 143, Dec Q 1865, Lewisham, Vol. 1d, p. 1361, Jan Q 1874, Bethnal Green, Vol. 1c, p. 426, Shaw's Union Officers Manual of Duties (1846), pp. 54–5; Surrey HC: CHY/4/2/7 Oct 1835; TNA: HO107/718/2, f. 20, p. 6; HO107/1698, f. 560, p. 43; RG9/70, f. 107, p. 18; RG10/304, f. 4; RG11/232, f. 61; RG14/895; RG14/4022/80/4022; University

College Hospital London Archives: Middlesex Hospital Medical Register 1874; Register of Deaths 1872–1874; Correspondence with and information relating to the East India Company is in IOR/B/233, p. 597; IOR/E/1/305, no. 3424; E/4/1102, p. 1170: E/4/1103 p. 1120; E/4/1105 p. 1051; E/4/1107, p. 56; IOR/L/AG/23/2/4; IOR/L/MIL/2/517, 556: L/MIL/3/1916, no. 86, 1919 no. 121; L/MIL/9/299, ff. 115, 455; L/MIL/12/70, f. 513; L/MIL/12/77/no. 262; L/MIL/12/78, no. 262; IOR/N/2/9, p. 460; The story of her adventure in the jungle is in Duberly, F. I. L. (1859) *Campaigning experiences in Central India*, London, pp. 106–7; with more of Mrs Duberly's notes at BL: ADD MS 47218C.

Chapter 31: William Cotgreve

His birth date is from CALS: EDC2/9, p. 340; His brother's job is in TNA: C3/35/63; His Freedom of Chester and election to the Council are at Bennett, J. H. E. (1906) *The Rolls of the Freemen of the City of Chester, Part I, 1392–1700*, Record Society of Lancashire and Cheshire, p. 42; CALS: ZA/B/1, f. 174; His activities on the Isle of Man are in *Monumenta de Insula Manniae*, Manx Society Vol. 9 (1862), pp. 68–9; A map of the Crow is at Braun, G. (1572–1617) Civitates Orbis Terrarum, Cologne; Property ownership and wealth is in Staffordshire RO: D593/P/2/1-6; BL: Harley MS 2150, f. 198r; 2131, ff. 187v, 190r; 2105, f. 160r; 2039, ff. 125, 129; 2063, ff. 23–4; 2067, ff. 32, 166r; TNA: CHES3/82; For his early civic roles and relationships see TNA: CHES38/2; CHES24/98/2; CALS: QJF 3/4, 4/1, 4/4, 5/2; ZSBC/21, 23; CALS: A/B/1, ff. 188, 217; EDC2/9, p. 340; BL: Harley MS 2025, f. 31r; 2125, f. 41r; Raines, R. F. (1853) *The Derby Household Books*, Chetham Society, p. 19 (the editor wrongly identifies 'Mr Cotgreve' as John Cotgreve [See Chapter 22] but he died in 1547); For his mayorality and mayors in general see *The History of Cheshire containing King's Vale-Royal Entire* (1778), Chester, p. 397; BL: Harley MS 2125, ff. 41v, 43; Bennett, J. H. E. (1906) *The Rolls of the Freemen of the City of Chester* Part I, pp. 67–8; Laughton, J. (2008) *Life in a Late Mediaeval City: Chester 1275–1520*, Oxford, p. 121; BL: Harley MS 1989, f. 393r; CALS: ZA/B/1, ff. 225–7; Z/M/PE/2/32; TNA: SP12/232, f. 92; SP12/233, ff. 42, 139; NLW: Hawarden MS 148; Wood, E. M. (2003) *A reappraisal of early modern Chester through a reading of the city's antiquarian collections*, Ph.D. Thesis, Birkbeck College London, p. 195; For his shrievality see CALS: Z/SB/13; Ormerod, Vol. 1, pp. 181–2; For the dispute with the bakers see Morris, R. H. (1894) *Chester in the Plantagenet and Tudor Reigns*, Chester, p. 113; BL Harley MS 2081, f. 108; CALS: G13/38, ff. 15–16; Z/A/B/1, f. 202; TNA: CHES14/58, ff. 150v, 151v, 153r; CHES15/13; CHES38/24; His will is at CALS: EDA 2/2, p. 155ff; His burial is as CALS: P51/1/1.

Chapter 32: Thomas Cotgreave

Correspondence with Henry Hulton is in York, N. L. (2010) *Henry Hulton and the American Revolution*, Colonial Society of Massachusetts, pp. 381, 385, 389; Houghton Library, Harvard: MS CAN 16; Civic, local and official positions are in *A list of the Governors and Guardians of the hospital for the maintenance and education of exposed and deserted young children 1767*, London, p. 15; Bennett, J. H. E. (1908) *The Rolls of the Freemen of the City of Chester, Part II, 1701–1805*, Record Society of Lancashire and Cheshire, p. 320; Land Tax Act 21 George II; CALS: CAS/2; DBN/B/9/6; HI/1; Z/A/B/4, f. 162; Z/A/B/5, p. 15; Z/CL/122(e), No. 4; Z/QRTC/3, 5, 7, 8; Z/M/AB/2/f. 56; Z/S/F/180; TNA: CHES21/7; *Chester Chronicle* 13 Feb 1789; *Derby Mercury* 17 Feb 1791; *London Gazette* 31 Mar 1789; References to trusteeships are in NLW: Caerhun 56, 78–80, 83, 84, 85, 88, 89, 93, 94, 98–100, 104, 106–15, 117; Chirk Castle/Part 2, no. 156; Part 7, nos 4514, 6488; Denbighshire RO: DD/GA/733; Flintshire RO: D/BC/738,739, 4126; CALS: Z/CR3/21-22; *London Gazette* 1 Apr 1755, 1 Apr 1765; Property and wealth is mentioned in LMA: A/FH/D/4/1/1; CALS: DPB/1021/15, p. 49; DSA/229; Z/A/B/5, p. 59; Z/CR49/72; Z/CR165/45; His will and associated proceedings are in CALS: WS Thomas Cotgreave 1815; CALS DPB/1021/11, p. 171; 12, p. 583; 13, p. 6; 15, pp. 48, 164, 370, 407; 16, p. 130; 19, p. 263; PROB 11/1208 quire 378; NLW: SA/1845/226; There is a brief obituary in *Chester Chronicle* 15 Apr 1791; *The Times* 22 April 1791; *Bath Chronicle* 14 April 1791.

Chapter 33: Sydney Cotgreave

Family information is from CALS: MFR13; P16/4/2; P29/3/4; P51/3/2; P65/1/2; Z/TCP/7/81; *Chester Chronicle* 27 Jul 1810, 4 Jun 1830; Chester Company of Cordwainers' private records; *Chester Courant* 31 Jul 1810, 18 Sep 1810, 9 Jul 1811; *Gentleman's Magazine* Vol. 29 (1759), p. 194; LMA: P89/MRY1/346; *Monthly Magazine* Vol. 13, Part 1 (1801), p. 368; Vol. 15, Part 1 (1803), p. 191; Vol. 30, Part 2 (1810), p. 380; *Morning Post* 8 Jul 1836; RDEW, Mar Q 1843, Marylebone, Vol. 1, p. 204; TNA: HO107/680/15, f. 17, HO107/739/5, f. 26; Information about the workhouse in Westminster is from Neate, A.R. (1967) *The St Marylebone Workhouse and Institution 1730–1965*, St Marylebone Society, London, pp. 17–18; LMA: WEBG/SM/38/1; 40/1; *Abstract of the Answers and Returns made Pursuant to Acts 3&4 Vic c99 and 4 Vic c7*, London, 1843.

Chapter 34: William Cotgreave

Family information is in College of Arms: Bigland Pedigrees Vol. III, p. 170; Berks RO: D/EN/20/4 Poll Book 1812, p. 19; D/P53/1/6, 8; DP53 vicar's rent book; Berkshire Archaeological Journal Vol. 45 (1941), p. 16; CALS:

DBW/L/F/20-1; DPB/1021/11, p. 179; P9/7/4, ff. 2–3; P45/3/1; QDV1/50–55; WS James Cotgreave 1827; WS Paul Miller 1793; WS Sarah Cotgreave 1831; WS Sarah Cotgreave 1832; WS Thomas Cotgreave 1803; WS William Cotgreave 1847; Information relating to his bank and financial difficulties is in Oxford History Centre: Hey/VIII/ix/7; *Oxford Journal* 15 Oct 1814, 14 Jan 1815; *Oxford University and City Herald* 24 Sep 1814; TNA: E144/64; *Law Times* Vol. 19, p. 49; *Rusher's Reading Guide and Berkshire Directory for 1808*, p. 208 [also editions for 1809–13]; *The Times* 15 Oct 1814; His time in Cumbria is detailed in Cumbria Archives: D/SEN/5/3/6; D/SEN/BOX48/6/2; Bishop's Transcripts of Maryport Parish, burial 18 Mar 1840; PR79/5; PR160/7; *History, Directory and Gazetteer of Cumberland and Westmorland*, W. White & Co (1829), p. 321; Leekey, G. (1813) *The Stamp-Office List of Country Bankers*, London, p. 31; RDEW: Mar Q 1840, Cockermouth, Vol. 25, p. 67; Mar Q 1847, Cockermouth, Vol. 25, p. 92; BT107/197/Whitehaven/35; *Carlisle Journal* 21 Sep 1833, 19 Oct 1833, 6 Sep 1834, 12 Dec 1835, 6 Apr 1838, 26 May 1838, 3 Aug 1838, 7 Sep 1838, 8 Aug 1840, 16 Jan 1841, 20 Feb 1841, 13 Mar 1841, 1 May 1841; *Westmorland Gazette* 24 Mar 1832; Biographical information is in *A meeting of the Commissioners for carrying into execution within the county of Chester the act lately passed for duties on income*, Chester (1799), p. 1; *Baldwin's Complete Guide to all Persons who have any Trade or Concern within the City of London and Parts Adjacent*, 11th Edition, 1768, London [and later editions]; *Chester Chronicle* 12 Sep 1791, 20 Apr 1798, 19 Sep 1800, 21 Sep 1804, 29 Oct 1813, 25 Feb 1815, 17 Mar 1815, 20 Jun 1815; *Chester Courant* 27 Oct 1795, 25 Jan 1803, 16 Oct 1804, 30 Apr 1805; *Gloucester Journal* 20 Nov 1797; Kent, H. (1767) *Kent's Directory for the Year 1767*, 34th Edition [and later editions]; Leigh, H. (1788) Miscellaneous Poems, Manchester; LMA: BT/T/1382; CLC/B/192/F/001/MS 11,936/255, no. 381334; MS 11,936/282, no. 426136; MS 11,936/303, nos 460860, 481510; MS 11,936/277, no. 418338; DW/MP/62, no. 120; P92/SAV/3008; P92/MRY/014; *London Gazette* 15 Jun 1790, 15 Nov 1814, 20 Sep 1814, 19 Nov 1814; *Morning Chronicle* 1 Apr 1852; *Pigot and Co.'s Directory of Cheshire, Cumberland, Derbyshire, Durham, Lancashire, Leicestershire, Lincolnshire, Northumberland, Nottinghamshire, Rutlandshire, Shropshire, Staffordshire, Warwickshire, Westmoreland, Worcestershire, Yorkshire, North Wales, 1828–29* [Part 1: Cheshire–Northumberland], p. 84; *Salisbury and Winchester Journal* 9 Jan 1815; Surrey History Centre: G/111/64/7-8; Tarvin Enclosure Act 31 George III, c.35; TNA: C13/2891; CHES18/15; HO107/1145/6, f. 49; PROB11/1132; *Whitehall Evening Post* 21 Sep 1780.

Chapter 35: Harriet Cotgreave

Family information is in CALS: WS Sir John Cotgreave 1836; P 29/2/1; P 29/3/7; Z/CCF13/81; *Chester Courant* 2 Mar 1819; Grosvenor Archives: Letter to S Cotgreave dated July 1989; RDEW: Dec Q 1876, Chester, Vol. 8a, pp. 260, 265; Burke, J. (1833–38) *A Genealogical and Heraldic History of the Commoners of Great Britain and Ireland*, London, Vol. 1, pp. 530–2; The bankruptcy and court case is described in *Chester Chronicle* 25 Aug 1848; *London Gazette* 17 Jun 1842, 13 Sep 1842; TNA: ASSI57/4, pp. 15, 17; C14/502/C110; C33/903, f. 149; C33/958, ff. 62r, 178r, 256r; Thomas's personality can be seen in NLW: Henry Robertson 27/13-27; *Cheshire Observer* 1 Sep 1866, 23 Jan 1869; *Chester Chronicle* 1 Sep 1866; Examples of fraudulent pedigrees are in Bedford RO: GY11/265; Bigelow, J. (1895) *The Life of Samuel J Tilden*, New York, Vol. 1, pp. 367–70; Bigg-Wither, R. F. (1907) *Materials for a History of the Wither Family*, Winchester; Burke's *Landed Gentry*, 2nd Edition (1847) Vol. II, p. 1150; Centre for Kentish Studies: U49 C13/69-71; Cornwall RO: PW/119; Cotgreave, P. (1995) Spence Pedigree Forgeries, *Family Tree Magazine*, July 1995, p. 3; Denbighshire Archives: PD/101/1/9; Fishwick, H. (1874) *The History of the Parish of Kirkham*, Chetham Society, Pedigree of Westby: *Genealogist*, New Series, Vol. 2, p. 239; *Genealogists' Magazine*, Vol. 6, pp. 292, 370; Hanson, G. A. (1876) *Old Kent: The Eastern Shore of Maryland*, Baltimore, pp. 303–4; Hertfordshire Archives: DE/Gd/27286; Kelly, S. (1854) *The Life of Mrs Sherwood*, London, p. 94; King, O. B. (1953) *The King Family, being its history from 1415 to 1953*, pp. 11, 14; Leicestershire, Leicester and Rutland RO: DE728/954; Lincolnshire Archives: THOR VI/XIII/4; *Miscellanea Genealogica et Heraldica*, 2nd Series, Vol. 5, pp. 228, 304; Norfolk RO: BUL4/324; *Notes & Queries* 1st Series, Vol. 9, pp. 221, 275; Vol. 10, p. 255; 2nd Series, Vol. 8, p. 435; Vol. 9, pp. 61, 131, 147, 149, 185; Vol. 10, p. 107; 3rd Series, Vol. 1, pp. 8, 54, 92; Vol. 7, p. 480; 5th Series, Vol. 9, pp. 189, 297; Ormerod Vol. 3, p. 37; Personal communication from Pat Graham, December 2004; Personal communication from Richard G. Grylls, Jul 1995; Rogers, J. (1846) *Pedigrees of Caermarthenshire, Cardiganshire and Pembrokeshire in continuation of Lewis Dwnn to about the years 1700–10*, Vol. 2, p. 152; Saleeba, L. (1999) The Usticks Come Unstuck, *Genealogist*, Sep 1999; Somerset RO: DD/WO/54/11/38-39, 45; Staffordshire RO: D(W) 1733/F/7; Terrill, A. E. (1887) *Memorials of a family in England and Virginia*, p. 323; *The Cheshire Sheaf*, 1st Series, Vol. 2, p. 372; 3rd Series, Vol. 5, p. 94, Vol. 28, p. 74; Warwickshire RO: CR0341/271/9.

Chapter 36: Jane Nickson Cotgreave

Family information and wills are in CALS: P 9/2/1; P 9/5/1-2; WS Sarah Cotgreave 1831; CGPA: Jane Nickson Cotgreave 21 Jul 1898, Mary Brown Nickson 21 Jan 1872; *Cheshire Observer* 29 Oct 1887, 16 Jun 1888; Shropshire Archives: 5168/2/67; 6241/1/155A/20-21; P303/A/3/4; TNA: HO107/1205/6, f. 45; HO107/1995, f. 69; PROB11/1604; PROB11/1829; PROB11/1888; RG9/1886, f. 42; RG10/2792, f. 42; RG11/2667, f. 81; RG12/2123, f. 73, p. 4; *Whitchurch Herald* 2 Apr 1898; *Worcester Chronicle* 12 Dec 1849; Holiday desti-nation are documented in *Aberystwyth Observer* 25 Jun 1870; *Aberystwyth Times*

26 Jun 1869; *Isle of Wight Observer* 27 Jun 1857; *North Wales Chronicle* 24 Jun 1865; *Cambrian News* 26 Jun 1869; *Rhyl Advertiser* 25 Sep 1880; The court case can be traced through TNA: C14/806/C95; C15/408/N38; C32/57 [1848 No. 95]; *Dormant Funds in Chancery: Supplement to the London Gazette*, 1914 edition, p. 1883; 1917 edition, p. 1; *Morning Post* and *Morning Chronicle* Mar 1853–Nov 1857, *passim* (repeated refs to Cotgreave vs Walmsley in the Chancery Court); *The Times* 11 May 1853; Charitable giving is recorded in *Ragged School Union Magazine* Dec 1859, Nov 1862, Oct 1886, Jul 1887; *London Standard* 18 Mar 1841, 24 Dec 1849, 21 Jan 1886.

Chapter 37: Richard de Malpas Cotgrave

His family is detailed in *Burke's Peerage* (online edition), Farmar of Millwood, accessed 8 July 2004; Mary Wesley's biography is Marnham, P. (2007) *Wild Mary: A Life of Mary Wesley*, London, p. 18; Information about his sons comes from *Roll of Honour of the Empire's Heroes* (no date, *c.* 1920), Queenhithe unnumbered volume; TNA: WO339/75112; Other family information is in BL: IOR/L/MIL/9/298; IOR/V24/3917-20; Gloucestershire RO: D4481; Legal matters are in TNA: C16/565/F25; *Law Reports*, In re Cotgrave [1903] 2 Ch. 705; *London Gazette* 19 Jul 1881, 29 Jul 1898; The controversy concerning the post in Cyprus is in TNA: CO512/3, General Letters 10139, Governor's Letters 13975; References to his whereabouts and occupation are in TNA: RG9/520, f. 100; RG10/1148, f. 24; RG13/2029, f. 97; RG14/12952/199; United Grand Lodge of England, Membership Registers: Stuart Lodge; LMA: MR/PEO; Newspaper reports of his activities and situation are in *Banbury Guardian* 10 May 1883; *Northampton Mercury* 13 Jan 1893, 11 Aug 1893, 29 Sep 1893; *The Star* (Guernsey) 13 May 1884, 27 May 1884, 12 Jun 1884, 17 Jun 1844; *The Times* 22 Jul 1901; *Western Morning News* 27 Oct 1921; *Western Times* 8 May 1899, 30 Nov 1899, 10 Apr 1901, 15 May 1902 [and many dates in the early twentieth century referring to sports events]; His grandfather's and wife's wills are in CGPA: Edward Stone Cotgrave 24 Nov 1868; Amelia Farmar Cotgrave 26 Jan 1936. His marriage and death are registered at RDEW: Mar Q 1926, Willesden, Vol. 3, p. 294; RMEW: Dec Q 1877, Kensington, Vol. 1a, p. 338.

Index